Date Due

Twelfth Century Studies

Twelfth Century Studies

Josiah C. Russell 1900 -

AMS PRESS
NEW YORK, N.Y.

Library of Congress Cataloging in Publication Data

Russell, Josiah Cox, 1900–
 Twelfth century studies.

 Includes index.
 1. Civilization, Medieval. I. Title.
 CB354.6.R87   909'.I   77-83792
 ISBN 0-404-16022-0

FIRST AMS EDITION: 1978

MANUFACTURED IN THE UNITED STATES OF AMERICA

AMS PRESS INC.
NEW YORK, N.Y.

Contents

Acknowledgments

The chapters in this monograph originally appeared as individual contributions in the following publications:

The Writing of History in the Twelfth Century, Chapter 4 (Renaissance of the Twelfth Century), *The Development of Historiography*, edited by Matthew A. Fitzsimons, Alfred G. Pundt, and Charles E. Nowell (Harrisburg, Stackpole, 1954), pp. 38-50.

The Short Dark Folk of England, *Social Forces*, 24 (1946), 340-347.

A Quantitative Approach to Medieval Population Change, *The Journal of Economic History*, 24 (1964), 1-21.

Tall Kings: The Height of Medieval English Kings, *The Mississippi Quarterly*, 10 (1957), 29-41.

Death Along the Deer Trails, *Mediaevalia*, Vol. I, No. 2 (1977), 89-95.

Allegations of Poisoning in the Norman World.

The Date of Henry I's Charter to London, *Dargan Historical Essays*, University of New Mexico Publications in History, No. 4 (1952), 9-16.

Gratian, Irnerius and the Early Schools of Bologna, *The Mississippi Quarterly*, 12 (1959), 168-188.

Ranulf de Glanville, *Speculum*, 45 (1970), 69-79.

Hereford and Arabic Science in England About 1175-1200, *Isis*, 18 (1932), 14-25.

Alexander Neckam in England, *English Historical Review*, 47 (1932), 260-268.

The Early Schools of Oxford and Cambridge, *The Historian*, 5 (1943), 61-76.

The Patrons of *The Owl and the Nightingale, Philological Quarterly,* 48 (1969), 178-185.

The Triumph of Dignity over Order in England, *The Historian,* 9 (1947), 137-150.

Social Status at the Court of King John, *Speculum,* 12 (1937), 319-329.

Attestation of Charters in the Reign of John, *Speculum,* 15 (1940), 480-498.

The Canonization of Opposition to the King in Angevin England, *Haskins Anniversary Essays,* edited by C. H. Taylor (Boston, 1929), pp. 279-290.

Introduction

This collection of studies is designed to help celebrate the fiftieth anniversary of the publication of *The Renaissance of the Twelfth Century* by Charles H. Haskins. "The absence of any other work on this general theme must be the author's excuse for attempting a sketch where much must necessarily rest upon second-hand information." But this hardly does justice to Professor Haskins' mastery of the subject—the Latin side of the great intellectual development of the period.

That Dean Haskins found time to do it at all is remarkable. His Harvard duties alone were extensive: dean of the Graduate School of Arts and Sciences, lecturer and supervisor of the very large beginning history course (old History 1), professor in charge of undergraduate and graduate instruction in medieval history and in charge of the course frequented by all graduate history students in bibliography and historical criticism. In addition he had large responsibilities away from the university campus, especially in the American Historical Association. He took all of these duties very seriously.

At registration he seemed to be giving the students ahead of me in other subjects the same sympathetic attention that he gave me who intended to work with him. Looking back from later experience as a graduate professor, I can see why he was pleased to have a candidate who knew several languages and had studied at a foreign university, but then I merely noticed that he seemed quite pleased that I was intending to study medieval history. He even admitted me to his course in Latin Palaeography.

That course had not been given for several years and so attracted an entire generation of medieval students, about a dozen. With my lack of graduate experience, I sought anonymity in the class by taking a seat behind a very large man and sitting well back so that I was as little in evidence as possible. I marveled at the level of knowledge that was shown by other students and the erudition of our professor. On only two occasions did I try to answer questions. One was on the method of naming early medieval and late Roman cities: a city name with the name of the tribe in the genitive plural: Lutetia Parisorum, for Paris. I have forgotten the other one. Of his course in bibliography and historical criticism I remember one comment upon the subject: "Bibliography is a very specious form of erudition." Very properly it discouraged the normal tendency of graduate students to proliferate footnotes rather than to concentrate upon criticism of evidence.

Professor Haskins had given up his connection with History 1 before I became an assistant in it. However, he gave a lecture in the New Lecture Hall for some worthy cause which I attended and was always happy that I had seen him there. It was one of his lectures upon the medieval university.

Haskins' seminar in the second year dealt with materials being prepared for his *Studies in the History of Mediaeval Science*. Instead of assigning topics for papers, he presented problems upon which he was still working, often in the form of the evidence itself. We devoted our time to looking up information in the library as well as trying to master the critical questions involved. The experience showed us how far we still had to go before we really understood processes of historical criticism. When we added a little, we were quite proud of it: an item about Daniel of Merlai stumbled onto in an English document was my one addition!

And then the doctoral examinations. One can admire the ease with which the professors moved through a field with questions designed to find out one's knowledge and ignorance and the subsequent digging in more deeply to find out just how well one understood the questions. The examinations on the top floor of Widener were not open to the public and thus the professors did not hesitate to ask many questions which the candidate could not answer or answered badly. Even then Professor Haskins on occasion protected his candidate. Professor Blake, substituting for Professor Ferguson, asked me about a certain document from Alexandria which utterly baffled me. Professor Haskins then asked, "Professor Blake, how long have you had that document?" Professor Blake, "Last Saturday" (this was on a Thursday). Professor Haskins, "Mr. Russell, have you seen the lost books of Livy?" "No." Professor Haskins, "They have not been discovered yet." And not a person smiled.

After the examination a search for a dissertation subject led to tentatively accepting the career and poetry of Master Henry of Avranches, a court poet of the first half of the thirteenth century. Professor Haskins left for Europe in the spring of 1925 and returned in September. By very good luck I was able to show that a large manuscript of poems were nearly all by Henry and added to it another collection so that I had more than a hundred poems, many of which furnished biographical information. Professor Haskins was interested in part because of the extensive patronage Henry had enjoyed from a long list of patrons from the pope to relatively minor bishops in several countries. When Professor Haskins returned, he arranged for me to see him in his Widener office once a week and to bring a chapter each time. He took the material and commented upon it page by page in his own hand. I remember one incident especially well. The opening paragraph of one chapter was particularly chaotic. Professor Haskins asked, "Russell, what were you trying to say?" I answered in a few simple sentences. "Why didn't you say it that way?" To this day when struggling with writing, I hear his "Why didn't you say it that way?"

Just before the final examination he dropped in to see me in the University infirmary where I had been forced to go for a number of days. Years later I heard that when some students who had been slow in finishing their graduate study had mentioned to him after my final examination that I had been in the infirmary, he said, "Some of the rest of you ought to go to the hospital." He did not believe that graduate study should be a life work and strongly urged students to finish as rapidly as they could.

Upon a few occasions that last year I did help with items in the *Renaissance*. One was about the alleged two heads of St. John the Baptist: at Constantinople and Saint-Jean d'Angely. The other was to look up the alchemical works ascribed to Michael Scot and Friar Elias of Cortona of which several turned up in the extensive collection of manuscript catalogues that the Widener possessed.

Professor Haskins' meticulous and sympathetic attention was given despite an uncertain state of health and his need for use of his time and energy for his own research and writing. He had given much to his graduate students.

Historically graduate study has been a quite personal matter. Men have been proud that they studied with famous masters of the past—a MacIlwain, a Ferguson, or a Haskins. They have been proud to carry on the traditions of research of these men and have felt enthusiastic that they were in the stream of academic movement in the advancement of knowledge.

The personal side of historical research and composition also has not been much discussed. The late Professor Notestein of Yale was deeply interested in all types of research and writing, not merely that of history. He found that many writers had very definite daily habits—writing early in the morning, resting after lunch and then meditating for a time before the activities of the rest of the day. In this way the mind was conditioned to react to daily conditions and to produce at the appropriate time creative activity. Now obviously since most historians are professors there has to be an adjustment to teaching and research, not to mention committee and faculty meetings.

Such orderly and daily schedules would naturally be best suited to long continued research and writing efforts upon a large topic—such as the *Renaissance of the Twelfth Century*. There have been later works upon phases of that movement, notably the recent and fine general study by Professor Packard, another student of Professor Haskins: *Twelfth Century Europe*. In such an effort, moving from one topic to another systematically brings contingent ideas to mind in the construction of topics.

History is sometimes called 'our memory of the past.' For the historian the historical process is one of constructing a synthetic memory of his own about the past, parallel to his own memory of the past derived from his experience and reading. Continuous reading and study tends then to a usable knowledge of the past, not merely for general works, but for comparison with other ideas about the past. It can result in new constructions of the past in a rather haphazard and un-programmed way. This collection of articles is of this character rather than a *synthèse* of the past. It is an "effort to advance knowledge at critical points." The technology of such intellectual action has not been much discussed and might be of interest in a few examples of how such writing develops.

In 1932 the editor of the *De Expugnatione Lyzbonienis* proposed an author on the basis of the opening phrase, "Ost. de Bald. R. salutem." as Osbert de Bawdsey. However, another reader and I, looking at the footnote, read the phrase, "To Osbert of Bawdsey, R. sends greetings." From our acquaintance with medieval letters we knew that, unless the sender of a letter was of much higher social status than the recipient, he would have put his name last. So the author probably had the initial "R," not very helpful since it might be Ralph, Richard, Robert, Roger or even others, such as Ranulph, as in the study included below. Our memories almost instinctively produced the reaction.

In the summer of 1953 at the city archives of Bologna, I looked over one of the manuscripts of the lists of city householders of the mid-thirteenth century. Somehow I had thought of Bologna then as a relatively small city in which the Law University was a vital, if not dominant, institution. However, by quickly multiplying the number of folios by the average number of names of householders, derived from a small sampling, I saw that Bologna must have been a city of at least 50,000 and was perhaps even larger. Now the professors of Civil Law in a city of that size should have been men of great wealth, as indeed their tombs showed. A Civil Law School in such a setting would be very different from a law school in a small city. One could at once understand why classes by distinguished and wealthy lawyers were held at hours which did not conflict with law court hours and why the students took over the administration of the schools. Lawyers might well have taught then, as many do today in Italy, a relatively light class schedule, deriving from it minimum salaries but maximum prestige for high fees.

Many years ago my father and I were invited by friends to watch a deer hunt and attend breakfast and lunch for the hunters near Myrtle Beach, S.C. One of the members of the party was Senator "Cotton Ed" Smith, a long time U.S. senator from South Carolina. As a historian I thought that it might be interesting to see the senator in an unusual setting. However, the format of the hunt proved interesting also: the deer moved along trails from swamp to higher ground while the hunters were assigned, one to each trail, to watch for them. While considering the series of deaths along deer trails in the period 1050–1150 I remembered this pattern and believe that it was in principle the same as the modern one. Of course, men were not stationed behind the hunters up front, as in the Norman days.

Or the time that Professor Callahan read a paper at Kalamazoo about the possible poisoning of Eustace, the son of King Stephen of England. The description of Eustace's symptoms reminded me strongly of how I had felt when I had had an attack of acute appendicitis some years earlier. It led me to consider the question of poison and appendicitis and to the idea that appendicitis, without operations, could have led to a considerable number of deaths of "acute stomach trouble," perhaps as many as four or five per cent, before modern diagnosis and surgery.

Between 1929 and 1931 I borrowed books from the medieval collection which James F. Williard had built up in the University of Colorado Library, mostly of documents whose charter witness lists I examined for names of writers of thirteenth century England. It was an efficient research venture since it enabled me to check documents for all 300 writers rather than to look at documents for just one or a few writers. As Charles Bémont remarked in a review of my *Dictionary of Writers of Thirteenth Century England*, it might well be done for other centuries of English writers and for other countries as well.

However, while looking at those lists I seemed to see that witnesses appeared in a definite order, even in the lists in small villages. Together with the dean of the school, New Mexico Normal University, we worked out a mathematical test and saw beyond doubt that there was a high degree of orderliness in all the lists. Undoubtedly people sat in definite order and were recorded in such an order. Eventually, however, it was clear that even people at a table could be recorded in two ways, by order (clergy-laity or subdivisions) or by dignity alone. That is, some high lay officials could have their names recorded before those of lesser clergy. One arrangement would account for the English House of Lords–House of Commons organization (essentially one of dignity) while most others were based on Estates or order.

Another case turned up with regard to the use of machines for statistics, which I was using in Chapel Hill in the laboratory of a tennis companion, Dudley Cowden, a distinguished statistician in the School of Business Administration there. He had just acquired a machine which made it easy to solve correlations by the "least squares" method. At the time I had found the percentages of men listed by height and by color (nigrescence) by county in the nineteenth century by Beddoe, an anthropologist. I also knew of the percentages by counties of the several classes of man in Domesday Book. Here was a chance to see if the anthropologists' principle of continuation of physical characteristics was true and also to have some fun with the machine. The well-known assumption that the English areas of the north with large numbers of Scandinavian immigrants (liberi) would have a higher percentage of tall blonds proved accurate: the correlation was good. Then we tried the correlations with the villani and the cottarii: there was little correlation so they were evidently economic groups rather than physical. Finally we ran a correlation between the servi and found an even higher correlation between numbers of these and shortness and darkness than with the tall light liberi. So the short dark folk had remained a separate group from neolithic times even into the nineteenth century: the persistence of physical type was no myth.

Not so pleasant was another unwitting adventure into

historical fact. When our family returned from a year in England, in 1939, we were welcomed by a host of fleas left by two dogs and three cats from our previous renters, three weeks before. This was time for the fleas to multiply into several hundreds and for them to become very hungry. However, they obviously preferred two of us and avoided, if possible, the other two, a fact of flea life that we later heard from many who lived in flea country. Now here was a possible explanation of why, if plague was 60 to 70% fatal, only a third of the people (or even less) died when presumably most would have been exposed. This was really learning history the hard way!

One can see that in these instances of origination of research, there is a large factor of chance or accident. Indeed it is doubtful if one can foresee and plan for all types or eventualities of study of historical sources. There is a further danger of being bound by historical conventions or fixed ideas, even among the most learned. It is, for instance, virtually impossible for one interested in extrasensory perception to get his articles published in reputable journals, so great is the antagonism against this field of study, even after the brilliant work of the Rhines in the field. Less antagonistic but still there, is the strong feeling against sociology. That field's special terminology is frequently defined as "jargon," while historical references to palaeography, diplomatic, prosopography and other rather unusual words are perfectly proper for historians to employ. Or try to get a textbook published which emphasizes population and see what happens. These imply definite limitations upon the study of history.

One method of passing beyond conventional limitations imposed by past graduate training is to get acquainted with literature in other disciplines. There is, of course, *The Journal of Interdisciplinary History*, which admits articles from many fields of study, but one who works in odd fields may find that he quickly runs out of journals that will publish his material. However, the study of nonhistorical or even nonmedieval materials often suggests new methods or new ideas that may be profitably used in medieval fields. Nearly all of my ideas about population came originally from acquaintance with courses and personnel in sociology at the University of North

Carolina, one of whose main interests was population. One need not apologize for work with Odum, Hagood and Vance: they were all presidents of the Population Association of America.

Every professor has at his disposal one great source of criticism of his work and even new ideas for research—his students. If he allows them to raise questions with no threats of reprisal should they disagree with him, he will usually be rewarded by very valuable hints in regard to his ideas and teaching. Even, or perhaps more often, freshmen give remarkably clever views. For one thing, they are usually not as inhibited or awed in class as upper classmen and, if they do not understand what is being said, do not hesitate to express their questioning. And just try to explain in detail feudalism, manorialism, or scholastic philosophy and find out what details you do not know or cannot explain properly.

Finally, one needs experiences to realize that even the greatest can make mistakes and that therefore every statement by no matter how great an authority is subject to criticism. Two instances of this as a graduate student shocked me at the time, but were valuable in reducing my respect for infallibility. There is a two-column life of William of Ramsey in the *Dictionary of National Biography* by a well known medievalist. In my study of Henry of Avranches I found that William never existed but was a result of a series of mistakes, all understandable, based in part upon a mistaken attribution of Henry's poems to the character. The great German historian, F. Liebermann, examined the manuscript of Henry's poems in the summer of 1877 and correctly reported in an article in the *Neues Archiv* (IV,1879,p.23) that most of the poems were by Master Henry. Fourteen years later in the same periodical (VIII,1893,p.227) he quoted information about the same manuscript, secured from a less-skilled friend in England, that the collection was mostly of the poems of William of Ramsey. He had either forgotten or mistrusted his earlier study.

One final word about the chronology of the enclosed studies. Like Professor Haskins's "twelfth century," it begins earlier, at Domesday Book of 1086 and continues later, generally through the reign of King John, although two, at least, continue through later centuries. I have not revised them nor added to them: surprisingly little work has been done in most of these fields. The first study seemed to provide a good introduction although it was written as part of a text for the history of history writing, but it includes some ideas not generally given in such books.

Many of these topics might well be subjected to further research. Charter witness lists still offer opportunities for identification of persons and of social status, even of political ideas. The clerks who wrote the charters which preserve such large amounts of information about medieval life deserve study. Prosopographical studies of medieval writers can still be useful. Some fine work is being written about canonization of opposition to later medieval English kings and even of royalty itself. Perhaps these studies may suggest and stimulate research in the great field of medieval life of which Charles Homer Haskins was a master.

CHAPTER 1

The Writing of History in the Twelfth Century

General Character of the Intellectual Revival

During the course of the tenth century, both the tempo and character of European civilization underwent significant changes. The population grew more rapidly than during the several preceding centuries. There was a notable quickening of trade and there were many evidences of growing intellectual and political interests and ambitions. The restless vikings left their mark on Iceland, Greenland, England, France, Southern Italy and Russia. Meanwhile, the cities of Italy and elsewhere grew rapidly in commercial and industrial strength as their merchants traversed the water and land routes of the known world. The thrust of these movements caused Christian Europe to shift from a defensive toward an aggressive position in its relations with the pagan and Mohammedan states of the Slavic northeast, in Spain, in Italy and especially in the Near East.

This expansive elan pervaded the European intellectual world as well. Since it was chiefly a Latin world, the revival of learning, usually called the Renaissance of the twelfth century, was actually a re-examination of earlier Latin literature accompanied by a modest literary development of its own. The Latin Classics aroused more interest than during the preceding millenium. Roman Law was studied ardently at Bologna and

1

influenced political thinking in many lands. The study of theology, particularly at the University of Paris, occupied many of the better minds of the day. Much rhymed poetry, expressive of deep emotions, was written. An interest in science led to extensive translations from the Arabic as well as from Greek in Spain and Italy. As one would expect, this intellectual enthusiasm institutionalized itself in an increasing number of schools of higher learning and eventually the university.

Inferior Status of Historical Studies

These developments were reflected in quantitative, if not qualitative, changes in the historiographical activities of the period. But in this period, no office of historian existed, nor did anyone devote full time to the teaching of history. This subject remained as it had been, a part of grammar, and was treated as such—hence, there was no historian to define the functions of his office or consider rigorously the implications of history as a field of knowledge.[1]

The writing of history was largely determined in the later medieval period by the patrons of the historians, the function and purpose of their writing, and by the personalities of the writers themselves. The chief patrons were monastic houses and reigning families. However, feudal lords and cathedral chapters often also fostered this work. Some of the rising communes patronized history but they did not wield an outstanding influence upon historical writing until the thirteenth century. The literary tradition also tended to remain unchanged although the growing influence of the classics appears in greater dependence upon them, resulting in an increase in the size of accounts. The subject matter tended to be general or miscellaneous, although such spectacular movements as the Crusades, the rise of the communes, and the development of national monarchy were bound to excite historical interest.

Patrons and Literary Centers[2]

Monasteries. The monasteries continued to be the great literary centers. More learned men lived together there than elsewhere, thus providing each other with an intellectual stimulus. They had access to history books and often also to extensive collections of documents, together with the leisure to read and study them. Furthermore, the officials of the monastery often travelled widely and all travellers usually availed themselves of monastic hospitality. The chronicler, Gervase of Canterbury, tells us that he wrote at the instance of fellow monks: he, like many other chroniclers, was a sacristan in charge of the books of the house.[3]

Monastic libraries were usually collections of books housed in a conveniently placed closet or press, often in the passage between the choir and the chapter house. Many medieval volumes still bear the press marks, usually of three characters (for instance, A II e), where the first indicates the tier of the press, the second, the shelf, and the third, the place in the division of the shelf. Occasionally an attempt at alphabetical arrangement was made, and the results recorded in a list or catalogue. As a rule, the monastic library had a collection of the Fathers, but rarely had the classical historians or books defining chronology and lengths of reigns or other books of ready reference.[4] "The work of the historians never attained the same degree of popularity in the medieval libraries as did other types of literature." Nevertheless, the ber of medieval histories in some libraries must have been considerable, to judge from the number of authors cited by some writers.

After 1050, there was a tremendous increase in the number of religious houses established. The great Cluniac Reform was followed by numerous foundations of Cistercian monks and Austin canons, and, to a lesser extent, of Benedictine and Premonstratensian houses. However, the number of chronicles did not increase in the same proportion. The newer houses were often smaller, poorer and, at least after the first generation, less attractive to intellectually gifted young men. The newer orders like that of Cluny, for example, either burdened their members with more religious services, or like the Cistercians, located them in country districts unfavorable to intellectual stimulus. So, while houses of all groups wrote chronicles, for the most part, they are the work of the great Benedictine houses, usually located in the urban centers.

Royal Courts. The royal courts often included men of learning as well as men of action. The court of Henry II of England, as well as the Norman court of Sicily, was famous for such groups. These courts were centers of the kinds of activity which would normally find their way into the chronicles. However, the medieval king and his court were usually migratory. At that time books were heavy and could not be readily transported with the court. The royal clerks were also usually too busy to write history on the move even if they were so inclined. Except for a few countries, records were seldom enrolled and properly recorded. Even the thought of attaining perpetual fame in this world *was* essentially a secular idea—the careers of few rulers were exemplary enough to justify their biographies as works of edification. Thus, clerks usually postponed their writing until they were away from the court.

The close association of the monastery of St. Denis with the French kings is paralleled by a series of chronicles emanating from that house, probably initiated by the great abbot Suger (*ca.* 1081-1151) and covering the history of France. This series continued into the fifteenth century.[5]

The only case in which a medieval European historian seems to have been expressly employed to write a history was that of William (1130-84), who became archbishop of Tyre and the greatest historian of the Crusades.[6] He was apparently chosen by King Amaury of Jerusalem about 1167 to write the record of the king's deeds, which were already noteworthy and promised to achieve even greater fame in the future. This effort was a spectacular success and suggests what might have been produced by similar encouragements. For the most part, such cases of association of prominent historians with great courts were more or less accidental. The court of Henry II of England was remarkable for its writing, but the two historians of his reign, Roger of Hoveden and whoever wrote the chronicle dedicated to Abbot Benedict of Peterborough, were only casually associated with it and received no known patronage.[7] A member of that court, the witty Welshman, Walter Map, wrote *Courtiers Trifles* giving a candid account of its activities[8] and explaining tacitly why so little writing was done there.

Cathedral Chapters. A third center of history writing was the cathedral. Learned men belonged to the Cathedral Chapters and, although frequently busy or even away from the cathedral, they often had much time at their disposal and could enjoy greater stability than the royal court. Moreover, the eleventh and twelfth centuries saw the chapters better equipped to serve as intellectual centers than a later date. The chapter, then, was closely knit, often eating together and drawing its expenses from common endowments. Subsequently, it became the practice for the common funds to be divided into prebends and for the chapter members to go their separate ways. Furthermore, their schools were at their height, during the eleventh and twelfth centuries, often drawing excellent teachers and students. Later, they were to be overshadowed by the rising universities. In this period, too, many canons and even bishops wrote history. Proportionately, they probably furnished as many historians as did the monasteries. Like the monasteries, they often had libraries and were located in situations favorable for the accumulation of news.[9]

The members of cathedral chapters occasionally made use of official journeys to seek information. Thus, Henry, Archdeacon of Huntingdon (d. *ca.* 1158), tells how he stopped at Bec in 1139[10] and was shown a copy of Geoffrey of Monmouth's book by another famous chronicler, Robert of Torigni. Henry apparently grew up in the episcopal family of Lincoln and was encouraged to write a history of the English from the time of Caesar. He commences Book III as follows:[11]

> Now (1088) I have to deal with events which have passed under my own observation, or which have been told me by eye-witnesses of them. I have to relate how the Almighty alienated both favour and rank from the English nation as it deserved, and caused it to cease to be a people. It will appear also how he began to afflict the Normans themselves, the instruments of his will with various calamities.

Henry's views are a characteristic rationalization of the ruling class, but Henry was also too honest to pass over certain obvious failings of the Normans.

Cities. Parallel to and part of the general growth in population was the rapid increase in the size of communes and cities
of Europe in this period. This development was more rapid in
northern Italy than elsewhere, producing, with the aid of
widespread lay education, the earliest civic chronicles. Most of
them were anonymous, even those of the great cities of Venice
and Florence in this period.[12] There were few civic chronicles
in the rest of Europe. The most remarkable achievement in the
encouragement of history writing occurred in Genoa.

On the basis of existing evidence the first official recogni-
tion of civic history was by Genoa, whose consuls and council
in 1152 honored the historian Caffaro of Caschifellone by de-
creeing that his history should be copied with care and preserved in the city archives. Caffaro was about 72 then, but
continued to write history until within three years of his death
at the age of 86. In addition to the annals, he wrote accounts of
two Genoese expeditions in which he participated. He was
apparently an able citizen who served his city well in many
ways. The city commissioned the chancellor Obertus (1164-
73), and later, the notary Ottobonus (1189-96), to continue *The
Chronicle.*[13] These writers were laymen who shared in civic life
and thus brought to their writing an exact and detailed knowledge of city life.

Papacy. Although the Church was the greatest European
institution of the period, no general church history was then
written. The chief focus of ecclesiastical interest was theological rather than historical. Instead of producing a great church
history, the ecclesiastical writers have left us a series of great
theological works. The most widely used of these was the
Sentences of Peter Lombard. There is little history in it, since it
is mainly devoted to theological relationships in which the
earth and its inhabitants occupy only a minor part.

Historical Tradition and Criticism

Medieval histories fall into three main types: past history
based upon earlier writings, general chronicles of miscellaneous subject matter, and specialized accounts. The first usually
took the form of a world chronicle, of which there were very

many. The second and third were often discussions or records of current events. The value of the first has been overlooked by modern historians who have emphasized the other types. However, in a study of historiography the former are also important, especially when studied for a critique of historical sources for a particular period.

Popular Histories. The study of past history naturally involved the composition of a pattern of universal history. This had been standardized for the Middle Ages by Eusebius and Jerome and placed into chronological periods for the six days of eternity of which the sixth began with the birth of Christ and continued to the present. The seventh began with the end of the Earth. As a pattern, it was an idea which was only occasionally followed. Within this framework there was room for individual differences. "It was not until the twelfth century that chroniclers began to copy standard epitomes of earlier history without reworking the material."[14] In England, however, the influence of Bede was very powerful upon the leading twelfth century historians,[15] while Orosius' *History Against the Pagans* set the pattern for ancient History.

The greatest twelfth century follower of Bede was William of Malmesbury (?-1142) whose chief works were: *Lives of the Kings of England* and *Lives of the Bishops and Abbots of England.* His easy running account may be illustrated by a paragraph about the well-known historian, Marianus Scotus:[16]

> During this emperor's reign (Henry IV, 1056-1106), flourished Marianus Scotus, first a monk of Fulda, afterwards a recluse at Mainz, who, by renouncing the present life, secured the happiness of that which is to come. During his long continued leisure, he examined the writers on chronology, and discovered the disagreement of the cycles of Dionysius the Little with the evangelical computation. Wherefore reckoning every year from the beginning of the world he added twenty-two, which were wanting, to the above mentioned cycles; but he had few or no followers of his opinion. Wherefore, I am often led to wonder, why such unhappiness should attach to the learned of our time, that in so great a number of scholars and students, pale with watching, scarcely one can obtain unqualified commendation for knowledge. So

much does ancient custom please, and so little encouragement, though deserved, is given to new discoveries,
however consistent with truth. All are anxious to grovel
in the old track, and everything modern is condemned:
and therefore as patronage alone can foster genius, when
that is withheld, every exertion languishes.

Marianus' attempt to revise chronology was not very successful, yet his work was immensely popular. He was used
and commented upon by a second great twelfth century historian, Ordericus Vitalis, whose work had very limited circulation. Ordericus was a monk of St. Evroul in Normandy (1075-
ca. 1141). In his first book, he includes material chronologically
up to his own day. The second book is concerned largely with
the apostles and the popes. The third book deals with St.
Evroul and Norman affairs. The other ten books, telling of
more recent centuries, are heterogeneous in character, but
present a tremendous amount of valuable information.[17]

Sigebert of Gembloux (d. 1112), has been called "the best
of the universal chroniclers of the Middle Ages," although this
claim is much disputed.[18] His *Chronographia* used more than
fifty other works as sources and in turn was copied by more
than that number of later writers.

Study of Classical History. The tradition, as presented by the
standard epitomes, could only be improved by a study of
classical and early medieval sources themselves and by the
development of historical criticism. There was much ancient
history reproduced in the writings of the chroniclers, some
directly; even more was probably taken from those collections
of excerpts called florilegia such as the *Liber Floridus* (1120),
canon of Lambert of St. Omer in Flemish Belgium.[19] It included maps, genealogies, and discussions of chronology
which might be useful to the historian. It is heavily local in its
choice of subject matter but draws from a very wide circle of
histories and other literature.

The study of the classics was hindered by the inaccessibil-
ity of some of the greatest historians, particularly of the
Greeks, and by the lack of interest in their study.[20] To this,
Lambert of Hersfeld[21] (d. ca. 1088), however, is an exception.
His works provide "An excellent illustration of the effective
use of Livy, Sallust, and Suetonius by a medieval scholar who

could profit both by their historical content and by their rhetorical values." Even Lambert's very marked bias with respect to the history of his own time had classical precedents.[22] Lambert illustrates what might have been done if the historical effort of his time had been organized professionally. The general tendency was to copy what one had rather than to seek for better authorities or for original sources.

In contrast to Lambert's historical achievement, may be placed the inaccuracy of Geoffrey of Monmouth's *Historia Regum Brittaniae*, if indeed that work is to be considered as history rather than propaganda or fable.[23] His account of the genealogy and succession of kings contradicted Bede's evidence. If Geoffrey's picture of Arthur was true, Arthur must have been a greater ruler than Alexander and a greater prophet than Isaiah. These are the criticisms which a canon of Newburgh in England, William (1136-*ca.* 1198), voiced in the last half of the twelfth century against the authenticity of Geoffrey's books. The brilliance of this insight into ancient history immediately arouses one's curiosity about what William might have done to vulnerable sources, but in settling the starting point of his excellent history within a century, of his own time, William did not seek the opportunity.[24] Of the two, however, Geoffrey's work was immensely more popular and was used by even reputable historians during the rest of the Middle Ages.

Historical Criticism. A penetrating historical critic of the twelfth century is Otto of Freising (*ca.* 1110-58). He records the story of the destruction of Mohammedan idols by Bishop Tiemo in the east, but doubts the story because Mohammedans do not have idols.[25] Indeed, his description of Mohammedanism is very fair considering the scope of knowledge in his day. Even more important is his denial of the validity of the Donation of Constantine. Imperial advocates, he states, point out that Constantine actually gave the western half of the Empire to his son, which would not have been done by so devout a ruler if he had given it previously to the Church, nor would the great Theodosius have appropriated it later if it had belonged to the pope.[26] Here, of course, the sharpening impetus of controversy to criticism is clear. Otto, a Cistercian monk and later bishop, was a member of the German imperial

house, and had studied at the University of Paris. There he
may have been a student of Hugh of St. Victor (d. 1143), whose
Book of the Three Most Important Factors in Events represented a
real, though not very influential attempt to inculcate accuracy
in describing historical incidents.[27]

The principles which had interested Hugh had already
been tried in a series of notable works by Gregory of Catino, a
monk of Farfa in Italy, just before the end of the eleventh
century. He drew up first of all a great register of the many
documents of Farfa, charters from popes, emperors and other
feudal lords, the famous Farfa Register, or, as he liked to call it,
the *Liber Gemniagraphus sive Cleronomialis Farfensis*. He was
very careful to copy correctly, even including all of the witnesses in the charters, and tried not to guess in regard to words
difficult to read in the text.[28] He followed this with another
register of temporary contracts and less important documents,
the *Largitorum* and a topographical index of the Register called
the *Floriger Cartarum*. On the basis of these great collections, he
wrote a *Chronicle of Farfa*, mostly about the monastery. The
idea of proceeding from a careful edition of documents to a
narrative history was excellent, even though in execution the
narrative tended to resemble a string of documents. This
promising development was followed only in a few places,
mostly in the south of Italy.[29]

Outside of strictly historical literature, historical criticism
of a high order was presented by Guibert de Nogent (1053-
1124), in his book on relics and their authentication. Again a
very practical matter had forced decisions and thus had neces-
sitated some method of criticism.[30] Guibert also wrote a story
of the First Crusade, *Gesta Dei per Francos*, and an autobiography.[31] All of these works were well done.

A serious deficiency of much of medieval historical writing
was the absence of historical sense.[32] Like the painters and
sculptors in dealing with Biblical characters, they imagined that
people of ancient times dressed as in their own time. Presumably they thought and acted much the same, and used the same
languages. The result was that anachronisms abounded.

The writing of contemporary history involved other types
of historical study. The sources were usually common information which was in circulation and which was known to the

historian in the monastery. The difference in the historians of that age lay chiefly in their instinct for accuracy; few of them apparently took the trouble to check their information. Some believed more easily than others; most of them accepted even Geoffrey of Monmouth uncritically. Then, too, some had better channels of news than others. One of the best contemporary statements of a sound historical approach appears in the chronicle of Helmold, Priest of Bosau (*ca.* 1120-72), entitled *The Chronicle of the Slavs.* [33]

> In portraying deeds of men, as in chiseling out the most subtle carving, there ought to be a sincere concern that one be not led from the way of truth by favor, by hatred, or by fear. (I dedicate this book to the venerable lords and brethren of Lubeck) in the hope of rendering honor to men of the present day and of contributing profit through the knowledge of facts to men of the future. And I hope that I shall not be without some little gain from the prayers of the great men who may read this little book.

Hagiography. The pattern of hagiography was well established so that a capable writer could produce a creditable biography with no great difficulty. The early life, miracles at conception or birth, schooling, and early temptations of saints seldom occupied much space. The adult life was usually given in detail, since normally much more was known about it in the twelfth century than had been the case earlier. The miracles performed or witnessed by saints are described in detail. The biography was nearly always a straight-forward account, which runs to many modern printed pages with a minimum of embellishment. As history they are often quite useful—much can be learned from even the shortest of them, because they frequently present information which chronicles seldom recorded. The miracles with their illustrations of psychoneurotic behavior, have not been sufficiently studied by modern historians. Of autobiography, there was little; what there was is interesting for the presentation had to be original as there was no tradition for the autobiographer to follow. [34]

Functions and Purposes of Historical Writing

Medieval historical writing was neither a full time occupation, nor professional. Some of it is definitely for edification, and probably all of it was considered so. Other writers were impressed by the greatness of such movements as the Crusades, particularly of those in which they participated. Occasionally the writing was used to defend a position or a course of action in the past. Finally, much medieval historical literature had no other object than to record current events of general interest. Naturally, the function and purpose of the writing influenced the author's form and the organization of his composition.

Recording of Current Events. The mind of the twelfth century was a good bit like that of the modern newspaper reader. It was interested in the lives and deaths of outstanding world leaders (popes, kings, lords), of important local characters, and in great and unusual events. These accounts were often arranged in approximately chronological order, particularly local events, since they were usually recorded in the more extensive chronicles not long after they happened. News items of distant events came in more slowly and might find their way into chronicles only after local events of earlier months. Within each year almost no attempt was normally made to arrange items by subject matter. Monks wrote surprisingly little about their own religious houses; their attention was largely centered upon the outside world.

An exception to this rule is the great historian of the mother house of the Benedictines, Monte Cassino, Leo Marsicanus of Ostia (*ca.* 1046-1117), keeper of the archives and librarian of his house. Abbot Oderisius first invited him to write a biography of the abbot who became Pope Stephen IX. This work was subsequently enlarged into a full length story of the monastery. Leo explained his method of collection:[35]

> Then I sought out such little writing as seemed to treat of the matter, composed in a ragged style and briefly, and chief of these the chronicle of the Abbot John—also I collected the books necessary for this task, namely the history of the Longobards, and the chronicles of the Roman emperors, and pontiffs; likewise searched diligently for privileges and charters as well as concessions and documents with various titles (such as those of Roman pontiffs, of various emperors, kings, princes,

> dukes, counts, and other illustrious and faithful men)
> that were left to us after the two destructions by fire of this
> convent although I could not find even all of them; lastly I
> questioned scrupulously all who had either heard of or
> seen any deeds of modern times or of abbots.

Such careful methods were characteristic of Leo, who produced an admirable and unusual work. He later became a
cardinal and a very distinguished churchman.

Unfortunately, this fine work did not necessarily establish
a tradition at Monte Cassino. A successor of Leo as keeper of
the archives and librarian was Peter the Deacon (*ca.* 1107-
1140), who continued the chronicle of the house and copied
out great cartularies of the documents of the house. He was
always interesting but frequently inaccurate, especially where
the interests of his family or the monastery were concerned,
and very gullible. Peter also wrote saints' lives and a series of
biographies of the great monks of Monte Cassino. He was thus
remarkable for his versatility. With him, outstanding historical
writing ceased at Monte Cassino.[36] Thus, the historical accounts of even one of the greatest of the medieval monastic
houses were incidental rather than a primary interest of its
librarians and keepers of archives.

Close to documentary history and its emphasis upon administration are treatises upon its practices, like the account of
English law, possibly by Ranulf of Glanvill, and of the Exchequer by Richard FitzNeal,[37] treasurer of England, 1158-98,
and bishop of London, 1189-98. Both of them give an intimate
view of the working of a remarkably efficient medieval government. They give, of course, a much better view than that
derived from occasional items and even running accounts of
important events in the chronicle of Roger of Hoveden, who
shared to some extent in the governmental machine of England. These two types of materials enable the historian to gain
a well-rounded picture of contemporary practical politics.

Those writings which were polemical and written to prove
a case often made important contributions to historical criticism. The long series of pamphlets which grew out of the
controversy between the emperor and the pope in the latter
half of the eleventh century stimulated political theory in a

14   TWELFTH CENTURY STUDIES

remarkable fashion.[38] The pity is that except in the case of
Thomas Becket the English were not aroused in the same way
in the twelfth century. Even polemical pamphlets illustrating
the trends of thought in the time of the formation of the
English constitution would have been invaluable.

Pride in Achievement. Pride in achievement was one of the
causes for the writing of history. Sometimes this pride is not
easily distinguishable from special pleading, as is the case of
Archbishop Romuald of Salerno (1153-1181), who, by virtue of
his high office, was a constant attendant at the court of the
Norman kings of Sicily. He was an outstanding diplomat and
participated in many of the great events of the period, such as
the diplomatic negotiations at Venice in 1177 involving the
emperor, the pope, the communes of northern Italy and his
own master, William II. Romuald of Salerno obviously had a
fine education and wrote in an eloquent style and for the most
part accurately, if from the royal point of view. His contemporary, Hugo Falcandus, wrote from the standpoint of the barons
of the kingdom, who, like most feudal barons, were frequently
in rebellion against the king and saw historical events in a quite
different light. He apparently came from outside of the Norman kingdom but had been well received there; he wrote
excellent Latin, was reasonably impartial and very discerning
in regard to events in that kingdom.[39]

Edification. The types of historical material suitable for
edification were several; prominent among them were the
saints' lives, the stories of missionary effort and of the crusades
and even the general chronicles. Indeed, one phase of scriptural interpretation practised constantly in sermons, as well as
in the theological classroom, was called the historical and
involved an historical explanation of the text. The methods of
interpretation naturally spread beyond Scriptural texts, and
thus the use of history was very practical.[40] Hagiography was
also used constantly in the monasteries, where private and
public reading of the lives of the saints was a constant form of
edification. The chronicles of Helmold, mentioned above, and
of Adam of Bremen tell of the advance of Christendom in
northern Europe.[41]

The Crusades naturally inspired authors to write; they

were important as wars and even more as holy ventures upon a vast scale in an ecclesiastical age. Each Crusade had its chroniclers as did usually each contingent within the Crusade. Most of the accounts were written by clerks accompanying the troops, who wrote them upon their return to Europe.[42] The most important and comprehensive was by William, Archbishop of Tyre (1130-84). Led for the most part by distinguished rulers or nobles, the Crusades, in many respects, resemble ordinary feudal wars and operations, but they were also a manifestation of expansion on the part of the dominant class, an expansion that failed.

While the greater crusading efforts were led by great feudal lords, at least two expeditions led by lesser people succeeded spectacularly: the Crusade of 1147 which captured Lisbon and that of 1189 which took Silves. Both cities remained permanently a part of Portugal.[43] In contrast to the heroics, the bitter hostility among Christians and the feudal instability of the Near East Crusades, these ventures were more sober and probably better organized; the chronicles about them are businesslike and detailed.

One purpose of historical study is to analyze the present in terms of the past, to try to see what has been the course of human events in order to understand the world today, and, perhaps, to gauge the possibilities of the future. This was not a medieval aim, because the Middle Ages had its own philosophy of history; it thought that it knew, as far as was necessary, what had happened in the past and that it could prophesy with reasonable accuracy about the future. Thus, it was only natural that Bishop Otto of Freising should include a book on the future in his great work on universal history. *The Book of Revelation* was of tremendous value because of its vivid picture of the future. In a sense, then, since the answers to the main questions about the past and future of the human race were known, the answers to the lesser questions of history were unimportant; therefore historical criticism was not particularly necessary.

Personality

The Twelfth Century Renaissance was not an individualistic age like the better known and later Renaissance. Rather conventional by tradition, its historians could not appeal to great audiences, and, thus, had no incentive for popular writing. The scholars, such as Abelard, who craved intellectual leadership or the admiration of even the academic audience, might better teach theology or the arts at the schools. History had few attractions for dynamic and vibrant personalities. The chroniclers wrote in terms of men or of incidents rather than of institutions or culture as a whole, while leaving relatively little information about themselves. A very large portion of the monastic chronicles and even of other historical literature is anonymous, and thus gives little idea of the writers or of the circumstances of writing. The tradition is one in which the subject matter is personal but authorship is quite impersonal. The few but rather well-known autobiographies include those by Peter Abelard, Guibert of Nogent, Gerald of Wales, and Jocelin of Brakelond.[44]

An Official as Historian. These, however, are not really typical twelfth century historians. The career of William, Archbishop of Tyre, can be cited as an example of the more professional historians. He was not trained especially as a historian, but had such a career offered him as part of an official and clerical career by King Amaury in 1167. His education as an historian was partly by experience in the diplomatic and clerical world of the day and partly by the reading of chronicles, both Latin and Arabic. His shift from theoretical to actual knowledge of politics seems to have been accompanied by a growing faith in the importance of mankind in his own history. His work then became characterized by six qualities which indicated an essential greatness of mind: objectivity, freedom from prejudice, critical attitude toward his sources, wide range of interests, analysis of cause and effect, and concern about style. His faults were carelessness about chronology and professional bias in favor of the Church.[45]

A Scholarly Historian. Interest in scholars and intellectual history appears in the chronicle of Robert of Torigni, who became Abbot of Mont Saint-Michel (1154-86). He is conventional in relying heavily upon Sigebert of Gembloux for history before his own time, but Robert's work records, as few others

do, events of consequence for intellectual history: the translations of James of Venice in 1128; Gratian's *Decretals* in 1130; the
death of Hugh of St. Victor in 1143, who left many books as a
monument to his knowledge; the death of Abbot Rogert,
"erudite in both Scriptures"; the law book of Master Vacarius
in England; the elevation of Geoffrey Arthur (of Monmouth) to
a bishopric in 1152, "who translated the history of the Kings of
Britain from Celtic to Latin"; the translation of a Greek book at
the request of Pope Eugenius in 1152; the death of Bishop
Gilbert of Poitiers, "who commented brilliantly upon the
Psalms and Pauline Epistles" in 1154; the long series of translations from the Greek by Burgundio the Pisan in 1181. The
chronicle, also, records the usual data, but was wide in its
reach. The Mount was a very revered shrine, visited by many
important people who became Robert's informants.[46]

The Typical Historian. What then was the twelfth century
historian? He was obviously not a professional; none was paid
for writing history and none taught history as a discipline. He
did not have even the idea of history as the changing, developing culture of the past. He had no function in society as a
historian; his history writing might interest or flatter or edify
but it conveyed little understanding of the past. In short,
history was essentially a pleasant hobby for a variety of men.
Some of these were men of importance in the world, some
were obscure monks in lesser monasteries. But even the historian's historian, Sigebert of Gembloux, was the author of a
rather meager chronicle in comparison with the fuller histories
of his own day. The brilliant and detailed accounts were written by men whose individual genius was not overcome by the
jejune tradition of the time or whose interest in a great en-
deavor led irresistibly to a full and interesting exposition.

Nevertheless, historical writing did advance in this period. The chronicles increased both in yearly material recorded
and in breadth of interest. The conception of a philosophy of
history was carried further by such writers as Otto of Freising.
Well organized biographies of saints and some good character
sketches of secular leaders appear. A beginning is made in the
keeping of archives and in the production of records. Even
criticism advanced occasionally in such writers as William of

Newburgh and Guibert of Nogent. And Geoffrey of Monmouth did appear then—well, he did help with a long and entertaining series of stories about King Arthur. With the growth of literacy and the appearance of advanced schools, history might expect a brilliant future, particularly if the processes of definition applied to theology would be applied to history.

Notes

1. On the place of history in the schools see E. M. Sanford, "The Study of Ancient History in the Middle Ages," *Journal of the History of Ideas,* V (1944), pp. 21–43, especially pp. 28–43. The finest study of this period is C. H. Haskins, *The Renaissance of the Twelfth Century;* see also Robert S. Lopez, "Still Another Renaissance," *The American Historical Review,* LVIII, No. 1 (October, 1951), pp. 1–22.
2. On intellectual centers see especially C. H. Haskins, *op.cit.,* pp. 32–69.
3. *Gesta Regum,* II, p. 3.
4. J. S. Beddie, "Libraries in the Twelfth Century: Their Catalogues and Contents," *Haskins Anniversary Essays,* pp. 1–24, especially p. 18.
5. A. Molinier, *Les Sources de l'histoire de France,* II, pp. 181–184; III, pp. 97–104.
6. A. C. Krey, "William of Tyre, the Making of an Historian in the Middle Ages," *Speculum,* XVI (1941), 149–166. William's chronicle is edited in the *Recueil des Historiens des Croisades,* Historiens Occidentaux I (1844); it is translated by A. C. Krey and E. A. Babcock, *A History of Deeds Done Beyond the Sea,* 2 vols.
7. C. H. Haskins, "Henry II as a Patron of Literature," *Essays in Medieval History Presented to Thomas Frederick Tout,* (1925), pp. 71–77.
8. Edited by M. R. James; translated by M. B. Ogle and F. Tupper, *Master Walter Map's Book, de Nugis Curialium.* Map lived through the reign of Henry II (1154–1189) and died about 1209; he was a clerk, precentor of London.
9. The French chapters seem to have produced little.
10. *Chronicles of the Reigns of Stephen, Henry II and Richard I,* IV, pp. 65–75.
11. Henry's chronicle is translated by Thomas Forester. The quotation is from p. 222. Another cathedral writer of England was Ralph de Diceto, who was dean of London, and thus in an excellent position to write his histories, edited by W. Stubbs, *Opera Historica.*
12. U. Balzani, *Early Chronicles of Europe: Italy,* pp. 293–315. For Castaro in Genoa, pp. 303–304.
13. These Genoese chronicles are edited by Pertz, *Cafart et Continuatorum Annales Januenses,* M. G. H. SS. XVIII.
14. E. M. Sanford, "The Study of Ancient History in the Middle Ages," *Journal of the History of Ideas,* V (1944), p. 32; H. Buttenwieser, "Popular

Authors of the Middle Ages: The Testimony of the Manuscripts,"
Speculum, XVII (1942), pp. 50–55.

15. H. Richter, *Englische Geschichtsschreiber des 12 Jahrhunderts*, especially emphasizes this influence.

16. Quotation from J. A. Giles, *William of Malmesbury's Chronicle of the Kings of England*, pp. 317–389. William's works are edited in the Rolls Series. The work of Marianus, the *Chronographia*, is edited by D. G. Waitz, M. G. H. SS. V, pp. 481–564 (without the first two parts). It is also edited in Migne, *Patrologia Latina*, CXLV.

17. Ordericus Vitalis, *The Ecclesiastical History of England and Normandy*, translated by Forester.

18. Statement of A. Molinier, *Les Sources de l'histoire de France*, I, iii, No. 2193. Thompson and Holm, *A History of Historical Writing*, p. 191, suggests Ekkehard of Urach, whose works are edited by D. G. Waitz, M. G. H. SS. VI, pp. 1–127. Sigebert's work is edited by D. L. C. Bethman, M. G. H. SS. VI, 300–374. He wrote much else, including a *De Scriptoribus Ecclesiasticis*. Sigebert's sources and users are given in the edition of his work, pp. 271–275.

19. E. M. Sanford, "The Liber Floridus," *Catholic Historical Review*, XXVI (1941), pp. 469–478.

20. J. S. Beddie, "The Ancient Classics in the Medieval Libraries," *Speculum*, V (1930), pp. 3–20, especially pp. 12–13.

21. Edited by V. C. L. Hesse, M. G. H. SS. V, pp. 134–263. Good short accounts of Lambert in Barnes, p. 83, and Thompson, p. 187.

22. E. M. Sanford, "The Study of Ancient History in the Middle Ages," *Journal of the History of Ideas*, V (1944), p. 23.

23. G. H. Gerould, "King Arthur and Politics," *Speculum*, II (1927), pp. 33–51. Geoffrey lived about 1100–1152 and was an archdeacon of Llandaff and bishop of St. Asaph. As the fountainhead of Arthurian romance, his history has a very large literature.

24. *The Chronicles of the Reigns of Stephen, Henry II, and Richard I*, ed. Richard Howlett, I, 11–19.

25. Translated by C. C. Mierow, *The Two Cities by Otto Bishop of Freising*, especially p. 412. Edited by A. Hofmeister, in *Scriptores Rerum Germanicarum*.

26. Otto, iv, 3.

27. The manuscript has not been published. For an edition of the prologue and a brief discussion of the work, see William M. Green, "Hugo of St. Victor, De Tribus Maximis Circumstantiis Gestorum," *Speculum*, XVIII (1943), pp. 484–493.

28. Cf. U. Balzani, *Early Chroniclers of Europe: Italy*, pp. 149–160; *Il Regesto de Farfa*, ed. I. Georgi and U. Balzani (1879–1888); *Liber Largitorius*, ed. G. Zuchetti; *Il Chronicon Farfense*, ed. Balzani.

29. At St. Vincent on the Volturno about 1119 (Balzani, pp. 159–160), Monte Cassino by Peter the Deacon (ca. 1107–1140).

30. C. H. Haskins, *The Renaissance of the Twelfth Century*, p. 235. Edited in Migne, *Patrologia Latina*, CLVI.

　　　　　　　　　　　　　　　　　TWELFTH CENTURY STUDIES

31.　*Gesta,* edited in *Recueil des historiens des croisades, historiens occidentaux,* IV (1879); the *Vita,* ed. G. Bourgin, *Guibert de Nogent: Sa Vie,* 1053–1124.
32.　T. F. Tout, *Collected Papers,* III, 7.
33.　*The Chronicle of the Slavs* by Helmold, Priest of Bosau, translated with an introduction by F. J. Tschan, pp. 251–252; edited by B. Schmeidler.
34.　See the excellent pages of Haskins on this topic, *The Renaissance of the Twelfth Century,* pp. 253–260; *The Confessions of St. Augustine* offered one model.
35.　Balzani, *Chroniclers of Early Europe: Italy,* pp. 169–170. His work is edited by W. Wattenbach, M. G. H. SS. VII, p. 574. Another exception was Jocelin of Brakelond of the Abbey of Bury St. Edmunds, England, whose chronicle covers the years 1173–1203 and is largely devoted to his house. It is edited by T. Arnold, *Memorials of St. Edmunds,* and J. G. Rokewode (Camden Society, London, 1840), and translated by T. E. Tomlins, *Monastic and Social Life in the Twelfth Century.* It is the basis for Carlyle's *Past and Present.*
36.　Balzani, pp. 174–180, for Peter the Deacon. Peter has been edited by W. Wattenbach, M. G. H. SS. VII, p. 727.
37.　Glanvill is edited by G. E. Woodbine, *Glanvill: De Legibus et Consuutudinibus Angliae.* FitzNeal is edited by A. Hughes, C. G. Crump, and C. Johnson; translated in E. F. Henderson, *Select Historical Documents of the Middle Ages,* pp. 20–134. *Chronica Rogeri de Hovedene,* ed. W. Stubbs, translated by H. T. Riley; Haskins, *The Renaissance of the Twelfth Century,* pp. 261–262.
38.　Edited in the M. G. H., *Libelli de Lite.* Discussed thoroughly by A. J. Carlyle, *A History of Medieval Political Theory in the West,* IV; C. H. McIlwain, *The Growth of Political Thought in the West.*
39.　Balzani, pp. 230–235; the works of Romuald and Hugo are edited in Muratori, VII; Romuald also by Ardnt, M. G. H. SS. XIX, p. 398, and by Hugo of Siragusa.
40.　Harry Caplan, "The Four Senses of Scriptural Interpretation and the Mediaeval Theory of Preaching," *Speculum,* IV (1929), pp. 282–290; F. Fellner, "The 'Two Cities' of Otto of Freising and its influence on the Catholic Philosophy of History," *Catholic Historical Review,* XX (1934), pp. 154–174.
41.　Adam of Bremen, remarkable for geographic information as well as historical, is edited by B. Schmeidler, *Gesta Hammaburgensis Ecclesiae Pontificum.*
42.　See Thompson and Holm, *A History of Historical Writing,* Chapter XVIII.
43.　C. W. Davis, ed. *De expugnatione lyxbonensi; narratio de itinere navali peregrinorum hierosolymam tendentium et sylviam capientium. Proceedings of the American Philosophical Society,* LXXXI (1939), pp. 590–676.
44.　On Autobiography see C. H. Haskins, *Renaissance of the Twelfth Century,* pp. 253–260.
45.　Krey (note 6), especially pp. 162–163.
46.　*Chronicles of the Reigns of Stephen, Henry II, and Richard I,* ed. R. Howlett, IV, pp. 114–299.

CHAPTER 2

The Short Dark Folk of England

The history of a subject class of people is usually less easy to follow than that of a dominant class. Such a class usually makes little effort to preserve memories of its existence in elaborate funeral monuments and seldom leaves records of its life in literature or enduring architecture. As an exceptional and interesting case we present the evidence about a sub-merged class of people in England—the short, dark folk. Their very inferiority worked to preserve their memory: their short size and dark color, their separateness as a class, and their simple duties to their lords. This study tries to bridge the gap between history and physical anthropology with regard to one racial group throughout many centuries. It is based upon rather unusual data: correlation of percentages of classes in Domesday Book with figures of average height and nigrescence in nineteenth century England, Domesday and other evidence about the condition of the *servi* (slaves), fourteenth century surveys of Welsh landholding, and patterns of land settlement. Ordinarily such disparate data must be used with caution, but in this case they seem to present a coherent picture of a social group which early found a way of life so humble that it has preserved a continuity since prehistoric times.

TABLE 1. Data Concerning Height, Nigrescence, and Domesday Social Classes, Counties of England

County	Height (inches over five feet)	Nigrescence	Percentage of each Class in county*			
			Servi-coliberti	Bordars-cotters	Villani	Freemen-sokemen
Bedfordshire	7	18†	12‡	30	47	2
Berkshire	7.5	11	12	41	42	0
Buckinghamshire	6.5	24	16	24	54	0
Cambridgeshire	6.5	15	10	42	36	4
Cheshire	6.5		8	27	34	2
Cornwall	7.5	28	21	43	32	0
Derbyshire	7.5	4	1	24	60	4
Devon	7	18	19	28	46	0
Dorset	7	19	16	43	33	0
Essex	7.5	12	11	50	26	5
Gloucester	5.5	19	26	22	44	0
Hampshire	7	9	18	38	37	0
Herefordshire	6		13	27	40	0
Hertfordshire	6	24	11	40	37	1
Huntingdonshire	6.5	18	0	17	66	1
Kent	7.5	10	9	28	54	0
Leicestershire	7	16	6	20	39	28
Lincolnshire	7.5	3	0	16	30	46
Middlesex	6	9	5	36	51	0
Norfolk	8	6	4	37	18	34
Northamptonshire	7	18	10	24	47	13
Nottinghamshire	7	6	0	19	46	27
Oxfordshire	6.5	7	14	28	52	0
Rutland	7	18	0	12	85	1
Shropshire	6		17	23	35	0
Somerset	7	13	17	37	38	0
Staffordshire	7.5	14	7	29	54	0
Suffolk	7.5	6	4	30	14	41
Surrey	6	12	11	28	54	0
Sussex	7	10	4	31	57	0
Warwickshire	7	13	13	27	53	0
Wiltshire	6	15	18	44	30	0
Worcestershire	7	15	14	39	33	0
Yorkshire	9	0	0	23	63	6

*The numbers in these four columns come from Inman, Domesday and Feudal Statistics (London, 1900), p. 3. In the calculations 1 is substituted for 0.

†These numbers are secured by adding 7.4 to the original numbers to eliminate minus numbers and using the nearest integer. The average for Bedfordshire, Huntingdonshire, Rutland, and Northamptonshire is an average for the four counties.

‡In the case of × 0.50 the nearest even number is used. For other fractions the nearest number is used.

I

In the latter half of the nineteenth century the anthropologist, Beddoe, published some statistics upon height and nigrescence of Englishmen.[1] These figures have had a curious history since then. Anthropologists, believing in the preservation of human types throughout long periods of time, have used them as evidence of early human settlement.[2] Historians have not received them so enthusiastically, possibly because they involve data of which they are suspicious and possibly because they involve statistics.[3] In their distrust they received encouragement from an eminent embryologist who after stating that the data are "no evidence at all" explains that there may have been other sources than a short dark race in England responsible for persons of these characteristics. He ends "Libertine Spanish seamen or prolific Jewish women may well be expected to have produced evidence of nigrescence during fourteen centuries."[4]

As so often happens the research for this study began with an accident. In the course of a study upon English medieval population the possibility of trying a correlation between the figures for height and nigrescence and the percentages of the freemen and sokemen of Domesday arose. These men were thought to be Danes for the most part and therefore tall and blond. There is a close correlation, as can be seen in Table 1. To control the results correlations were then attempted between the figures of height and nigrescence and other classes mentioned in Domesday in large numbers, *villani* (peasants), cottars, and *servi* (slaves).[5] The assumption was that these were social rather than racial groups and would, therefore, produce no correlation. This is true of the villains and cottars, but the *servi* show a quite high correlation (Table 2). This naturally demanded an explanation. This statement is given in part to show that there was originally no bias in favor of the thesis of the study.

The situation then is that the freemen-sokemen were, in general, a tall, light Danish group. The coloring and the height of the free Celts and the Anglo-Saxons were about the same. As Hodgkin has written, "The darkness of the British population must have varied in different districts according to the proportion of the pre-Celtic races with which it had been fused."⁶ The same would be true with respect to height. Thus the conclusion emerges that the *servi* were a short, dark group, a racial rather than a social group primarily. A "slave" group which is also a racial group may have a quite different history from such a group which is merely economic and social in its classification.

II

The short, dark people are apparently of Mediterranean descent and developed in Europe in the neolithic period. It apparently came to England as several migrations and with differing types within the general group.⁷ Some of them were responsible for Stonehenge and other megalithic monuments. They submitted to the invading Celts probably because they had inferior tools and weapons. If the *servi* of Domesday can be identified with the subordinate groups (*nativi*) which existed among the Welsh in the later Middle Ages, the history of the group can be carried back through Roman times to the era of Celtic control of England. The Romans imposed upon the existing set-up only a superstructure which apparently did not disturb the social arrangments there.

The evidence for Welsh society comes from surveys of the lands of the Prince of Wales taken by the English at the end of the thirteenth century and in the fourteenth century after the deposition of the last native princes.⁸ The use of these data as evidence for Welsh society over several centuries presumes a very static state of affairs, but this was precisely the condition of Celtic culture. The lands of the prince were among the more primitive of the Welsh territories located in the extreme northwest and west where the influence of the English was least powerful.

The pattern of settlement among the Welsh was different from that of the Anglo-Saxons. It was a hamlet culture almost entirely whereas, as we shall see, the Anglo-Saxon favored the large village. The Welsh pattern usually shows only one type of status for each hamlet: it is either a free hamlet or a serf hamlet. While the services of the two types of hamlets vary within each type, the differences between the obligations of the two types are quite marked. It ought to be possible to determine if the services of the *nativi* of the Welsh bore a resemblance to the services of the *servi* of Domesday.

Each village, native or free, seems to have had a very direct relationship to its lord. The free hamlets paid quarterly payments to their lord, were required to do suit at the lord's court, went to war, paid relief (an inheritance tax) and fees for marriage of their daughters, but were free from most other services. The unfree hamlets owed much heavier quarterly payments as well as relief and fees for marrying their daughters. In addition the inhabitants had to take their grain to the lord's mill, pay for grazing rights (usually an animal annually), sell the lord a certain number of animals at a fixed price, and carry stone and other materials for him at his wish. Certain groups of servile hamlets were required to go to war and do court service but these were not usually servile obligations or privileges and they may have been developed in the constant fighting in the Welsh mountains. It will be noticed that no farm labor at so many days a week is mentioned, but there is a heavy service of hauling entailed.

TABLE 2. Correlations of Data in Table 1

	Height	Nigrescence
Height		—.465
Servi-coliberti	—.444	.594
Freemen-sokemen	.847	—.531
Bordars-cotters	.019	.012
Villani	.124	.014
Numbers of counties in correlation	34	31
Statistical degrees of freedom	32	29
Confidence limits, five percent	.340*	.325
Confidence limits, one percent	.437*	.456

*Estimated as half way between the limits for 29 and 35.

III

The Anglo-Saxons had a quite different pattern of land settlement. They preferred to live in large villages which might include several social classes. Whether the social classes were marked off by different divisions within the villages is not known but it is quite likely. The Anglo-Saxons also preferred to live lower in the valleys. Their use of a more powerful plow enabled them to till heavier soils than the Celts had done and thus they opened up much land in the clay soil area of England. Obviously if the Anglo-Saxons conquered a Celtic people a considerable adjustment might be required at the time of settlement, an adjustment which should be seen in the plan of settlement of manors.

The value of the knowledge of the patterns of landholding was demonstrated by August Meitzen[9] many decades ago, but the English map evidence has never been collected and has not been studied except for one essay upon English land systems.[10] The historical implications which might be realized may be illustrated by two maps. The first is that of Crawley which has been discussed in a careful study by Professor and Mrs. Gras.[11] The second is that of Hitchin which formed a part of the evidence upon which Seebohm wrote his famous book, the *English Village Community*.

Crawley was a double village, North and South Crawley, situated on each side of the main street of the village. The size of the holdings can be determined exactly by an extent of the lands of about 1280 which also records the services that the inhabitants of Crawley owed at the time. The whole village was in the demesne of the Bishop of Winchester which would tend to have preserved the ancient conditions perhaps longer than if the village had been under secular lords. The inhabitants of both parts of Crawley would have been considered villains according to the standards of the thirteenth century.

The people of North Crawley as well as those of the hamlet of Woodcote usually held a house and lot (messuage) and ten acres of land, although there were variations. These peasants worked two days a week on their lord's land, harvested in season, and harrowed if they had horses. If they had certain duties with the animals they were exempted from their regular duties. They had to have a license to marry their daughters or to free their sons. They were responsible for suit at court: this is usually a sign of Anglo-Saxon tenure. Their duties in general seem to be those which are attributed to the *gebur* by the treatise known as the *Rectitudines Singularum Personarum*[12] and are much like those of the ordinary serfs of the thirteenth century.

In the southern part of Crawley the peasants usually held a half-virgate (15 acres) or its multiple. They returned quarterly payments to the lord and had to have his license to marry a son or daughter or to sell any of the larger animals. The lord indeed might buy certain of them at a stated price. They might have to work in the lord's meadow and do boon work (extra work) during the harvest in the autumn. In addition a considerable amount of carrying might be required: grain, stones, wood, wool, cheese, and even letters for the lord. They might be asked to make a hedge for the deer park. The similarity of the work of these peasants to that of the *nativi* of Wales is quite marked.

If we turn to Domesday we find that Crawley then had 6 *villani*, 25 *bordarii* (cottars) and 20 *servi*. If we compare the populations in 1086 and about 1280 we have the following:

	Domesday, 1086	About 1280
South Crawley	6 villani	25
	20 servi	
North Crawley	25 bordarii	19 North Crawley
		6 Woodcote

The assignment of the various groups in 1086 is based upon the following principles. The *villani* would certainly have virgates (30 acres or its divisions) and must therefore be placed in South Crawley. The tenures for North Crawley and Woodcote are practically the same and must be considered together. Bordarii usually held less than half-virgates and must be placed in North Crawley and Woodcote. Indeed *bordarii* were usually ordinary *villani* with less than the normal villain holding. This leaves the *servi* in South Crawley. There are two possible objections to this identification of these persons with the in-

habitants of South Crawley in or about 1280. Both are raised by
Professor and Mrs. Gras. The holdings in North Crawley, they
say, are Celtic farthinglands and therefore should belong to
the lesser class which would be the slaves. However, a study of
extents of the period shows no one division which can be
called Celtic and all sorts of units of five acres appear among
purely Anglo-Saxon inhabitants. If, as we have shown, the
servi are a racial group, it is quite possible for their economic
status to have been better than that of the poorest Anglo-
Saxon peasants. Indeed, the very high amounts which
"slaves" occasionally pay for freedom indicate that they were
not all poor.[13]

When we consider the question of the time of the establishment of the pattern at Crawley we are almost inevitably
driven to the conclusion that it occurred at the time of the
Anglo-Saxon settlement. It is very unlikely that Celts living
there earlier would have dwelt on only one side of the street.

Another interesting case is that of Hitchin. Domesday
says that this village had 79 *villani*, cottars, and bordars, but
only 12 *servi*.[14] The eighteenth century enclosure map shows a
small hamlet named Walworth in the manor with its own
green and herdsman.[15] It is thus possible that the *servi* lived at
Walworth rather than in the village proper. Here, again, if we
make this identification, it is very unlikely that the *servi* received their lands after the Anglo-Saxon conquest.

If Crawley and Hitchin are fair samples of what occurred
at the Anglo-Saxon conquest, the short, dark folk settled
alongside the new dominant race or remained in separate
hamlets nearby. The name of the community would be
Anglo-Saxon and the weight in numbers and prestige of the
conquering group would cause the extinction of the Welsh
language. Known as Wealh or Bret or *servi* they might leave
their influence only in such terms as "merchet" and "wedd,"
maiden and pledge.[16]

Both cases also would seem to show that the Anglo-
Saxons respected the rights of the submerged group of pre-
Celtic *servi* if we may so identify them. The lands of the *servi*
would then be land "in domanio" and owe special duties to the
lord. The Anglo-Saxon land would be the folkland. What

happened to the free Celt is not of primary importance since we are dealing with the submerged pre-Celt but it is a major mystery.[17]

IV

The Danish and later the Norman invasions set up above both Anglo-Saxons and pre-Celts other dominant groups. In the eyes of these groups the two submerged groups might easily tend to lose their racial distinction and form one group marked only by social status. The term *servi* had apparently disappeared largely in the Danelaw by the time of Domesday. Their number was probably small in most of the Danelaw counties anyhow. However, in the case of Huntingdonshire where average height is low and nigrescence high (indicating probably the presence of many of the early Mediterranean people) there are no *servi* in Domesday. After the time of the Norman invasion the term *servi* disappears from all of England. In the case of Crawley it seems possible to identify the Domesday *servi* with a group of about 1280. In several other early surveys similar identifications are possible, notably in the surveys of lands of Shaftesbury and Peterborough Abbeys.

One unpublished survey of Shaftesbury Abbey comes from the early years of the twelfth century and is thus within a few years of Domesday. In it the evidence about Stokes, Dorset shows the following coincidences:[18]

Domesday Book		Extent	
villani	7	half-virgaters	9
bordarii	4	cottars	9
servi	4		

In this case the *servi* would seem to be comprehended among the cottars. In Henleigh we have[19]

Domesday Book		Extent	
villani	30	half-virgaters or more	25
bordarii	15	less than half-virgaters	15
servi	4	bubulci (herdsmen)	4

The *servi* would seem to be represented by the bubulci (herdsmen).

Series of comparisons of terms may be made with the data
of the Peterborough extent of the 1120s.[20] Here the *servi* are
sometimes to be identified with persons called either *bubulci*
(herdsmen) as in the Shaftesbury Survey or more commonly
bovarii. At Pytchley the one reference to *bubulci* occurs:[21] "In
the court are four plows with thirty oxen and eight *bubulci*,
each of whom has a half-virgate (15 acres) of demesne." These
are obviously parallel to the *bovarii* who possessed a varying
number of acres: five at Ashdon and Fisherton, nine at Glin-
ton, and ten at Castor and Scotter.[22] At Oundel there is the
following coincidence:[23]

Domesday Book		*Extent*
villani	23	25
bordarii	10	10
servi	3	6 (bovarii)
burgenses	?	15

The survey states, "the men of the village along with the *bovarii*
pay for head tax five shillings each year." We shall find in
Domesday a notable connection between these two conditions
in their close relationship to the lord.

The *bubulci* and *bovarii* are set off carefully from the villains, cottars, *bordarii* and the *sokemen* (a class of freemen with
special legal obligations), but they are occasionally associated
with the shepherd or the swineherd.[24] One might have expected that the *vaccarius* (cowherd) would be the same as the
bovarius except that the two are separated at Castor.[25] The
wives of these persons usually have some stated duties as
winnowing the grain or helping with the harvest.[26] Since the
week work on the fields is very carefully stated and was quite
valuable it seems clear that the *bovarii* did not have to share in
that obligation.

Thus the Domesday *servi* seem to appear in the Shaftesbury and Peterborough extents (descriptions of landholdings
with their services) as cottars or as a class including the *bovarii*,
bubulci, and *vaccarii*. They were bound closely to the lord and
often paid a special sum which was classed with burgess
payments. They had land, from five to fifteen acres, from
which they received income located on the lord's demesne.
These extents seem to make certain that they had no regular

week work but were associated in some way with the animals of the demesne. There is no mention of carriage services directly but care of the animals probably implied its existence.

With these duties may be compared the services of a class called the *geneat* in an eleventh century document, the *Rectitudines Singularum Personarum*.[27] The other two classes mentioned, the *cotsetla* and the gebur are easily identified with the later cottar and *villanus*. The duties of the geneat follow:

> Geneat-right is various according to the rule of the estate: in some places he must pay land-rent, and a swine yearly for grass rent, and ride and carry with his beasts, and haul loads, work and provide food for his lord, reap and mow, cut deer hedges, bring travellers to the townships, pay church scot and alms-money, keep watch and guard the horses, and go errands far and near, wherever he is ordered.

Since the word, *geneat*, seems to be pretty close to *bovarius* in meaning[28] it is not difficult to identify the geneats as among the *servi*. The geneat is identified also with the radmen or radknichts appearing in Domesday in the southwest of England.[29]

V

In Domesday the *servi* constitute about *nine* percent of the recorded population. Of them the latest authority writes:[30]

> The *servi* and *ancillae* of Domesday are undoubtedly male and female slaves. They are normally regarded as part of the equipment of the lord's demesne, and in most entries they can be distinguished clearly enough from the general body of the manorial peasantry. The *coliberti* can be no other than freedmen, who have received holdings from the lord of the estate.

The *servi* then had no holdings of their own. If they had families we are to envision about 100,000 of them being supported as agricultural slaves on the demesne.[31] Could the relatively primitive medieval economy have supported such a large number of slaves? Usually agricultural slavery must be supported by an economy based upon *well paid* cash crops rather than upon the subsistence economy of the Middle Ages. Furthermore, the group evidently preserved its identity over the centuries, an achievement which the disturbed family to which slaves are usually confined often prevents. Maitland questioned the possibility of such a type of slavery.[32]

The distribution of the *servi* had also been remarked upon by Maitland.[33] It can be illustrated anew by the use of samples: cases in the right hand column of every tenth page of the first volume of Domesday.

Number on each manor	*Number of instances*
1	17
2	33
3	12
4	16
5	11
6	13
7	7
8	4
9	6
10	2
11	2
12	1
13	1
14	2
15	2
17	1
20	3
Total	133

Since there are 633 *servi* in the whole series the average to a manor is a little less than five. If the *servi* lived at all separately they existed in a distinctly hamlet culture.

The close relationship of *servi* to the lord can be illustrated by the following items:

> Ruislip.[34] "And four *servi* and four freemen who hold three hides and one virgate."
> Stanwell. "And eight *servi* and two knights who have under them six *bordarii*."
> Risendune. "There are eight *servi* and *ancille* (female *servi*) and a mill with ten shillings and a burgess in Gloucester who pay three pence."
> Berwetun. "There the king had 28 *villani* and 26 *bordarii* and 4 *coliberti* and 5 *servi* and 5 burgesses."

In each case the *servi* are listed with groups which bring an income to the lord but who do not fit into the conventional pattern of land holding. The case of Stanwell is repeated elsewhere in that the *servi* never seem to hold of any but the principal lord. This is peculiar if the *servi* were but a class of farm labor.

Earlier we have showed cause for believing that the *servi* were equivalent to the *geneat* who might be identified with the *bovarii* or even the class appearing occasionally as the *radmen* or *radchenisti*. Let us note the occurrence of these groups in Domesday since they are largely limited to a few counties located in the west of England:[35]

County	Bovarii	Radmen	Radchenisti	Servi
Cheshire	172	145		193
Gloucestershire			137	2,044
Herefordshire	104	24	47	691
Shropshire	384	167		871
Worcestershire	73	33		677

It is difficult to believe that these classes were peculiar to this one group of counties. Probably here the method of classification was different and thus revealing. Plainly there was a choice between classifying men as *servi* (by race) or *bovarii* (by economic status). Thus this revelation tends to confirm the belief that the *servi* of Domesday included many more than the household slaves or even the agricultural slaves without holdings. The *coliberti* need only to have been freed from the status of slavery: their holding of lands need not have changed at all.

There is one more problem to examine. In Domesday for Middlesex the actual size of landholdings is given but the *servi* seem to have none. Take the case of Harrow:[36]

> There are 13 *villani*, each with half a hide (60 acres), and 28 *villani*, each with one virgate (30 acres) and 48 *villani*, each with a half-virgate (15 acres) and 13 *villani* with four hides (480 acres) altogether and two cotters with 13 acres together and four *servi*.

From the evidence above it would seem that the lands of the
servi if, in this case, they had any were on the demesne which
had a special relationship to the lord of the manor. It was
indeed rather a political relationship than an economic one and
was probably the result of a continuing race distinction based
upon the Anglo-Saxon conquest.

VI

Of course, if races are easily mixed, they naturally disappear and it is useless to attempt to trace their passage through
history. However, two conditions exist which make it clear
that anthropologists are correct in their belief that types do
persist century after century. The first is that in the smaller
places population is replaced faster than in the larger ones.[37]
Thus if on the average a population is just holding its own, it is
actually increasing in the smaller places but is diminishing in
the larger places which are the melting pots of humanity. The
second is that humanity is inclined to mate with persons of
similar physical and mental characteristics.[38] Both of these
conditions show why characteristics once located in small
country settlements persist until the people are uprooted.
Since conquests are usually by conquering groups which ad-
just themselves as easily as possible to the preexistent population such uprooting seldom occurs.

The course of the short, dark folk of England may be set
out as the following hypothesis. The folk submitted to the
Celts or perhaps its own dominant group was driven off by the
Celts or earlier invaders. It lived in small hamlets with special
duties (heavy payments in kind or money, care of animals,
carriage and messenger services, and direct service to the lord
of the district) under the Celts during the Celtic, Roman, and
post-Roman periods. The Anglo-Saxons forced them to reset-
tle in or near the new large villages but retained their land in
demesne: their services to their new lords remained much the
same. The Danes and the Normans tended to confuse the
status of the short, dark folk with that of the lowest of the
Anglo-Saxon group, although the old distinctions of service
and demesne died out slowly. Eventually the society of late

medieval England shows free, serf, and cottar. However, assortative marriage and the settlement of the short dark folk in small villages has preserved the type as an anthropological element in the modern English population. Then the industrial revolution caused a great increase of population in some of those areas in which this racial element was numerous.

Notes

1. Beddoe, *The Races of Britain* (Bristol, 1885). Beddoe's comments upon the data are given on pp. 143−144. The data are given on pp. 190−191 and on a map on p. 192. The evidence upon height appears in his 'On the stature and bulk of man in the British Isles,' *Memoirs of the Anthropological Society of London*, III (1867−9), pp. 384−575. His remarks on the average height of the English in some of the counties appear on pp. 542 ff.

2. C. S. Coon, *The Races of Europe* (New York, 1939), pp. 300−334. He gives a good bibliography upon English anthropology. To him and to R. B. Vance I am indebted for advice.

3. It is not even mentioned in F. M. Stenton, *Anglo-Saxon England* (Oxford, 1943). "Attempts to argue from craniological evidence or from statistics of pigmentation in the modern population seem to have resulted in complete scepticism." R. Lennard, "From Roman Britain to Anglo-Saxon England," *Wirtschaft und Kultur*. Festschrift zum 70 Geburtstag von Alfons Dopsch (Leipzig, 1938), p. 67.

4. Quoted by R. H. Hodgkin, *A History of the Anglo-Saxons* (Oxford, 1935), I, 382d−e.

5. With the *servi* are included the *coliberti*, a small group identified with the *servi* in that they are a freedman group. Thus if the *servi* constitutes a racial group, the *coliberti* obviously belong to it.

6. Hodgkin, *op. cit.*, p. 173.

7. Coon, *op. cit.*, pp. 109−113.

8. For the surveys see those of the *Record of Caernarvon* (London, 1838, Rolls Series). In the introduction is a long discussion of the services and obligations listed in the body of the returns. Less satisfactory evidence appears in P. Vinogradoff, *The Survey of the Honour of Denbigh* (London, 1914), but the commentary is much better, particularly pp. lxxxvi−xcvii.

9. *Siedlung und Agrarwesen des Westgermanen und Ostgermanen*, etc. (Berlin, 1896).

10. H. L. Gray, *English Field Systems* (Cambridge, Mass., 1915).

11. N. S. B. and E. C. Gras, *The Economic and Social History of an English Village* (Cambridge, Mass., 1910), pp. 183−186 for Domesday and pp. 229−238 for the extent (description of land holdings) of about 1280.

12. Translated in W. Stubbs, *Select Charters*, etc. 9th ed. H. W. C. Davis (Oxford, 1921), p. 89. See also F. Liebermann, *Die Gesetze der Angelsachsen* (Halle, 1903−16), I, 444−453; III, 244−252, for an edition and exposition of this treatise.

13. F. W. Maitland, *Domesday Book and Beyond* (Cambridge, 1897), p. 33, esp. note 3.

14. D. B. I, 132b.

15. Seebohm, *op. cit.* (1926 edition), pp. 12−13.

16. These Celtic words were picked out of a list of common constitutional and other terms by my colleague, Professor Urban T. Holmes. The frequent appearance of the root "Wal" in connection with hamlets has been commented upon by Lennard, *op. cit.*, pp. 64−66. See *ibid.*, pp. 67−68 for other evidence about loan words.

17. It might easily be assumed that the free Celts were driven out to Cornwall or Brittany or destroyed by the Anglo-Saxons because of the few traces left of them in later times. However, the anthropologists insist (Coon, *op.cit.*, p. 384) that the Celtic type is even more predominate than the Anglo-Saxon. If this is true the result may have been produced by (1) Celts as wives of the Anglo-Saxons (Coon, p. 210 gives an example); (2) inclusion of many persons of Celtic type among the Anglo-Saxon invaders; (3) survival of large numbers of Celts as cotters and bordars. Since the Celtic free hamlet was small even in its association with the Anglo-Saxon in a large village the Celtic element would be submerged. Possibly all of these occurred and the combination produced the result.

18. D. B. I, 78b2; British Museum, *MS Harley* 61, fo. 52^{rv}.

19. D. B. I, 78b2; British Museum, *MS Harley* 61, fo. 54^{v}-55^{r}. The term *bubulci* appears also on fo. 374^{r-v}.

20. *Chronicon Petroburgense*, ed. T. Stapleton (London, 1849, Camden Society), pp. 157−173 from the "Liber Niger."

21. *Ibid.*, p. 162. Other less revealing references to *bubulci* occur at Aldewinkle and Irtlingborough on p. 166.

22. *Ibid.*, pp. 162 and 164 for five acres; p. 163 for nine; pp. 163 and 165 for ten.

23. *Ibid.*, p. 158; D. B. I, 221b. "Et homines ville cum vi bovariis reddunt de chewagio per annum v sol." Five shillings would seem to be the total.

24. *Chronicon Peterburgense*, p. 166 for shepherd, p. 163 for swineherd.

25. *Ibid.*, pp. 163−164. The *vaccarius* is also mentioned at Eye, p. 165.

26. *Ibid.*, pp. 164 and 165 for harvesting; two references to winnowing on p. 163.

27. Translated in W. Stubbs, *Select Charters*, etc. 9th ed. H. W. C. Davis (Oxford, 1921), p. 89. See also F. Liebermann, *Die Gesetze der Angelsachsen* (Halle, 1903−16), I, 444−453; III, 244−252 for an edition and exposition of this treatise. Compare another definition of the geneat: 'His geneat shall work either on the land or off of the manor, wherever he is told to go, ride, drive (horses), carry loads, drive herds and do many other things? J. Earle, *A Handbook to the Land Charters* (Oxford, 1888), p. 377.

28. So my colleague, Professor E. E. Ericson tells me.

29. Professor Stenton prefers to translate the term; 'follower' and regards to the geneat as an aristocrat among the peasants. The difficulty of following his identification is that for a class which is obviously regarded as a large one his identification offers so few examples. F. M. Stenton, *Anglo-Saxon*

England, pp. 465–468. See also Liebermann, *op. cit.,* I, 97, 99; 197; II, 94, for other references and geneat.

30. Ibid., pp. 469–470. With him Vinogradoff agreed: *The Growth of the Manor* (London, 1920), pp. 333–334. This is not to deny that there were some personal slaves among the Anglo-Saxons.

31. My estimate of Domesday population is 1,100,000 for England alone.

32. *Domesday Book and Beyond,* p. 28.

33. Maitland, *op. cit.,* pp. 17–21. That geneat land was distinct from the lands of the nobles (thegns) is clear from Liebermann, *op. cit.,* I, 197.

34. D. B., I, 129 b2; 130 al; 168 2; iv, 83 respectively.

35. H. Ellis, *A General Introduction to Domesday Book,* etc. (London, 1833), II, 511. If these other classes are added to the number of *servi* and *coliberti* the resulting percentage is closer to the position which the average height and nigrescence of the counties entitle them in the cases of Cheshire, Gloucestershire, and Shropshire.

36. D. B. I, 127a.

37. This is a well known situation in modern population. That this is true of medieval English population is shown in my as yet unpublished *Medieval British Population.*

38. See, for instance, Burgess and Walter, "Homogamy in social characteristics," *American Journal of Sociology,* XLIX (1943), 109 ff: C. A. Anderson, "Our present knowledge of assortative mating," Rural Sociology, III (1938), 296–302.

CHAPTER 3

A Quantitative Approach to Medieval Population Change

Geographers and city planners, endeavoring to explain or foretell changes in urban population, sometimes use an approach called basic-nonbasic.[1] A basic factor is one which brings in money from outside of the city and which usually sells its products beyond the city limits. The nonbasic factor furnishes services and supplies to the city. Thus a factory would normally be a basic factor, while grocery stores, barber shops, and similar institutions, together with most professional groups, would be nonbasic. A factory employing a thousand workmen would add to the city not merely the workmen's families but about an equal group of nonbasic families, perhaps a total of six or seven thousand persons. This concept is a very useful one in modern society and is worth testing for its possibilities for medieval settlements.

In the Middle Ages life was simple. Instead of a thousand-employee mill as a possible basic factor, there were fairs, markets, fisheries, and guilds which attracted buyers from the countryside; and castles, courts, and monasteries where people were supported by outside money. The question is whether nonbasic groups appeared inevitably alongside or near these basic factors and, if they did, what size did they attain with respect to the basic groups. Should we be surprised at the appearance of a village under a castle, explaining it as existing under the protection of the lord, or should we learn to expect it as a normal nonbasic complement to the basic castle? This study will consider the hypothesis of a basic-nonbasic pattern, largely from the evidence of Domesday Book of England of 1086.[2]

Domesday Book provides a very large amount of data about villages and market towns in the rather primitive eleventh century. The principles of local organization thus stand out with some clarity. The second volume, concerned with Norfolk, Suffolk, and Essex, often presents information for three times: that of King Edward just before 1066 (TRE), that just after the Conquest, and that of the Survey in the reign of King William (TRW). The first, second, and third times are referred to frequently in Domesday as then *(tunc)*, after *(post)*, and now *(modo)*. From these data in some instances short-period changes can be seen. Unfortunately, Domesday Book does not present detailed information about the boroughs; and even when a city such as Colchester was included, little besides the agricultural holdings of the inhabitants is given. Its information about monasteries and monastic villages will be supplemented by data of later periods.

The boroughs and market towns were set amid agricultural villages whose size varied with local circumstances but in general was small.[3] The surplus grown in the villages was the ultimate support of the larger settlements which were scattered over the countryside. The map of Domesday Leicestershire (p.00) illustrates the pattern. At a distance of eight to twelve miles from the county borough, Leicester, there appears a series of market towns of a few hundred people. Other boroughs, comparable to Leicester in size, occur approximately twenty-five to thirty-five miles away. However, there were exceptions to this pattern, such as the large villages of Aystone, Oadby, and Wigston Magna, within a few miles of Leicester. That such patterns of population distribution should exist should not be surprising, especially to those who know

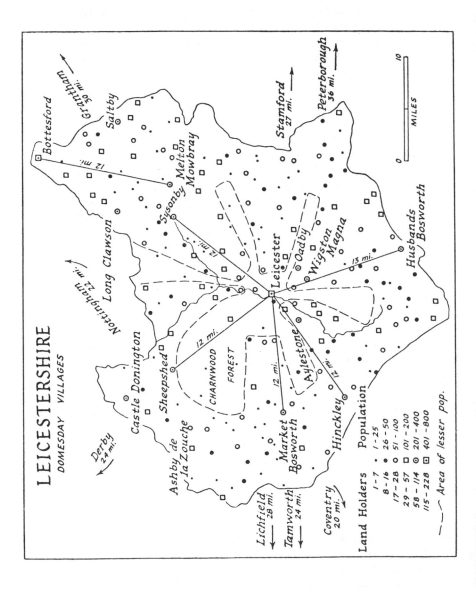

something of the literature illustrating the distribution of modern population.[4]

The agricultural population, being largely a subsistence group, is regarded as neither basic or nonbasic but a neutral factor. It has to be isolated and subtracted from village total population in order to identify the basic and nonbasic elements. This can probably be done satisfactorily for Domesday evidence by using the number of plows as an index of the agricultural element, since nearly all tillage then characteristic of England was based on plows. The number of landholders to the plow varied from 2.1 in Herefordshire and Gloucestershire to more than 5 in East Anglia.[5] The latter was a populous and fertile area where the large number to the plow would suggest a high percentage of persons supported by nonagricultural activities. We assume that there were about 2.1 persons to the plow. In some cases Domesday indicates that there were more plows in use than were actually necessary: in those cases the lesser number would be the more correct number. The normal working team was apparently four animals handled by two men.[6]

A test of the number to the plow may be illustrated in the cases of Gorleston and Eye in Suffolk in the times of King Edward (1066) and William (1086).[7] For Gorleston and its member, Lowestoft:

	TRE	TRW
Villani	25	15
Bordars	15	15
Servi	10	7
	50	37
Plows	14	9

The decline was 5 plows and 13 persons, an average of 2.6 to the plow. The loss was caused apparently because 24 persons attached to the manor were fishing at Yarmouth.

The situation at Eye was more complicated:[8]

	TRE	TRW
Villani	39	20
Bordars	9	16
Servi	12	0
Burgesses	0	25
	60	61
Plows	23	11

Here there was a decline of 24 persons and 12 plows in the course of a few years, 2 to the plow. The appearance of the 25 burgesses raises the question of whether they were a basic group or nonbasic. If basic, is the nonagricultural group (presumably 13—that is, 36 less 23 for the 11 plows) enough as a nonbasic group? If nonbasic, where is the basic element, assuming the hypothesis of basic-nonbasic factors? Actually, William Mallett built a castle at Eye in the period, but he was a minor lord who can hardly have built a very large one.[9] In addition, a priory of perhaps four monks was established there before 1086 but after the Conquest.[10] These are obviously basic factors: between them the need for a nonbasic group would arise.

Fortunately there is considerable evidence in Domesday and later documents to determine the number of persons about the monasteries of the time and near the castles.

Domesday Book provides detailed information about Bury St. Edmunds, one of the wealthier houses of the time. It had "75 bakers, ale-brewers, tailors, launderers, shoemakers, robemakers, cooks, porters and *dispensatores*, who daily ministered to the needs of the abbey."[11] This would be about the same as the number of monks.[12] The abbey also supported "thirty priests, deacons and clerks as well as 28 nuns and some poor people,"[13] who are hard to define in terms of basic and nonbasic. In the thirteenth century, Bury St. Edmunds had 80 monks and 21 chaplains served by 111 servants and others.[14] The matter is complicated because the borough was a sizable place, and it cannot be certain that others than those mentioned served the abbey.

Unlike St. Edmunds, Ely was a peculiarly isolated monastery although farmland was nearby. In 1086, 40 villeins each had 15 acres of his own; together they had 14 plows, and there were 5 plows in demesne. This complement of plows (19) was just about right for the 40 villeins. In addition there were 28 cottars and 20 *servi* in the village.[15] One suspects that they were "ministering to the needs of the abbey": but there is a problem of the number of monks in 1086. In 1093 and again in 1108, Ely had 72 monks. However, Ely was made the episcopal chapter for the new bishop of Ely in 1092:[16] probably the monastic chapter was enlarged then, so that the previous number of monks (in 1086) may have been considerably less. If, as we shall see, the ratio of one servant to one monk held then as later (and the cottars and *servi* were servants) there should have been about 48 monks in 1086. The establishment of Ely as a bishop's see seems to have stimulated the borough's growth: Cambridge demanded of Henry I (1103-35) that its monopoly of commerce in the county be not disturbed, and by 1377 Ely was about as large as Cambridge.[17]

The monastery of Abingdon, Berkshire, had 78 monks in 1117, which was probably about the number for the entire twelfth century.[18] Two lists of abbey servants remain, both for the third quarter of the century.[19] The lists include personnel of the bakery, cellar, and infirmary, and also maintenance men for the plants, and employees in the garden, the mill, and the pasture. There were 76 altogether, thus about equaling the number of monks. This was probably a minimum, since Oxford was only six miles away and doubtless provided for some of the abbey's needs. Most of the servants were probably married, but enough might have been single to keep the average nonbasic family small: probably about 3.5 would be a maximum multiple to estimate the total population represented by the servants. This would mean, including the monks, that there would be a multiple for either monks or servants of about 4.5 for the whole village. If true, the number of monks at Abingdon can be estimated as about 46 in 1086.[20]

The community about the abbey of Ramsey, Huntingdonshire, can be estimated for the late thirteenth century from
information compiled apparently while William of
Gomecestre was abbot (1267-85).[21] About 121 persons were
then in the employ of the house. These included some agricultural workers who probably should be excluded as a neutral
factor. Eliminating about twenty of these would leave about a
hundred, which would still include some poor people and
seven *prebendarii* (pensioners) in the hospital. The number of
monks has been estimated as about eighty.[22] At about the
same time, Evesham in Worcestershire included sixty-seven
monks, three clerks, five nuns, and three poor, together with
sixty-five servants and dependents. This would again give
about one servant for each monk.[23] Evesham's monastic population of 1086 probably was about twenty.[24] About 1328,
Winchcombe Abbey in Worcestershire drew up a list of the
abbey's and abbot's servants, unluckily specifying merely a
plural in some cases.[25] Assigning two for the plural, one gets
thirty-five servants for the abbey and eighteen for the abbot, a
total of fifty-three. The number of monks for the thirteenth and
fourteenth centuries has been estimated at fifty to sixty, which
is what the wealth of the monastery would suggest.[26] Toward
the end of the century, Meaux in Yorkshire drew up a similar
list. The number of servants, setting aside the purely farming
element, was about forty.[27] In addition there were some dozen
legal advisors and fifteen holders of corrodies (right to live at
the monastery): the former probably did not live at the house.
In 1393, Meaux had twenty-eight monks:[28] these together with
the corrody holders would about equal the number of servants.

The evidence then suggests that there would be near the
abbey gates in the local village or city about as many families as
there were monks, the result of the presence of the house. This
was naturally not true of the Cistercian monasteries with their
lay brothers to handle the needs of the abbey. These houses
were able to remove even farming populations from their
manors because they could substitute these brothers for the
manual labor. However, even that system seems to have bro-

ken down by the end of the thirteenth century. Perhaps before the Conquest monks did much of the work in the house, but it is unlikely that they did the specialized work, such as the care of the roofs. Furthermore, heavy farm labor has always been incompatible with long sustained religious or intellectual activity.

The cathedral constitutes a somewhat different problem, largely because of the migratory character of the episcopal retinue and the possibility of nonresidence even of the canons of the cathedral chapter.

A study of the bishop's household, dealing primarily with the more literate members, does note in passing that "Pope Alexander III in the Third Lateran Council (1179) thought it necessary to restrict archbishops, journeying on their canonical visitations, to a retinue of forty to fifty horse and bishops to twenty or thirty."[29] And there were others who kept up the episcopal palace while the bishop was away. The Bishop of Hereford, Richard of Swinefield, of the late thirteenth century, had forty paid servants: squires *(armigeri)*, serving valets *(valletti* or *vadletti de ministerio)*, servants *(garciones)*, and pages *(pagii)* in addition to clerks.[30] If we can assume that the first two groups, totaling about twenty, were married and had sixty dependents and the others (about twenty) were single, we have a basic group of about one hundred. The cathedral chapter of St. Paul's, London, in 1381 had 108 persons paying poll tax—102 priests and 6 clerks—but it was a very wealthy chapter. However, the influence upon the cities is difficult to estimate in nonbasic terms.

Domesday presents one case where such influence may be estimated. In 1075, the Bishop of Selsey moved to Chichester and presumably his chapter with him. Unfortunately, the information about the land held *communiter* by the canons at Selsey does not give details about its inhabitants.[31] However, the number of houses (haws) in Chichester increased by another sixty from the time of King Edward to 1086.[32] If we assume that half of the increase consisted of canons and their clerks supported by the cathedral endowment, their number should have been about thirty. A small cathedral, such as that

of Chichester, should then have had about fifteen to twenty
canons. The bishop probably had a very modest retinue.

Among the basic factors in population change was the
activity of the ruling class, which drew its income from wide
areas but disbursed it in small ones. They spent time in some of
their favorite castles or cities or hunting lodges, even though
much of their life, especially that of royalty, was migratory.
Since their dignity normally found one expression in the size
of their retinues, this was a factor in population. The appearance of even a baron would crowd a village, and the coming of
a king and his retinue would overwhelm any but a sizable
borough. Large-scale castle building brought extensive
changes in cities, where great sections were torn down to make
room for them, especially following the Conquest. The addition of even a small castle, as at Eye, might affect the economy.

The changes in the village of Clare, in Suffolk, illustrate
what could be the result of constructing a castle which was the
head of a great honour. Its owner in 1086, Richard of Bienfaite,
had shared the justiciarship in 1075 and had built up a great
complex of estates in the eastern counties.[33] The changes recorded in Domesday are:[34]

	TRE	1067	TRW		TRE	1067	TRW
Villeins	40	35	30	Plows	48	36	31
Bordars	10	10	30	Sheep	60		492
Servi	20	20	20	Swine	12		60
Socmen	5	5	5				
Burgesses			43				
In castle	—	—	?				
	75	70	128				

The change from arable land to pasture for the many more
sheep and swine would account for decline in the number of
villeins. In the castle there were 7 secular canons[35] and, of
course, the staff of the castle. Subtracting 65 as the farming
group (31 x 2.1) would leave 63 to be accounted for. If there
were 25 in the castle besides the canons, there would be a basic
group of 32, which would still not account for 31 of the 63

persons. However, Clare was actually far enough away from its sizable neighbors, Bury St. Edmunds, Cambridge, Colchester, and Ipswich to be a tertiary center, a market town which would create another group of basic persons, merchants selling to the surrounding areas. The establishment thus of the *caput* (head) of a great honour probably triggered a potential development so that it became a market town of perhaps five to six hundred.

The castle of Clifford in Herefordshire, which was built on wasteland by order of King William, would seem to have been organized as follows:[36]

	In castle		Farming		Borough
Men	4 (or 5)	Bordars	13	Burgesses	16
Servi	6	*Bovarii*	4		
Ancille	4	Welsh	5		
	14 (or 15)		22		
				Value	60s
		Plows	12		

The four men holding large tracts of land were evidently the custodians of the castle: the *servi* and *ancille* (men and women slaves?) were probably associated with them in the castle.[37] This would leave about the right number of plows, twelve, for the other twenty-two persons. In two ways the number of burgesses seems correct: they are equal to the people presumed to have been in the castle and their value should be about five shillings a person. The actual value is a little low but that might be expected on the Welsh border. On the basis of the hypothesis, a village of about 150 should have been near the castle.

Using the hypothesis and on the basis of rather scant evidence in Domesday Book, a very conjectural estimate of the number of people in and about the castle of Wigmore can be made.[38] This castle was built on waste land at Merston and thus no earlier settlement was there. At Wigmore there were only four *servi* and two hides of land: no plows are mentioned so presumably the *servi* were herders. The *burgum* was worth only seven pounds: if it was rated like the Clifford community not far away there should have been about twenty-eight "merchants" there. This was the *caput*, head castle, of the Mortimer family which at the time was a relatively modest noble family: their acquisition of great holdings came later. One might well expect a retinue of twenty to thirty for such a family, which would thus match the hypothetical group of merchants. The castle and village may be estimated conjecturally as about 55 to 65 families and about 200 to 250 in total population.

In view of these examples of the size of settlements in and about castles of baronial lords of importance, the population near small *castella* must have been quite small. Domesday Book has no regular way of presenting evidence about this type of settlement, and so the data are not easy to interpret. Many of the castles in the boroughs were essentially shire-houses (county court houses) whose complement of shire officials was about eight to twelve.[39] With an equivalent nonbasic group, the county officialdom would augment the population of a borough by about fifty to one hundred in addition to what was produced by the custodians and any other residents of the castle.

The royal castle of Windsor provides a problem, since it is not certain whether the Windsor of 1086 was the old city or the new, or both. In a sense it makes little difference, since even old Windsor was only two miles from the castle: the 95 haws recorded as being there would be expected near a great royal castle.[40]

Fortunately the number of persons in the household of Henry I can be estimated very roughly at about 172, from the *Constitutio Domis Regis*.[41] This does not include the king's judicial courts, which often accompanied him on his journeys, nor such lords as might be with him as members of his council. Many of them might have been married, with families settled in London, Westminster, or Windsor; but a good part of them went with him. Walter Map asserted that on one occasion twenty ships were required to carry the court across the Channel:[42] unfortunately he did not designate the occasion, so that a clearer picture of the fleet is unavailable. When the king and his court (with their families) were in London it must have been a basic factor of at least five hundred.

Earlier, the large size of certain villages near Leicester was mentioned. All three were seats of great lords. Two were relatively simple in structure:[43]

Oadby (held by Countess Judith)		Wigston Magna (by Hugh de Grantesmil)		
Socmen	49	Priest	1	Socmen	31
Bordars	11	Knights	2	Freemen	4
	60	Clerk	1	Villeins	32
			4	Bordars	12
Plows				Servi-e	3
(9 at 2.1)	19				82
	41				
		Plows (17 at 2.1)			36
					46

The socmen and bordars at Oadby were unlikely to have been members of Countess Judith's retinue and were presumably a nonbasic group (except for the farmers) of the village. Forty would be about right for the retinue of a wealthy and powerful countess. On the other hand the priest, knights, and clerk were probably part of Hugh's retinue and thus of the basic group. A retinue of about forty-six would be appropriate for the seat of a great landholder whose holdings lay in many counties.

Not far away from these villages was Aylstone, a more complicated settlement.[44] There a lesser countess, Alveva, had a seat, and the Earl of Mellent a prosperous milling center together with lands of two of his vassals, Turold and Ulnod:

	The Countess	The Earl	Turold	Ulnod
Socmen	1		5	
Villeins	18	24	1	2
Bordars	8	5	2	3
Servi	1	1		
Total	28	30	8	5
Plows		Plows		Plows		Plows	
(8 at 2.1)	17	(7 at 2.1)	15	(2 at 2.1)	4	(2 at 2.1)	4
	11		15		4		1

It would appear that the Countess had a retinue, according to the hypothesis, of about eleven; rather small, but in spite of her title she was a minor landholder. The Earl had four mills worth forty-eight shillings. If we assume one man for each five shillings, there would be about ten basic persons, leaving five to be accounted for. It seems likely that the Countess had a larger retinue, supported by the extra-sized nonbasic extra of the earl and his men. At least it is clear that there were good reasons why villages of a larger size should have been so near Leicester.

The evidence about the castles and monasteries seems to fit the basic-nonbasic hypothesis well. Only occasionally have other basic factors, such as mills and markets, been mentioned. We have mentioned without explaining that we have assumed one basic person for each five shillings value of these. This is assumed partly because it represents a 5 per cent return upon what a skilled workman would then make in a year (that is one hundred shillings, or three hundred days at four pence a day), and partly because it seems to work out satisfactorily in practice.[45] We consider the hypothesis now with respect to economic factors.

Perhaps the best example in Domesday of something approaching an industry is the salt works at Droitwich near Worcester.[46] The salt came from brine in three great springs and some minor ones. The brine was evaporated in wooden sheds called *saline*. Domesday shows about 150 of them held of the king:[47] of these, a variety of lords had about 100 and the rest were presumably used by local operators.[48] The burgesses (112) and houses (38), together with 18 bordars in the adjacent manor of Wycelbold and 3 *salinarii*, given in Domesday Book, would suggest a population of about 170 families, about the same as the 151 families of the four parishes in 1563.[49] In the interval both the process of producing the salt and the volume of production remained much the same,[50] so it is reasonable that the population would remain as it was. With Worcester only four miles away and Wycelbold even closer (with certain merchants as citizens), Droitwich might well develop almost entirely through its salt works, since its weekly market and annual fair may also have been primarily for the sale of salt.[51]

The question is whether the salt workers as a basic group included a proper proportion of the population.

One of the king's manors had attached to it in Droitwich thirteen *saline* and three *salinarii*.[52] Presumably the *salinarius* was a master workman, since salt making was a highly specialized operation at Droitwich, producing a very high grade of salt of which the city was proud.[53] If the ratio of *saline* to *salinarii* was typical: the 150 *saline* of the city should have been worked by about forty *salinarii*. However, some holdings had ratios of one burgess or house to two *saline*:[54] or about one half of the other ratio. This suggests that each master had an assistant to help him, as we should expect, bringing the salt workers as a group to about eighty, or half of the population. The number of persons paying the lay subsidy was 87 in 1276 and 90 in 1327.[55] These were the more substantial persons of the town, presumably the *salinarii*, which we have estimated as about forty, and a roughly equal number of nonbasic persons of some means. The full population thus can be accounted for on the hypothesis that the salt making industry supplied the basic factor for an equally sized nonbasic group.

A second industry was fishing, of which one large center in 1086 was Wisbech in Cambridgeshire. Its quota of 33,260 eels was probably the largest in England: the village quite appropriately was held by Ely Abby.[56] The composition of the village by classes was:

Villani	15	Total	65
Socmen	13	Plows (10 at 2.1)	21
Cottars	17		44
Fishers	20		

The plows would have been used by the villani and socmen (a special type of freeman). Wisbech was a small village in which there would be few basic operators besides the fishers.[57] The twenty fishermen plus three others (perhaps merchants) are by our estimate just about half of the forty-four in the nonagricultural group.

Another place, Seasalter, Kent, called in Domesday Book a little borough *(parvum burgum)*, was apparently based upon oyster fisheries.[58] Domesday says that the place belonged to the kitchen of Canterbury (Christchurch) Abbey and had eight fisheries. Its recorded population consisted of a priest (presumed because a church is mentioned), the feudal holder, Blize, and forty-eight bordars; a total of fifty families. The two plows mentioned would probably require the work of only four or five men. If the basic industry, here fisheries, would require as we believe the work of half of the nonagricultural people, the eight fisheries would employ about twenty-two persons, or about three to a boat. The value of the fisheries had risen from twenty-five shillings to five pounds and was thus worth, in 1086, about five shillings a fisherman or about the average for a skilled workman. The nearness of Canterbury (five miles) must have limited the functions of Seasalter very largely to fishing: its claim to being a borough presumably rested upon its nonagricultural character.

The herring fisheries off the east coast seem to have been growing in the eleventh century, as in France.[59] Beccles, Suffolk, had the following population:[60]

Burgesses (at market)	26
Freemen	12
Villeins	7
Bordars	26
Socmen	20
and their bordars	30
	121
Plows (16 at 2.1)	34
	87

Half of these 87 should be basically employed, or about 44. If we assume that these were fishermen, there would be a quota for more than a thousand herring apiece, since they owed sixty thousand. As this was probably in the nature of a tax, the total catch must have been several times larger.

The situation at Kessingland and thirteen nearby villages in 1066 suggests that villagers fished at one place and lived at others.[61]

	Men	Plows	Farmers	Nonagri- cultural	Herring quota
Kessingland	7	3 at 2.1	6.3	.7	22,600
Other villages	51	14.5 at 2.1	30.5	21.5	8,660

There were more plows in the villages in 1066 (18) than twenty years later. Kessingland apparently was the best fishing site: some of the villages were not on the sea. It would seem that many of the men from the villages spent at least part of their time fishing at Kessingland, and in increasing numbers.

After all, these were small fishing ports. It is unfortunate that there is so little information about the greater centers: Dunwich and Yarmouth, among others. One recalls the twenty-four men from Gorleston who were fishers at Yarmouth: were they organized as a boat company? The twenty ships of Dover which were manned by twenty-one persons apiece (the captain and a crew of twenty?) were required for royal service only fifteen days a year.[62] Were some of them fishing boats the rest of the year? No wonder the king had a sergeanty for a man to hold his head while he crossed the Channel. Few landsmen enjoy the smell of fishing boats! The herring were running heavily in the Channel at the time and must have been one of the chief sources of income for the Cinque Ports and other Channel ports.

Mills and markets were the most common form of business activity, although even about these the detailed information is limited. With mills are often associated fisheries, presumably because of the millpond. The information is presented in Table 1. Columns (a), (b), and (c) isolate the farming population which is estimated in (c). On our hypothesis, about half of the nonagricultural people should be nonbasic and are given in (d). The basic group is estimated from the values given for market, mills, and other "industries," by dividing the values by five shillings, as explained above. The data give the strength as well as the weaknesses of Domesday data, as the

TABLE 1. Estimate of Basic and Nonbasic Factors in Certain English Villages, 1086

| Village (pages D.B.I.) | Farming | | | Nonbasic (d) (a−c) (2) | Basic (e) (f+g) (5) | Value in shillings and pence of: | |
	Persons (a)	Plows (b)	Farmers (c) (b×2.1)			Market (f)	Mills (g)
Alcester, Beds. (210b, 212, 214b, 218)	42	14	29	6.5	9	10	36
Basingstoke, Hants. (39, 43)	52	20	42	5ᵃ	16	30	50
Bolingbroke, Lines. (351)	33	5	11	22	2ᵇ	??	10
Buckland, Berks. (58b)	23	4	9	7	6.5	20/6ᶜ	12/6
Cheshunt, Herts. (137)	78	21	44	17	15ᵈ	10	10
Cosham, Berks. (56b)	70	23	48	11	11	20	35/10ᵉ
Faversham, Kent (2b)	75	17ᶠ	36	19.5	20	80	20
Middleton, Leics. (235b)	40	10.5	22	9	9	20	25
Milverton, Somst. (86b, 87, 94)	150	50ᵍ	105	22.5	27	60	77/6
Newenden, Kent (4)	29	5	11	9	8	39/7	
Okehampton, Devon. (105b)	55	24	50	2.5	2.5	5	6/8
Oundle, Nhants. (221)	36	9ʰ	25	8.5	9	25	20
Spalding, Lincs. (351b)	74	17	36	19	18	40	50ⁱ
Tischfel, Hants. (39)	33	9	19	7	12	40	20
Ilchester, Somst. (86b)	108	28	59	54	48	220	20

ᵃApparently merchants and millers were not listed.
ᵇThe value of the new market is not given.
ᶜIncludes value of the dairy.
ᵈThe list includes ten merchants who are added to the total presented by the market.
ᵉIncludes value of the fishery.
ᶠUsing farm plow potential rather than listed 26 plows.
ᵍUsing farm plow potential rather than the listed 69 plows.
ʰUsing farm plow potential rather than the listed 12 plows.
ⁱIncluding fisheries and salt works.

notes indicate. The basic figures confirm, in the cases of Faversham, Milverton, and Oundle, the correction of the actual number of plows to a smaller figure indicating the number really needed on the manor. To fulfill our hypothesis, the numbers of nonbasic in column (d) should be somewhat near the basic in (e), as is the case for most of the examples. Some other interesting cases besides these may be considered.

The Lincolnshire village or market town of Louth presents an unusual picture of a milling center in Domesday with its eighty burgesses, forty socmen, two knights, and two villeins.[63] Eighteen plows of the village were presumably worked by the socmen and villeins. Thirteen mills were worth sixty shillings, or about five shillings apiece, about as one might expect. Assuming this represents thirteen men basically employed, there should be about twenty-seven other basically employed persons, that is, half of the eighty burgesses. However, the market was said to be worth only twenty-nine shillings, which is both a very small and a very unusual number. One suspects then that twenty-nine merchants were each charged a fee of a shilling apiece. The distance of Louth from other centers encourages one to assume that it was becoming a market town as well as a mill center.

Two other illustrations may be given. Walton in Norfolk, not far from Wisbech, belonged to a variety of lords.[64] Its 233 inhabitants, assuming that all the items are from one village, used only 29 plows which should have indicated about 61 persons, leaving 172 for other pursuits. For the basic industries, half (86) should be employed in its 39 salt works and one fishery, which would be about two persons apiece. This would follow the Droitwich pattern, although the type of salt was different. The mill at twenty shillings should add another four persons. This total would not be much different from the eighty-six estimated for either basic or nonbasic. Another case is that of Otterton, Devon, a holding of St. Michael's Mount in Cornwall, which had thirty-three *salinarii*. The other classes recorded are fifty villeins, and twenty bordars, alleged to have forty plows in addition to the six plows in demesne.[65] The "forty" plows arouses suspicion, since the land is said to be able to use only twenty-five plows! The chances are that the

"xl" was a misreading of "xi" and that there were seventeen
plows in use. Subtracting 36 persons, assumed to be using the
plows, 34 are left, which is very near the 33 *salinarii*. However,
there were three mills at Otterton valued at forty shillings total,
which should have meant another basic group of eight. This
casts suspicion at those large round numbers of fifty and
twenty which may well have been approximations, under-
estimating the labor force.

The effect of an addition of a market can be seen in the case
of *Caramhalla* (Kelsale, Suffolk)[66] from the following data:

	TRE	TRW
Freemen	25	25
Villeins	15	22
Bordars	11	26
	51	73
Plows	32	32

The ratio of men to plows in 1066 was very low, about 1.5 to the
plow instead of the expected 2.1. The increase of men from 51
to 73 might be in part the result of more men to the plows. This
would depend upon the size of the market. Unfortunately, its
value is not known. However, there were two manors there:
the smaller had sixteen men in 1086 and was valued at eight
pounds, while the second had fifty-seven men and was worth
sixteen pounds. If the purely agricultural manor saw a ratio of
one half pound value to a man, the larger might have the same
and thus have 48 agriculturists, which would leave 9 for the
basic-nonbasic group with half of them, or about 5, merchants.
Subtracting 9 from 73 would give 64 for the 32 plows, a much
more normal ratio.

The effect of change of basic elements is evident in the case
of two settlements in Wiltshire—Brokenborough and Malmesbury, slightly more than a mile apart. Brokenborough was
probably a century older than its neighbor: in the reign of
Eadwi (955-959) it apparently had a hundred houses, which
might be expected of a small borough then.[67] At the site of
Malmesbury was set up a large monastery and then a royal

castle,[68] both on what had previously been unsettled land. By 1086, Brokenborough had declined, although it was still a milling center.[69] Its neighbor then had at least 91 houses,[70] of which at least 25 were held of the king, an appropriate non-basic housing near a small castle, and the remaining 65 houses would be the proper support for a large monastery of perhaps 40 monks and for the millers who apparently worked but did not live at Brokenborough.

The hypothesis of a basic-nonbasic explanation thus seems to be satisfactory for explaining population and population change from the Domesday evidence and related data. For monastic houses there seem to be about as many monks as persons holding land in the adjacent villages. This is to be expected, since monasteries were substantial buildings of considerable value. Other basic factors, such as mills and fisheries, show also about one nonbasic landholder for each workman in the basic industry. The merchants vary in classification as in function: if they are primarily buying and selling to out of town persons they would be basic: if dealing primarily with and for the townspeople, probably nonbasic.

The basic-nonbasic approach should be valuable in at least two ways. For the earlier Middle Ages it enables one to conjecture with some certainty upon the population near castles, monasteries, and other basic factors. For the later period it may be applied to study of the larger boroughs where data exist, to estimate numbers in guilds and in occupational groups. The approach makes clearer the relationship of population to the basic groups and gives a certain reasonableness to its distribution.

Notes

1. For modern use, see, for instance, J. W. Webb, "Basic Concepts in the Analysis of Small Urban Centers of Minnesota," in *Annals of the Association of American Geographers*, XLIX (Mar. 1959), 55−72, especially 61−63; J. W. Alexander, "The Basic-Nonbasic Concept of Urban Economic Functions," *Economic Geography*, XXX (July 1954), 246−61.
2. References "D. B.," following, are to *Domesday-book seu Liber Censualis Willelmi Primi regis Angliae* ... (London, 1783, 1816). A series of geographical studies of Domesday is referred to as follows (each being published at

58   TWELFTH CENTURY STUDIES

Cambridge by the Cambridge Univ. Press in the year indicated): Darby, *Eastern England*, for H. C. Darby, *The Domesday Geography of Eastern England* (2d ed., 1957); Darby and Terrett, *Midland England*, for Darby and I. B. Terrett, *The Domesday Geography of Midland England* (1954); Darby and Maxwell, *Northern England*, for Darby and I. S. Maxwell, *The Domesday Geography of Northern England* (1962); Darby and Campbell, *Southeast England* for Darby and Eila M. J. Campbell, *The Domesday Geography of Southeast England* (1962).

3. The size of English villages of Domesday can be seen in my *British Medieval Population* (Albuquerque: Univ. of New Mexico Press, 1948), pp. 306–14, and may be compared with the larger villages of Spain in my "The Medieval Monedatge of Aragon and Valencia," *Proceedings of the American Philosophical Society*, CVI (Dec. 1962), 500–1.

4. The map was originally published in and is reproduced by permission of the *Journal of Regional Research*: it was drawn by Jerold G. Widdison. For these, see my "The Metropolitan City Region of the Middle Ages" in that journal, II (1960), 55–70.

5. A. H. Inman, *Domesday and Feudal Statistics* (London, 1900), p. 14.

6. *Ibid.*, p. 22. H. G. Richardson, "The Medieval Plowteam," *History*, XXVI (Mar. 1942), 287–94. F. W. Maitland, *Domesday Book and Beyond* (Cambridge, 1898), p. 403.

7. D. B., II, 283, 283b. There were also four freemen of the king there; p. 284b. The *villani* were serfs, bordars were small holders much like cotters, and the *servi* were supposed to be slaves; but see my "Short, Dark Folk of England," *Social Forces*, XXIV (Mar. 1946), 340–47.

8. D. B., II, 319b–320. There are other references to Eye which bring the number of landholders to about 145 or 147. See Darby, *Eastern England*, pp. 169, 195.

9. D. B., II, 379. He also set up a market, but no value is given.

10. *Victoria County History*, "Suffolk," II, 72–73; D. Knowles and R. N. Hadcock, *Medieval Religious Houses, England and Wales* (London: Longmans, Green, 1953), p. 65. It was established about 1080 and had four monks in 1279.

11. D. B., II, 372 ff.; M. D. Lobel, *The Borough of Bury St. Edmunds* (Oxford: Clarendon Press, 1935), pp. 12–13; Darby, *Eastern England*, pp. 197–99.

12. Knowles and Hadcock, *Religious Houses*, p. 61.

13. Lobel, *Bury St. Edmunds*, p. 12.

14. Knowles and Hadcock, *Religious Houses*, p. 61; *Victoria County History*, "Suffolk," II, 69.

15. D. B., I, 192.

16. Knowles and Hadcock, *Religious Houses*, p. 65.

17. F. W. Maitland, *Township and Borough* (Cambridge, 1898), p. 213; Russell, *British Medieval Population*, p. 142.

18. Knowles and Hadcock, *Religious Houses*, p. 58.

19. *Chronicon monasterii de Abingdon*, J. Stevenson, ed. (Rolls Series; London, 1858), II 237–43. Less helpful data are given in II, 299 ff. This and subsequent references to the Roll Series pertain to *Rerum Britannicarum*

medii aevi scriptores, printed in London for the Public Record Office of Great Britain in years as designated.

20. By subtracting as follows from the 136 (*D. B.*, I, 58b, *Bertune*): 78 agriculturists (37 plows at 2.1); one basic group of 12 for 58½ shillings for mills and fisheries and another 12 as nonbasic; then some 36 persons, together with 10 merchants, or a total of 36 to 46, is left as support for the monks of Abingdon Abbey, who should number about the same. Presumably Abingdon was too close to Oxford to have more than a rudimentary market.

21. *Cartularium monasterii de Rameseia*, W. H. Hart and P. A. Lyons, eds. (Rolls Series; London, 1893), III, 236–41. The date is the commonly held one shared by the editors. The settlement at Ramsey is apparently not included in *Domesday*. Darby, *Eastern England*, p. 321.

22. Knowles and Hadcock, *Religious Houses*, p. 74.

23. *Ibid.*, p. 65.

24. *D. B.*, I, 175b, offers some interesting data for conjecture. The 27 bordars should include 15 agriculturists (for 7 plows) and 12 others (6 basic for mills worth 30s and their 6 nonbasic). This leaves those paying 20s for *census*. If the *census* was a shilling a piece (often the tax of burgages, or city lots), there should have been twenty persons, which should have been nonbasic for an equal number of monks.

25. *Landboc sive Registrum...de Winchelcumba* (Exeter, 1892), I, 363–66.

26. Knowles and Hadcock, *Religious Houses*, p. 81.

27. *Chronica monasterii de Melsa*, E. A. Bond, ed. (Rolls Series; London, 1868), III, lxvi–lxxii.

28. Knowles and Hadcock, *Religious Houses*, p. 111. In 1336, it had 42 monks and 7 lay brothers.

29. C. R. Cheney, *English Bishops' Chanceries, 1100–1250* (Manchester: Manchester Univ. Press, 1950), pp. 1–21, especially 5.

30. *A Roll of the Household Expenses of Richard de Swinfield, Bishop of Hereford*, John Webb, ed. (London: Camden Society, 1855), especially pp. 166–72, 194–97.

31. Russell, *British Medieval Population*, p. 136.

32. *D. B.*, I, 17, 23. Fishburne manor was very close to the west of Chichester, so that the city's agricultural population was small. See also Darby and Campbell, *Southeast England*, pp. 463–66.

33. Under "Clare, Richard de" in the *Dictionary of National Biography* (London: Smith, Elder & Co., 1908). He was also known as son of Count Gilbert or FitzGilbert and even as Richard of Tonbridge.

34. *D. B.*, II, 389b.

35. Knowles and Hadcock, *Religious Houses*, p. 84.

36. *D. B.*, I, 183.

37. The *bovarii* were oxherds or cowherds. On Clifford, see also Darby and Terrett, *Midland England*, pp. 73, 103. A very small mill was there.

38. *D. B.*, I, 179b, 180, 183b. For Ralph de Mortimer's career, see account in *Dictionary of National Biography*. Darby and Terrett, *Midland England*, p. 104.

39. Mabel H. Mills, "The Medieval Shire-House," in *Studies presented to Sir Hilary Jenkinson*, J. Conway Davies, ed. (London, New York: Oxford Univ. Press, 1957), pp. 254–71; G. H. Fowler "Rolls from the Office of the Sheriff of Bedfordshire and Berkshire, 1332–4," in *Quarto Memoirs of the Bedfordshire Historical Society*, III (1929), especially 2–8.

40. *D. B.*, I, 56b, 62b; Darby and Campbell, *Southeast England*, pp. 279–80.

41. *Red Book of the Exchequer*, Hubert Hall, ed. (Rolls Series; London, 1896), III, cclxxxix–ccxciii, 809–13. It is translated in *English Historical Documents*, D. C. Douglas and G. W. Greenaway, eds. (New York: Oxford Univ. Press, 1953), II, 422–27 and bibliography. See also G. H. White, "The Household of the Norman Kings," *Transactions of the Royal Historical Society*, 4th series, XXX (1948), 127–55.

42. *English Historical Documents*, II, 390.

43. *D. B.*, I, 232b and 236 for Oadby; I, 232 and 236b for Wigston Magna.

44. *D. B.*, I, 231b, 237.

45. See Table 1 and explanation upon it. Five per cent would be a shilling in a pound.

46. On Droitwich, see E. K. Berry, "The Borough of Droitwich and its Salt Industry, 1215–1700," *University of Birmingham Historical Journal*, VI (1957–58), 39-61. Darby and Terrett, *Midland England*, pp. 251–56.

47. The earl is said to have had 51½ (*D. B.*, I, 172b), which should have been a third, as in a *wich* in Cheshire (*D. B.*, I, 268).

48. Evidently carried away to their own landed property; it was stated as belonging to certain manors of the lords.

49. *Victoria County History*, "Worcestershire," III, 78. Two parishes in Wich; the others at Witton and Gosford.

50. Berry, *Borough of Droitwich*, pp. 42–43, 51. The vats increased from between 310 and 320 in 1086 to 400 in the sixteenth century.

51. *Lay Subsidy Roll for the County of Worcester, circ. 1280*, J. W. Willis Bund, ed. (Worcester: Worcestershire Historical Society, 1893) pp. 7–8, 23–24; *Lay Subsidy ... for 1327*, F. J. Eld, ed. (1895), pp. 15–16, 37–38.

52. *D. B.*, I, 172. The volume of the product of these was a little above average: 23 mitts of salt to the *salina* when the average was 19.

53. *D. B.*, I, 265b. A Cheshire place, Actun, had a "quiet house" for making salt crystalize properly. For conditions, see Berry, *Borough of Droitwich*, pp. 48–51. The customs of salt making in Cheshire are given in *D. B.*, I, 268; they are probably much like those of Droitwich.

54. Osbert Fitz Herbert had 13 burgesses with 26 *saline*. Gilbert Turoldi had 1 burgess to 2 *saline*. *D. B.*, I, 176b, for both. Berry, *Borough of Droitwich*, pp. 48–49.

55. *Victoria County History*, "Worcestershire," III, 78. Also n. 51.

56. *D. B.*, I. The list of persons or religious houses to which eels were owed included: 6 fishers owing 3,500 to William Warenne (196b); 1 fisher for 5,000 to Bury St. Edmunds (192); 8 fishers for 5,260 to Ramsey Abbey (192b); 3 for 4,000 to Croyland Abbey (193); 2 for 14,000 to Ely (192); and a miscellaneous obligation for 1,500 (probably to Ely; 192).

57. King John arranged for some shipping by sea there just before his death. J. C. Holt, "King John's Disaster in the Wash," in *Nottingham Medieval Studies*, V (1961), 75–86.
58. *D. B.*, I, 52. Tait knew that it was an oyster center but called it largely agricultural. James Tait, *The Medieval English Borough* (Manchester: Univ. of Manchester Press, 1936), p. 67.
59. For the herring fisheries off the coast of France from 1030 to 1170, see M. A. Valenciennes, "Histoire naturelle du hareng," extract from *Histoire naturelle des poissons* (Paris, 1847).
60. *D. B.*, II, 283b, 369b.
61. Kessingland, *D. B.*, II, 283, 407; for others, 407, 407b. Southwold also seems to have had too few men for its quota of 25,000. *D. B.*, II, 371b.
62. *D. B.*, I, 1.
63. *D. B.*, I, 345.
64. *D. B.*, II; Ely Abbey, 213; Earl Alan, 149b; William de Warenne, 160; Roger Bigot, 173; *R. de Bello Fago*, 226; Robert Toni, 236; Hermer de Ferrers, 274b. The proportions of the Ely holding to the others are about the same.
65. *D. B.*, I, 104; III, 177.
66. *D. B.*, II, 330b. Kelsale is suggested by Darby, *Eastern England*, p. 202.
67. *Registrum Malmesburiense*, J. S. Brewer and C. T. Martin, eds. (Rolls Series; London, 1880), II, xxxi. Its alternative name was Kairdunburgh.
68. *Ibid.*, II, xxxi. The editors note that Bishop Leuterius granted the site as "terra illa que vocabulum est Maeldunesburg" rather than as manor. *Eulogium Historiarum*, F. S. Haydon, ed. (Rolls Series; London, 1858), I, 225.
69. *D. B.*, I, 67a. It had 64 villeins, 7 cotters, 15 *cosces* (cotters), 16 *servi* for a total of 102. The 64 plows would more than employ this group. The eight mills were valued at £ 8 12s. 6d. which should have indicated the employment of at least 34 millers who probably lived in Malmesbury.
70. *D. B.*, I, 64b. Long afterward, the inhabitants of Malmesbury were to keep up the borough wall. *Registrum Malmesburiense*, I, 136.

CHAPTER 4

Tall Kings: The Height of Medieval English Kings

Before the battle of Stamford Bridge in 1066 the messenger of Harold Godwinson, King of England, was asked what his master would give Harold the Tall, King of Norway, to avoid a battle. According to the saga the reply was, "Seven feet of English ground or as much more as he may be taller than other men."[1] This was a bold taunt to hurl. England made good his threat but not before his enemy had said of him, "That was but a little man, but he sat firmly in his stirrups."[2] Yet the English King was regarded by some of his contemporaries as tall,[3] and the Bayeux Tapestry would show him as about the same height as William the Conqueror.[4] Looking down from his great height, the Viking could refer to most men as short. Obviously height was a factor which was noticed and commented upon by medieval men.

Human height assumes an unreal importance because our eyes are near the top of our bodies, and thus they detect easily relatively slight differences in stature. Today a few inches seem to confer some advantage in securing positions of leadership,[5] and they were probably even more impressive in the Middle Ages when personal loyalty was a basic factor in feudal relations. But even if height had no influence, it would be intrinsically interesting. There is a surprising amount of information available about the height of medieval English kings, some of it quite accurate. It enables us to add greater precision to our knowledge of these men. Furthermore, the descriptive terms applied to some of them by chroniclers indicate what the medieval mind regarded as tall, medium and short, at least with respect to royalty. The only survey of this topic was made by Polydore Vergil who scattered the information in the form of descriptions of kings throughout his *English History,* published in 1534, from William II to Henry VII.[6]

This Anglo-Italian historian used good sources for much of his history, and some of them about royal height can be traced. Thus he quoted virtually verbatim from an early writer a description of Henry III, applying to his height his favorite term 'just' as a synonym for ordinary (mediocris).[7] Henry III was probably about 5-9 (five feet, nine inches) tall, but some of the other kings assigned this height may have varied from this figure. However, Vergil's information would be valuable primarily about those kings for whom we have no other information, especially for the more recent monarchs whose size might have been known to the historian personally or through his contemporaries. The only king earlier than A. D. 1400 about whom information from seals alone remains is Stephen, but Vergil's description of him as having a most appropriate stature looks like a cover for ignorance.[8]

His information about one of the more recent kings is corroborated strikingly by the measurement of his skeleton. Edward IV, according to Vergil,[9] exceeded all in height and was actually about 6-3.[10] He says that Henry VI was of noble stature,[11] which overestimates that king's 5-9 or 5-10.[12] He adds of Henry VII that his stature scarcely exceeded a just height.[13] Henry's funeral effigy was 6-1 in length, but, as we shall see, this could be several inches too long.[14] Probably a recent historian's statement that he was 5-9 is not far wrong.[15] Vergil, who knew the king, thus does not seem to exaggerate the king's height in spite of his predilection for him. This lack of bias with respect to stature is important for evaluating his description of Richard III whom he did not like. He says that Richard was undersized (*pusilla*),[16] a statement which might be discounted somewhat if Vergil had shown bias here.

Vergil's testimony with regard to the two predecessors of Henry VI is of some value, especially since Henry V's tomb effigy in Westminster Abbey is so mutilated that its length is uncertain. However, Henry IV's tomb effigy is about 5-9 which should be reasonably accurate.[17] His stature is described by Vergil's favorite word, just.[18] Since Vergil allows Henry V a "more than just" stature, it would seem that the son was taller than his father.[19] But with Henry IV Vergil's information would seem to fade: he says that Henry's predecessor, Richard II, was graceful,[20] which hardly does credit to his six feet.[21] His references to Richard's immediate predecessors likewise lack precision.

Richard II's tomb effigy measures about six feet in length. The exact length is difficult to measure, since his shoes are hidden by his costume.[22] The tomb effigy is thus approximately the same length as the king's height. The same seems to be true for the effigy and skeleton of King John: the former is said to measure 5-5 while the latter is about 5-5 or 5-6.[23] These are the only two cases where the two may be compared, and they show a reasonable similarity of length. We thus assume that for the period after John that the tomb effigy gives a fairly accurate estimate of height. Earlier it is not so certain. Obviously the seven foot effigies of Henry II and his queen, Eleanor of Aquitaine, at Fontevrault in France are much too long even though Eleanor was quite a woman.[24] The statue of Henry I at Rochester Cathedral is only 4-10 and thus is much too short.[25] These statues are of the twelfth century, which is alleged to have been less sensitive to this world and somewhat indifferent to actuality.[26] But even at the end of the century Richard I's tomb which is also at Fontevrault is only six feet long.[27]

This may not be an exaggeration. Two contemporaries comment upon his height. One says that it was noble (*procerus*) and very grand (*pregrandis*).[28] The second, Gerald of Wales, states that in stature Richard I and his older brother, Henry, were "great, a little more than ordinary."[29] Henry's height is also described by Gervase of Tilbury as great.[30] Gerald also indicated that Henry II's height was between that of his two tall sons just mentioned and that of his two short sons, Geoffrey and John.[31] Two literary figures of his reign, Walter Map

and Peter of Blois, describe Henry II in terms which suggest
that he might be closer in height to his tall sons than to the
shorter pair.[32] Peter, indeed, says that Henry II was neither
gigantic among short men nor insignificant among tall men, an
idea which he borrowed from the earlier and great chronicler,
William of Malmesbury. If Richard I was about 6-0 and John
about 5-6, their father may well have been about 5-10 tall.

For information about the height and other physical
characteristics of kings earlier than these, William of Malmesbury is largely responsible. According to him, William the
Conqueror was of just height and of great weight.[33] His son,
William Rufus, was very strong but not of great height.[34] His
son, Henry I, was medium, so that he was larger than the
smallest and smaller than the largest,[35] an idea used by later
writers of other sovereigns. On the basis of evidence presented
earlier it would seem that a just or average height would be in
the eyes of chroniclers about 5-9. The Conqueror and his son,
Henry I, would then be of about that height while William
Rufus would be shorter.

For these early kings the great seals of England offer one
possibility for providing evidence of height. They are continuous since Edward the Confessor. On one side of these early
seals the king is shown seated on a throne usually holding a
sword in one hand and an orb and cross in the other. Such care
is shown in detail and such a variety of measurements appears
for kings, thrones and swords that drawing from life is suggested. Since several different thrones appear, the orb and
cross seem standard and are of the same length in the seals of
William I and II and Henry I and II. The other side of the seal
shows the king riding and thus could hardly have been drawn
from life since the horse is usually in full gallop. The measurements are shown in Table 1.[36]

These measurements, if they were meant to indicate size,
seem to show that William I[37] and Henry I were about the same
height and slightly shorter than Henry II. They also seem to
parallel the chroniclers in their estimates. William II seems
distinctly shorter and thus conforms to the description that he
was "not of great height." This coincidence gives one some
confidence in the seals' evidence for height, at least in this

TABLE 1. Comparative Measurements of Objects on the Great Seals of a
Number of English Kings

King	Height of Throne	Torso and Head	Lower Leg	Orb and Cross	Sword
Edward the Confessor	9	23	12		14
William I	8	20	10	8	14.5
William II	7	19	9	8	12
Henry I	8	20	10	8	14
Stephen	10	23	14	6.3	8
Henry II	8	20	13	8	17.2

early period. Both Edward the Confessor[38] and Stephen appear definitely taller than the others and may well have reached nearly to six feet. The anonymous biographer of Stephen compares him to Saul in ambition and may have had a comparison of height in mind also.[39]

After the early period the seals seem to lose value in depicting size and proportion. They become more official and conventional and less personal. Some seals of Henry III, Edward I and Edward II are practically identical.[40] The same holds true for the next group of three: Edward III, Richard II and Henry IV[41] and even for a third trio: Edward IV, Edward V and Richard III.[42] In the last trio the same figure does for the tallest of medieval English kings, his young son and his short brother. In a sense the development of the seal is the reverse of the tomb effigy where the earlier ones seem to have no relation to reality and the latter do.

Fortunately estimates can be made of the height of thirteenth and fourteenth century kings without the help of seals. Henry III was stated earlier to have been 5-9, which is the length of his tomb effigy in Westminster Abbey. This figure might be questioned since his tomb is only half an inch longer than that of his short father.[43] However its 6-1½ is still long enough to hold him, while the great height of his son, Edward I, rather encourages one to attribute to Henry as many inches as possible, even though his second son, Edmund, seems to have been only 5-7 or 5-8 in height.[44] Edward I's skeleton has been measured and is that of a man of 6-2 in stature.[45] At the end of the Middle Ages it was customary to place upon the coffin of the deceased at his funeral his effigy. Several of these, made in part of leather and wood, remain in Westminster Abbey and were for a long time in such condition that they were known as the Ragged Regiment. The effigy of Edward I seems to be among these and is 6-5½ long which indicates some exaggeration.[46] Edward was said to stand head and shoulders over the common people, a veritable Saul over Israel.[47]

The son of such a tall man as Edward I might well be a tall man himself. One is not surprised to find that Edward II's tomb effigy in Gloucester Cathedral is about 5-11 in length.[48] He is said to have had an elegant body and great strength.[49] Edward III, his son, does not seem to have been quite as tall. A chronicler says that he did not exceed a just height nor yield to a depressed height and thus repeats an idea expressed about earlier kings.[50] His funeral effigy, which might be expected to exaggerate his height, was 5-10½.[51] Probably he was a little shorter, perhaps about 5-8. His son, Edward the Black Prince, was apparently about six feet tall.[52]

From this information the stature of the kings stands out with some clarity. Two of them, Edward I and IV, were tall by any standards. One, John, was quite short and a second, William II, may not have been much taller. A third, Richard III, was described as undersized, which seems slightly curious since he was a brother of the tallest of the group. Three, Richard I, Richard II and Edward II were about six feet tall, while Edward the Confessor, Stephen and Henry V may not have been much shorter. The others seem to have fallen within what the chroniclers call a just or ordinary height, apparently in the neighborhood of 5-9. These definitions are rather interesting in the scale which they suggest: tall about 6-0, medium about 5-9, and short about 5-6.

This standard may be compared with what is known of the ordinary stature to see whether it was a special standard of royal value or whether it conformed to the normal standards for the whole people. Unfortunately the evidence is rather slight and most of it comes from ossuaries (collections of bones) in cemeteries at Hythe in Kent and Rothwell in Northamptonshire. The information about height is given in the reports upon them:[53]

> (Hythe) A preliminary measurement of 155 femurs points to the men having averaged five feet five and a third inches, while the women were about five feet one inch.
>
> (Rothwell) The Rothwell men, judging from the measurement of 65 femurs no two of which belonged to the same body, were only five feet six inches. After measuring 38 female femurs, no two of which belonged to the same individual, I estimated the Rothwell women at five feet two inches.

One must bear in mind that this information comes from only two samples and that it represents height at death which in many cases must be many years or even decades after the individuals commenced their decline from full height.

In his survey of height in the British Isles of last century, Beddoe included Kent among the counties where the average height was 5-7½ and Northamptonshire where it was 5-7.[54] There were twelve counties where the average was below 5-7 and only two counties which had a higher average than 5-7½. Thus his average was only an inch higher than that of the ossuary in Northamptonshire and two inches higher than that of Kent. The difference in age would explain a part of the difference. However, it is obvious that even the modern height average was not near the 5-9 which medieval evidence would indicate was regarded as an ordinary height for royalty. There were then two standards, one for the mass and one for the leaders of the country.[55]

The attitude of the chroniclers is rather instructive. There was an interest in height, especially in the twelfth century and again at the beginning and in the middle of the fourteenth century. On the other hand few chroniclers of the thirteenth and fifteenth centuries (even that most prolix of all the chroniclers, Matthew Paris), seem to be interested in stature, although they describe other physical characteristics. When they do describe height, they define a tall man as noble (*procerus*), as if they expected all nobles to be tall. Richard I is said to have had an imperial presence while Edward the Confessor was kingly. There is a tendency to avoid the direct attribution of shortness. William II was not of great height; and John and his brother, Geoffrey, were below the height of their father. Richard III was harshly treated, but this was by men enjoying the patronage of his enemies, two generations after his death. This shows some attention by clerical writers, who probably had less interest in height than did others, and suggests that the high average stature of the medieval English kings did probably benefit them in public estimation.

The English kings, like most medieval royalty, had their enemies. In England a series of them was canonized, either regularly by the Church or popularly by the English people, as a sort of political sainthood. They gave the anti-royal forces a kind of religious sanction, a valuable support in the struggles of the time.[56] These included three archbishops of Canterbury, Thomas Becket, Stephen Langton and Edmund of Abingdon; two bishops of Lincoln, Hugh of Avalon and Robert Grosseteste; Bishop Thomas de Cantilupe of Hereford; Simon de Montfort, Earl of Leicester; and Thomas, Earl of Lancaster. What height did they attain? About three of them (Stephen Langton, Thomas of Cantilupe and Thomas of Lancaster), nothing seems to be known with respect to height.[57] The father of Simon de Montfort was said to be "tall and of a commanding appearance,"[58] which leads one to believe that the son may have been tall also. The height of three of the others is known, and a good guess can be made about the other one.

The guess concerns Bishop Hugh I of Lincoln, who was said to be shaped so like Henry II that he was thought to be his son.[59] If his height was similar, as seems likely, he was about 5-10. The greatest of these saints was Thomas Becket. His remains are thought to be in Canterbury Cathedral, although this has been questioned.[60] Two contemporary descriptions give his stature as noble[61] and eventually he was thought to be "seven foot save an ynche."[62] In height, if the remains are of the saint, he outranked any king after the Conquest before Edward IV with his 6-2 or 6-3. Another archbishop-saint, Edmund of Abington, seems to have been 5-11 tall.[63] In spite of pictures which seem to indicate that he was small,[64] the skeleton of Robert Grosseteste shows him about 6-1 in height.[65]

These anti-royal saints may be compared with their opposite royal numbers. Thomas Becket, if properly identified, obviously towered above Henry II. Hugh of Avalon, as has been stated, looked much like Henry II and thus would have been shorter than Richard I. Although the height of Stephen Langton is unknown, it could hardly have been shorter than that of King John. Both Edmund of Abingdon and Robert Grosseteste must have been taller than Henry III, and Simon Montfort may well have been also. Edward II was relatively tall and may have been taller than Thomas of Lancaster. In the struggle for inches, Richard I is probably the only king who had an advantage over his saintly antagonists. The other four kings probably suffered defeats in the struggle. This is a coincidence and probably has no significance, but the lack of height was probably no help.

The evidence about the height of the women of the royal families is naturally less than for the men and consists of the lengths of funeral and tomb effigies. Four tombs would indicate that Eleanor of Castile, queen of Edward I, was about 5-9 or 5-10,[66] that both Philippa of Hainault, queen of Edward III,[67] and Anne of Bohemia, queen of Richard II,[68] were about 5-6, while Joan, the second wife of Henry IV, was several inches shorter.[69] Among the funeral effigies, which usually exaggerate height, one supposed to represent Katherine of France, queen of Henry V and widow of Owen Tudor, is about 5-4,[70] and a very tall one of 5-11½ is alleged to be that of Elizabeth of York, queen of Henry VII.[71] If her son, Henry VIII, really reached 6-4 (which may be doubted),[72] it can be seen where he got his height. The women are about the height which the stature of their male relatives would lead us to expect.

There is even less information about royal children, but what remains is available for studying the mystery of Edward V and his younger brother, Richard. They were murdered in the Tower of London either by their uncle, Richard III, in 1483, probably in August, or just about two years later by Henry VII.[73] The weight of historical evidence favors the first date. Now the skeletons of the children have been measured and might be expected to throw some light upon their age at death. If the boys died in 1483, they were 13½ and 10 years of age respectively; if two years later, they would have been 15½ and 12 years. Their heights have been estimated at 4-10 and 4-6½.[74] Fortunately there are two of them which offsets the wide variation in rate of human growth exhibited by groups and individuals. Now the average American boy reaches the height of 4-10 just before 14 years and 4-6½ at about eleven.[75] This average falls just about in the middle of the ages of the boys. This raises the question whether the boys would probably be taller or shorter than children of men growing toward an average adult height of about 5-8. Since their father, Edward IV, was the tallest of medieval English kings and their sister, Eleanor of York, was also quite tall, we should expect them also to be taller than the average and to have reached their height in 1483 rather than two years later.

The bones of these children thus furnish evidence about one of the ugliest of medieval mysteries and tend to corroborate a commonly held opinion. The reverse is true of the even more commonly held notion that medieval man was notably shorter than modern man. This belief is usually said to be based upon the small size of surviving armor which, or course, was worn by the knightly class in the Middle Ages. This study has shown that English royalty was not short and that the descriptions of types of stature imply a high standard not merely for royalty but for the nobility as well. That it had some influence in giving a popular respect is probably offset by the equally unusual height of the popular and antiroyal saints. The chroniclers have been more generous in giving details of other physical and mental characteristics of the kings. This study thus adds precision about one of the more obvious and important factors in their personality.

Notes

1. *Heimskringla* iv, 44. *Heimskringla, the Norse Sagas by Snorre Sturlason*, trans. by S. Laing (London, 1930), p. 230.

72

TWELFTH CENTURY STUDIES

2. *Heimskringla* iv, 45; Laing, p. 230.
3. *Dictionary of National Biography* under Harold (VIII, 1302). The source is not given. Perhaps it is "Haroldus procerior statura fratris," *Lives of Edward the Confessor,* ed. H. R. Luard (London, 1858, Rolls Series), p. 409.
4. *English Historical Documents,* ed. D. C. Douglas and G. W. Greenaway (New York, 1953), II, 251. This assumes that the makers of the tapestry endeavored to indicate height. At least the figures are not given the same height. William the Conqueror appears in one place as taller than his brother, Odo, and his son, Robert. *Ibid.,* II, 264.
5. (There is a) "low positive relationship between height and leadership." R. M. Stogdill, "Personal Factors Associated with Leadership: a Survey of the Literature," *The Journal of Psychology,* XXV (1948), 41 and literature there cited.
6. *Polydori Vergilii Urbinatis Anglicae Historiae Libri XXVI* (Basel, 1534), one book to each king. He was copied by other chroniclers.
7. "Erat autem staturae mediocris, compacti corporis, alterius oculi palpebra demissiore, ita ut partem nigredinis pupillo celaret." He could have found this in the following three chroniclers. William Rishanger, *Chronica et Annales,* ed. H. T. Riley (London, 1865, Rolls Series), p. 75; Nicholas Trivet, *Annales,* ed. T. Hog (London, 1845), p. 280; Thomas of Walsingham, *Historia Anglicana,* ed. H. T. Riley (London, 1863, Rolls Series), I, 8.
8. "Statura corporis decentissima," Vergil, bk. x.
9. "Edouardus corpore procero, ac eminenti quippe qui omnes excederet statura." Vergil, bk. xxiv.
10. His tomb was opened and his bones examined on March 13, 1789. J. C. Wall. *The Tombs of the Kings of England* (London, 1891), pp. 349–50.
11. Vergil, bk. xxiii.
12. Professor Macalister's description of his remains is, "Fairly strong man, aged between 45 and 55, who was at least five feet nine inches in height (he may have been an inch taller, but I give the minor limit)." *Archaeologia,* LXII (1911), 536.
13. "Statura quae parum iustum excederet." Vergil, bk. xxvi.
14. W. H. St. John Hope, "On the Funeral Effigies of the Kings and Queens of England," *Archaeologia,* LX (1907), 551. Hereafter this is referred to as Hope. See also note 46.
15. C. Markham, *Richard III, His Life and Character* (London, 1906), p. 246.
16. Vergil, bk. xxv.
17. C. A. Stothard, *The Monumental Effigies of England* (London, 1836), p. 140. See below for evidence about accuracy of length of effigies. Stothard's scale of length for each illustration is assumed to be accurate.
18. "Honesta et justa." Vergil, bk. xxi.
19. "Fuit statura corporis quae justum excederet." Vergil, bk. xxi.
20. "Fuit formae gratia." Vergil, bk. xx.
21. "Judging from the length and size altogether of the male bones, there can be no doubt that they belonged to a man nearly six feet in height." *Archaeologia,* XLV (1880), 323.

22. T. and G. Hollis, *The Monumental Effigies of Great Britain* (London, 1840–2), pt. 1, nos. 9–10.

23. Stothard, *Monumental Effigies*, p. 29 for length of effigy. The length of the body was stated to be 5-6½ in Valentine Green, *An Account of the Discovery of the Body of King John* (London and Winchester, 1797), p. 4. Nash, *Worcestershire*, quoted in J. H. Ramsay, *The Angevin Empire*, p. 502 gives 5-6. A. L. Poole, *From Domesday Book to Magna Carta, 1087-1216* (Oxford, 1951), p. 486 gives 5-5.

24. Stothard, *Monumental Effigies*, pp. 13–14, 16.

25. Hollis, *Monumental Effigies*, pt. 1, no. 1. His wife's effigy is 5-6.

26. Lynn White, Jr., "Natural Science and Naturalistic Art in the Middle Ages," *American Historical Review*, LII (1947), 421–35.

27. Stothard, *Monumental Effigies*, p. 19; Ramsay, *op. cit.*, p. 367 gives 6-2.

28. Richard, Prior of Holy Trinity, London. "Erat quidem statura procerus, elegantis formae," *Chronicles and Memorials of the Reign of Richard I*, ed. W. Stubbs (London, 1864, Rolls Series), I, 144. "Erat itaque elegantis formae, statura praegrandis et omnium membrorum decentissimus." *Ibid.*, I, 197.

29. "Ambo staturae grandis, pauloque plusquam mediocris et formae dignae imperio." *Giraldi Cambrensis Opera*, ed. G. F. Warner (London, 1891, Rolls Series), VIII, 248. "Ambo hi staturae modicae, pauloque mediocre plus pusille. *Ibid.*, V, 199.

30. "Hic statura procerus," excerpt from Gervase in *Radulphi de Coggeshall Chronicon Anglicanum*, ed. J. Stevenson (London, 1875, Rolls Series), p. 447.

31. "Staturae vir erat inter mediocres; quod nulli filiorum contingere potuit; primaevis ambobus paulo mediocritatem excedentibus; junioribus vero duobus infra subsistensibus." *Giraldi Cambrensis Opera*, VIII, 215.

32. "He was a little over medium height," quoted from *De nugis curialium*, *English Historical Documents*, II, 389; Peter of Blois, Letter no. 66, quoted by K. Norgate, *England under the Angevin Kings* (London, 1887), I, 409.

33. "Justae fuit staturae, immensae corpulentiae." *Willelmi Malmesbiriensis monachi de gestis regum Anglorum*, ed. W. Stubbs (London, 1889, Rolls Series), II, 335. The French standard was somewhat lower apparently, for a monk of Caen wrote of him that William was "great in body and strong, tall in stature but not ungainly." *English Historical Documents*, II, 280.

34. "Praecipuo robore, quanquam non magnae staturae, "William of Malmesbury, *op. cit.*, II, 374. "The king's tomb, whatever it was, was crushed by the fall of the steeple in 1107 and all that remains of his bones now rests in one of the relic chests on the north side of the presbytery." *Archaeologia*, LX (1907), 521. See also, *Ibid.*, XLII (1869), 309–21.

35. "Statura minimos supergrediens, a maximis vincebatur." William of Malmesbury, *op. cit.*, II, 488.

36. These are given in sixteenths of an inch taken from the pictures in the *Pictorial History of England* (London, 1838–9): Edward the Confessor, I, 203; William I, I, 358; William II, I, 392; Henry I, I, 405; Stephen, I, 420; Henry II, I, 438. For the difficulties of the measurements see also J. H. Bloom, *English Seals* (London, 1906), ch. II and especially pp. 68–79.

37. On his seal William I's arms seem to be long with respect to his legs even when compared to other early kings. This physical characteristic was noted when his tomb was opened in 1562. *Archaeologia*, LX (1907), 520–1.

38. The Bayeux Tapestry also seems to show him as a tall man. *English Historical Documents*, II, 239, 253. He is described by a contemporary, "persona erat decentissima, discretae proceritatis reliquo corpore toto integer et regius homo." *Lives of Edward the Confessor* (Rolls Series), p. 396.

39. The author of the "Gesta Stephani," *Chronicles of the Reigns of Stephen, Henry II and Richard I*, ed. R. Howlett (London, 1886, Rolls Series), III, 5. He was also stated to be a man of great energy and boldness. William of Malmesbury, *Historia Novella* (Rolls Series), II, 539.

40. *Pictorial History of England*, I, 671, 689 and 731 respectively.

41. *Ibid.*, I, 748, 781 and II, 5 respectively.

42. *Ibid.*, II, 99, 117 and 123 respectively. See also J. H. Bloom, *English Seals*, ch. II.

43. J. C. Wall, *Tombs of the Kings of England*, p. 251 and note 7; *Archaeologia*, XLV (1880), 320; Stothard, p. 52.

44. Stothard, p. 73.

45. Joseph Ayloffe, "An Account of the Body of King Edward the First, as It appeared on opening his Tomb in 1774." *Archaeologia*, III (1776), 385.

46. Hope, *Archaeologia*, LX (1907), 517. The attributions are thought to be quite correct. Cf. *Ibid.*, pp. 565–70. Ayloffe, p. 386.

47. "Elegantis erat formae, staturae procerae, qua (ab) humero et supra communi populo praeeminebat." Rishanger, p. 76: Trivet, p. 281; Walsingham, I, 8 (See note 7). "Statura ejus procera et decens singulis membris ejus, ut incedendo cum populo facies ejus supereminentibus ceteris resplenderet, prout Saul quondam electus Domini animos inspicientium regem incidendem gratus laetificaret." *Chronicles of the Reigns of Edward I and Edward II*, ed. W. Stubbs (London, 1883, Rolls Series), II, 5.

48. Stothard, p. 78.

49. "Fuit corpore quidam elegans, viribus praestans," *Chronicles of the Reigns of Edward I and Edward II* (Rolls Series), II, 91.

50. "Corpore fuit elegans, statura quae nec justum excederet, nec nimis depressioni succumberet." Thomas Walsingham, *Historia Anglicana*, ed. H. T. Riley (London, 1863, Rolls Series), I, 328.

51. Hope, *Archaeologia*, LX (1907), 548–9, 551.

52. Stothard, p. 120.

53. F. G. Parsons, "Report on the Hythe Crania," *Journal of the Royal Anthropological Institute*, XXXVIII (1908), 422–3; "Report on the Rothwell Crania," *ibid.*, XL (1910), 493–4.

54. J. Beddoe, *The Races of Britain* (Bristol, 1885). The data are given on pp. 190–1 and comments on pp. 143–4. The evidence upon height also appears in his "On the Stature and Bulk of Man in the British Isles," *Memoirs Read Before the Anthropological Society of London*, III (1867–9), 384–573, especially p. 542 ff.

55. Somewhat the same kind of distinction can be seen in J. S. Brewer and J. S. Rodrigues, "Some Determinants of Apparent Size," *The Journal of*

Abnormal and Social Psychology, XLVIII (1953), 17–24.

56. My "Canonization of Opposition to the King in Angevin England," *Haskins Anniversary Essays* (Boston, 1929), pp. 279–90.

57. For the first see F. M. Powicke, *Stephen Langton* (Oxford, 1928), p. 1.

58. M. Creignton, *Life of Simon de Montfort* (Oxford, 1876), p. 15. His source is not given.

59. "Nisi esset iste filius ejus, quod etiam corporis forma consimilis fateri probatur." *Magna Vita S. Hugonis Episcopi Lincolniensis*, ed. J. F. Dimock (London, 1864, Rolls Series), p. 76. Both were quite fat.

60. W. P. Thornton, "Surgical Report on a Skeleton found in the Crypt of Canterbury Cathedral," *Archaeologia Cantiana*, XVIII (1889), 257–260; C. F. Routledge, "The Bones of Archbishop Becket," *ibid.*, XXI (1895), 73–80.

61. *Memorials of Thomas Becket* (Rolls Series) II, 302; III, 17. His height is not mentioned in III, 164; IV, 5, 8, 82 and 269.

62. G. G. Coulton, *Life in the Middle Ages*, II (Cambridge, 1929), p. 117. This was in the time of the very tall king, Edward IV.

63. W. Wallace, *St. Edmund of Canterbury* (London, 1893), p. 94.

64. S. H. Thomson, "Two Early Portraits of Robert Grosseteste," *Medievalia et Humanistica*, VIII (1954), 20–1. A third and later portrait is reproduced in A. C. Crombie, *Robert Grosseteste and the Origins of Experimental Science* (Oxford, 1953) on frontispiece.

65. See picture and diagram opposite p. 249 of *Robert Grosseteste, Scholar and Bishop*, ed. D. A. Callus (Oxford, 1955). The assumption is that the inside length of the tomb is approximately the height of Robert Grosseteste.

66. Stothard, p. 56.

67. Hollis, pt. I, no. 9.

68. Hollis, pt. I, no. 10.

69. Stothard, p. 140.

70. Hope, *Archaeologia*, LX (1907), 549.

71. *Ibid.*, p. 550.

72. In his teens "well over six feet, though not yet six feet four." F. Hackett, *Henry the Eighth* (Garden City, 1931), p. 37. No evidence given. A flatterer said that he was tall as Francis I. However, all that another said was that he was "above the usual height." A. F. Pollard, *Henry the Eighth* (London, 1930), pp. 39, 86. His armor is in the Tower of London and is described as for a man about six feet in height and well proportioned. *Archaeological Journal*, LXX (1913), 75.

73. On this controversy see J. Gairdner, *Richard III* (Cambridge, 1898), pp. 118–29 and C. R. Markham, *Richard III* (Cambridge, 1908), pp. 250–85.

74. *Archaeologia*, XXIV (1834), 5.

75. C. V. Millard, *Child Growth and Development* (Boston, 1951), p. 78.

CHAPTER 5

Death Along the Deer Trails

The death of King William Rufus in A.D. 1100 is still controversial: was it accidental or the result of a plot? The factor of motivation has been thoroughly explored by Professor Hollister, whose conclusion is that it was an accident.[1] At least four other persons of the Anglo-Norman nobility died in the period 1050-1150. Since fatal hunting accidents seldom occurred in hunts before or after this time, at least in England, some particularly dangerous form of the sport must have been practiced then. A very elaborate study of Rufus' death fails to suggest a reason for such danger.[2] The problem is to work out from the sources just how hunting was conducted at the time. There is a literature on deer hunting, but for western Europe it does not begin before the middle of the thirteenth century.[3] Several factors need study: the purpose of the hunt (pleasure, exhibition of personal prowess, meat), the weapons used, the kinds of dogs and horses employed, and the location of the action—in general, the technology of the particular type of hunt. Conditions were changing rapidly in western Europe, and hunting probably changed as well.

Of the five fatal accidents, four were caused by arrows striking the victim. The fifth was the death of Richard, son of William I, perhaps about A.D. 1075, who "while he was galloping in pursuit of a wild beast had been badly crushed between a strong hazel branch and the pommel of his saddle and mortally injured."[4] Richard's death occurred in the New Forest, as did the deaths of Richard, son of Duke Robert

Curthose, and that of William Rufus. One can assume that the type of hunting was the same. No details on the deaths of the two Richards are known beyond those mentioned above. The deaths of Milo, Earl of Hereford, and Malcolm Morville happened about 1143, but little is known beyond the fact that they were killed by arrows.[5] The type of hunting must be reconstructed from the much more extensive evidence about the death of the king. It seems clear that the hunters were not stalking the deer. This was below the dignity of kings and nobles. Slipping up on deer was a sport of lesser people, more frequently illegal than respectable.[6] Perhaps the most characteristic statement is that one might be killed by his "man" by accident.[7]

The treatises on royal hunting, beginning about 1250 in the west with *La Chasse dou Cerf,* tell of hunts in which the stag is pursued until it comes to bay.[8] By 1250 the hunt had become quite formal, but earlier it had probably been more of a rough-and-tumble chase of the deer, such as is told of Charlemagne's court.[9] The hunt now required an extensive personnel. In 1322 the royal hunter of King Edward II, William of Twici, was required to assemble a company including a lardener, two berners, four ventrers and a page, together with twenty-four greyhounds and forty staghounds. It was emphasized that at that time of year (July 21), the deer were fat and that the venison should be salted and put into barrels. No wonder the lardener was the second-best-paid man in the company. The best paid, of course, was Twici, who even wrote a treatise on the practice of hunting.[10] The writ to Twici was only one of twenty-one orders to huntsmen in several counties and royal forests. By fourteenth-century standards, royal hunting was a considerable business.

The professional hunters and foresters knew their chases and forests and prepared seriously for the formal hunts. They chose specific stags and would show the howmets (dung) of the chosen stag which they wished to capture to royal or other masters of the chase. On the appointed day, usually in the morning, the company of hunters assembled, and the hounds who did the scenting were turned loose, presumably near the intended victim of the hunt. When the stag was unharbored (started), the regular staghounds were unleashed and sent after the stag. Apparently the hunters followed on horseback. Horns sounded the signals for the participants. The stag was fast and durable, so it often took the better part of a day to bring it to bay. Sometimes relays of hounds were used. When the stag was finally brought to bay, it was recommended that it be hamstrung before its throat was slit. Then the remains were to be divided among the dogs, hunters, royal kitchen and guests. The sport consisted of following the hounds and stag and watching it at the end. Only occasionally are archers mentioned,[11] and they do not seem to have been nobles. Participants seldom died in this type of hunt.

In contrast to this complicated and ceremonial display, there was a much simpler hunt based on the habits of the deer, especially the red deer, and on personal prowess with bow and arrow. In the forest and clearings, the deer normally drank in one place and ate in others, a typical situation being swamp for the one and higher ground for the other. The deer, creatures of habit, tended to run at particular times of day (often in the morning and evening) from one area to the other along well-marked paths. Taking advantage of these habits, the huntsmen would take posts across the several trails and wait on foot for the deer to appear. Of course the deer can be hurried by professionals who unharbor the animals. This type of hunting was still being used in South Carolina in the 1930's.[12]

Theoretically, the hunters are in no danger of shooting each other, since each hunter shoots along one trail only. Thus far there seems little danger to the archers. But if a second line of hunters were to be posted behind the first line, its arrows might easily endanger the line ahead. The idea would be for this second line to stop or chase wounded deer not killed by the first line. But deer often move very fast: an archer would usually have only one shot. He might even tend to shoot at anything up the trail which moved, particularly if his eyesight were poor (eye-glasses were invented only at the end of the thirteenth century). This type of hunt then emphasized personal prowess of the archers rather than interest in following the stags. As can be seen, it was very different from the more formal type of hunt.

The fatal hunt in which King William died began in the evening, an apparently rather impromptu affair.[13] Three bits of information were known by the court. The first was that a parcel of five or six arrows was handed to the King and Walter Tyrel, as the King praised Tirel for his skill in archery.[14] Second: the King and Tirel with a very few others went to one site. Third: after some time it was known that the King was dead and that Tirel had fled to the continent; he was French. Presumably the King's man or men reported on William's death. Yet it is possible that, hidden by vegetation, he or they did not actually know what had occurred other than the royal death. No wonder then that the word spread that Tirel had killed the King!

Eventually, more accurate information came back to the English court from Tirel or from his men on the continent. This would explain how more details were added: "The King and Walter de Poix posted themselves and a few others in one part of the forest and stood with their weapons watching for the coming of the game."[15] Medieval custom would prescribe that the King and Tirel have the best places, watching adjacent trails near each other. However, if the deer were wounded, the lesser hunters farther along the trail would shoot the deer or pursue them. (Perhaps the Conqueror's son was doing this when he ran into a tree and was crushed.)[16] From this point there is confusion in the accounts. The King injured or missed a deer, and stepped out from his post. The deer ran between the King and another archer farther along the trail. The latter then shot. His arrow either missed the deer or caromed off the deer's back. In either case the arrow then hit the King, killing him instantly or a second later when he fell on the arrow.[17] The accounts mention no professional hunters: if they participated they probably unharbored the deer.

Who killed the King? The arrow should have come from the second line of archers—presumably men of either the King or Tirel, since Tirel was probably on the trail next to that of the King. Tirel's man could have shot the arrow, especially if the deer broke from the King's trail and swerved into the next one. Tirel claimed under impressive circumstances before a high church official that he did not kill the King and was not even in that part of the forest.[18] This might mean only that he was posted along another trail from that of the King.

Now Gerald of Wales, who was often at court and picked up information there, heard that a certain Ralph de Aquis, who had originally received the package of arrows, was the culprit.[19] The probability, then, is that Ralph was Tirel's man and that it was Ralph's arrow that killed the King. Since he was Tirel's man, Tirel was morally if not legally responsible for Ralph's action. The chances are that only the archer and Tirel knew what happened, and they did not stay to tell.

After the death of the King, Tirel and his men had a quick decision to make. The knight who had killed the son of Duke Robert not long before had dashed to the Priory of Lewes and had become an instant monk.[20] After all, the Duke was still alive and so were numerous relatives and friends of the deceased. One could never tell what quick revenge might be taken. Tirel had advantages that the earlier archer did not have. The "king's peace" still died with the King and was not in force until the coronation of the next king. Tirel and his men thus had time to escape from nearby Southampton. Henry, brother of William, hurried to Winchester, which was farther away; he was more intent on taking over the treasury than he was in finding those responsible for his brother's death. If Tirel's party escaped, Henry had an easy excuse for not pursuing the matter.[21]

The danger of the type of hunting that the King engaged in was recognized. The deaths in the twelfth century of Milo of Hereford and Malcolm Morville in Scotland brought on no legal difficulties from relatives, although gifts of land were set up for the soul of Morville by relatives of the archer who killed him.[22] The feudality of the time apparently regarded death in the hunt as an occupational hazard of their order.

Questions remain. Why did the second line of archers stay so close to the first? Had the range of the arrow increased while custom kept the second line where it had been earlier? Did the introduction of faster horses (perhaps a result of the Crusades) make the pursuit of deer on horseback more attractive?

Deer hunting by posting along deer trails did emphasize personal prowess and individual skill, even if it did result in the death of a king and series of nobles. It was appropriate to Norman culture. The arrow had been a very important factor at the Battle of Hastings—particularly in Harold's death. Its decline on the royal level was symptomatic of a more sophisticated age which preferred semi-spectator sport where men on horseback watched hounds chasing deer or falcons pursuing game.[23]

Notes

1. The literature on the subject is given conveniently in C. W. Hollister, "The Strange Death of William Rufus," *Speculum*, 48 (1973), 637–653.
2. D. Grinnell-Milne, *The Killing of William Rufus* (Newton Abbot, 1968).
3. Recently, for history of hunting, see Marcelle Thiébaux, *The Stag of Love* (Ithaca, 1974), or an earlier article, "The Mediaeval Chase," *Speculum*, 42 (1967), 260–274. Most of the early treatises have been edited by Gunnar Tilander in *Cynegetica*.
4. Ordericus Vitalis, *Historia ecclesiastica*, ed. A. Le Prévost, 5 vols (Paris, 1838-55), 2:391, *The Ecclesiastical History of Orderic Vitalis*, ed. M. Chibnall, Oxford Medieval Texts (Oxford, 1972–   ), 3:114–115. For the death of Richard, son of Robert Curthose, see Ordericus Vitalis, *Hist. eccl.*, ed. Le Prévost, 4:82–83.
5. *Gesta Stephani*, ed. K. R. Potter (London, 1955), p. 16: "And Miles...had his breast pierced with a comrade's arrow while hunting and died immediately." For Malcolm, see *Liber S. Marie de Dryburgh*, ed. J. Spottiswode (Edinburgh, 1847), pp. 68–69. The relatives included the mother of the Scotch king.
6. Lines 6311–6318 of Geoffrey Gaimar suggest that the king and his court saw deer and stopped, a form of stalking; but his account is very late and differs from more contemporary data. On stalking see D. P. Blaine, *An Encyclopaedia of Rural Sports* (London, 1840), pp. 530–537.
7. For Richard, son of Duke Robert, "a suo milite sagitta percussus interiit" (Florence of Worcester, *Chronicon ex chronicis*, ed. B. Thorpe [London, 1846–49], 2: 45); for William Rufus, "suorum unus militum...eadem in corde percussit" (*Chronicon monasterii de Abingdon*, ed. J. Stevenson, [Rolls Series, London, 1858], 2: 43) and "quidam ejus miles...pro cervo ipsum regem occidit" (William of Poitou, in *PL*, 149, col. 1271).
8. Thiébaux, *The Stag of Love*, pp. 17–58, and article in *Speculum*, (1967), 260–274.

9. Thiébaux, *The Stag of Love*, p. 25, citing Notker, tr. L. Thorpe (Baltimore, 1969), pp. 165–166.

10. *Calendar of Close Rolls, Edw. II (1318–1323)*, p. 578. Twici received 7½d. a day in 1322 and 9d. in 1325 (Alice Dryden, *The Art of Hunting* [Northampton, 1908], p. xi, from P.R.O. Exchequer Accounts Q.R. 279/16 and 361/18; in the latter account the lardener, Little William, got 3½d. a day while the better paid of the others only received 2d.). Dryden edited the work of Twici (*The Art of Hunting*, pp. 27–45; *La Chasse dou cerf*, pp. 119–130).

11. Dryden, *The Art of Hunting*, p. 55, from Twici.

12. I saw such a hunt near Myrtle Beach near the coast, as a nonhunting guest. The deer were started by the professional hunter with dogs. The deer came very fast, but only two, both does, were shot, bringing heavy fines on the hunt. The hunters were lined up across the deer trails, only one to a trail.

13. Ordericus Vitalis, *Hist. eccl.*, ed. Le Prévost, 4: 86. On evening as a favorite time for hunting since the deer were hungry then, see Blaine, *Encyclopaedia of Rural Sports*, p. 529.

14. Six arrows, two to Tirel (Ordericus Vitalis, *Hist. eccl.*, ed. Le Prévost, 4: 86); five arrows, all to Ralph of Aquis (Gerald of Wales, *De principis instructione*, in *Opera*, ed. G. F. Warner, [Rolls Series, London, 1891], 8: 325).

15. "Is (Tirel) ceteris per moram venationis, quo quemque casus tulerat, dispersis, solus cum eo remanserat" (William of Malmesbury, *De gestis regum Anglorum*, ed. W. Stubbs, 2 vols., [Rolls Series, London, 1887], 2: 378; Ordericus Vitalis, *Hist. eccl.*, ed. Le Prévost, 2: 375, and ed. Chibnall, 3: 95).

16. For the death of the Conqueror's son, see Ordericus Vitalis, *Hist. eccl.*, ed. Le Prévost, 2: 391, and ed. Chibnall, 3: 114–115.

17. Ordericus Vitalis, *loc. cit,;* Eadmer, *Historia novorum in Anglia*, ed. M. Rule, (Rolls Series, London, 1884), p. 116. William of Malmesbury (*De gestis*, 2: 378) adds a second deer to the confusion, which is, of course, possible. Grinnell-Milne (p. 100) assumes beaters, as on his map, and that Ralph de Aquis was the chief hunter and the man who killed the king. The author probably picked the right man but for the wrong reason.

18. Abbot Suger, of Saint-Denis, *Louis VI*, p. 12, in *PL*, 149, col. 1031.

19. Gerald of Wales, *Opera*, 8: 325.

20. Ordericus Vitalis, *Hist. eccl.*, ed. Le Prévost, 4: 82; William of Malmesbury, *De gestis*, 2: 332; Florence of Worcester, *Chronicon ex chronicis*, 2: 45; *Gesta normannorum ducum*, p. 279.

21. As Hollister points out (p. 652), apparently nothing was done about the matter by Henry I. Considered with the other cases of hunting deaths, this is not remarkable.

22. *Liber S. Marie de Dryburgh*, pp. 68–69.

23. From the number of references in the records, falconry might seem even more important than hunting. On the sport see Robin S. Oggins, "Falconers in the English Royal Household to 1307," *Studies in Medieval Culture*, 4 (1974), 321–329.

CHAPTER 6

Allegations of Poisoning in the Norman World

Sudden death was so traumatic in the Middle Ages that, unless its cause was obvious, it aroused suspicion of an unnatural cause, sometimes poison. Among the Normans several unexplained deaths in the ruling class were alleged to have been poisoning.[1] Many of these came from one writer, Ordericus Vitalis,[2] but there were other stories from later writers. These statements should be examined with regard to their accuracy: what poisons might have been used, what chances were there to administer them, and what illness might have been mistaken for poisoning—even what attitudes and biases might have existed toward the question.[3]

The historical literature on poisoning in the Middle Ages is not large and tends to skip from Nero to the Borgias, or a little earlier to the fourteenth century, and thus avoids the period of the Normans (A.D. 1000–1250).[4] The reigns of John and Henry III (1199—1272) occasionally figure, with, as might be expected, King John as the villain.[5] Earlier than this, Eustace, son of King Stephen, has been considered a victim.[6] The most serious accusations of poisoning constitute an appendix to D.C. Douglas's *William the Conqueror,* leading the author to consider the possibility of poison as a policy. Later than the reign of the Conqueror another alleged case involved the court of his son, Robert Curthose.[7] There are others, enough to make the question of poisoning important enough to consider

as a distinct problem. The brutal treatment of the conquered
English by the Normans, worse almost than that accorded any
other conquered group in the Middle Ages, casts an unfavorable light on the Normans to start with.

The Dukes of Normandy were not immune, according to
eleventh century sources. Richard III was poisoned about
1027, while his successor, Robert I, died similarly while on a
pilgrimage in the east about 1035.[8] Others also died abroad,
allegedly from poison. On a visit to Rome about 1050–1056 a
monk, Gunfred, treasurer of a group of pilgrims, died under
suspicious circumstances.[9] Gunfred was a monk of St. Évroul,
of which the chronicler, Orderic Vitalis, was a member and the
other pilgrims were well known to the chronicler. Alan, Count
of Brittany, fell to poison even earlier, while a later count,
Conan, was poisoned by none other than William the Conqueror, according to the source.[10] William, it was alleged,
entertained Walter of Pontoise, nephew of King Edward of
England, and Walter's wife, Biota, and murdered them both
with a poison draught.[11] These were all very important persons, both alleged poisoners and victims. No wonder then that
Professor Douglas could consider "poisoning as a method of
political action".[12] Nor did it end there. Many years later,
Sibyl, the wife of Robert Curthose, was alleged to have been
poisoned by Agnes, widow of Walter Giffard, an ambitious
woman at Robert's court. Even in southern Italy the Normans
were involved. Sikelgaita, wife of Robert Guiscard, is said to
have caused both her stepson, Bohemund, and her husband to
be poisoned. And yet no one was tried for poisoning in the
proper courts!

Let us look at the more detailed actions. Orderic Vitalis
tells a long story of Sikelgaita's unsuccessful efforts to destroy
Bohemund and her success with her husband.[13] She was said
to have arranged for doctors at Salerno, the already famous
medical center, to give Bohemund poison which she sent to
them. Bohemund, recuperating from wounds at Salerno, recognized the poison and wrote his father about it. Robert
threatened Sikelgaita who then sent an antidote to the Salernitan physicians who gave it to Bohemund. Later she poisoned
her husband, Robert. This tragedy in slow motion is extremely

unlikely and other sources suggest more natural causes for Robert's death. The accused was a woman and Italian, enough to arouse suspicion in a northern monk.

A second story deals with a noble, Robert de Gere. "One day when he was sitting happily by the fire, he watched his wife, Adelaide, holding in her hands four apples. He playfully snatched two of these from her and, ignorant that they were poisoned, despite his wife's protests, ate them." The poison, according to the story, soon took effect and after a few days he died. Douglas calls this "the overhasty eating of rotten apples", an obvious guess. More likely they were green apples. Even half a century ago children were warned against eating green apples, because they might cause "cholera morbus."[14] If Adelaide held four of them in one hand, they must have been small.

Now most of these accounts are by Orderic Vitalis and few occur in other sources of that period. One can then focus on the accuracy of one man. "Ordericus, if credulous, was neither malicious nor a liar, and these accounts concerned persons of whom he had special knowledge," according to Professor Douglas.[15] Yet the chronicler's experience may have affected his point of view. His father, a Norman near Shrewsbury, England, sent him to the monastery of St. Évroul in Normandy at the age of ten. "I never saw him again after he sent me into exile for love of his Creator as if I had been a rejected stepson." There, because his English name sounded barbarous, the monks changed it and thus subtracted another point of identity. Perhaps in partial revolt, he remained intensely interested in England and called himself *Angligena*.[16] In the case of his most famous charge of poisoning there are other factors.

The fifth book of Orderic's history is devoted to the monastery of St. Évroul, its founding and illustrious history and continuing gifts from neighboring lords. In this euphoric account there is one jarring note: that of the hostility of Mabel Bellême, wife of Roger de Montgomery. Mabel, through her father, William Talvas, had inherited lands which had belonged to the founders of St. Évroul. According to Orderic, she misused her rights of patronage of the Abbey, requiring it to entertain too many knights for too long, causing the abbot to object. This produced a celebrated altercation and permanent bad feelings.[17] "She was powerful and secular, callous and loquacious and too cruel." Unluckily for St. Évroul, she and her husband were in the good graces of William the Conqueror. She escaped from her dinner with the abbot after the altercation ill with something which might be interpreted as poison.[18]

Orderic went farther than this. After all, he was writing at the request of his superiors and for their benefit. According to him, Mabel came to a proper end. As revenge for taking a castle (just how is not stated) of a certain Hugh, that man and his three brothers crashed into her home near Bures near Troarne and cut off her head. "But in the end the just judge, who mercifully spares penitent sinners and sternly smites the impenitent, allowed that cruel woman, who had shed the blood of many and had forcibly disinherited many lords and compelled them to beg their bread in foreign lands, to perish herself by the sword of Hugh. When the murder of this terrible lady had been accomplished, many rejoiced at her fate."[19] What had happened was that Duke William had driven out these lords for rebelling against him and had given their lands to his faithful subjects, Roger and Mabel.

Orderic accused Mabel of preparing a poisonous draught for Arnold Échauffeur, but unluckily her husband's brother, Gilbert, came in first on horseback and drank the draught with fatal effects. This attempt failing, she persuaded Arnold's servant to give Arnold poison which she prepared which not only poisoned Arnold but two of his fellow guests, who, however, managed to survive. Now the odd thing is that none of the relatives of Arnold or the others chose to accuse Mabel of poisoning. The stories turn up a half century later, when Arnold's youngest son, still a monk of St. Évroul, told marvelous stories of the Bible and of what he had heard and seen.[20] He was probably the source of many of Orderic's stories.

Mabel was murdered near the Abbey of Troarne "where Durand was abbot [who] buried the mutilated corpse on 5 December (1077?) and, more through the partiality of friends than because of any special deserts of hers, inscribed this epitaph over her tomb:"[21]

> From the high stock of nobles sprung,
> Mabel, great lady, lies beneath this tomb.
> She among famous women showed most worth,
> Known for her merits over all the earth.
> In mind most keen, alert, tireless in deed,
> She spoke with purpose, counselled well in need.
> In stature slight, but great in probity,
> Lavish in spending, dressed with dignity;
> The shield of her inheritance, a tower
> Guarding the frontier; to some neighbors dear,
> To others terrible; she died by the sword,
> By night, by stealth, for we are mortals all.
> And since in death she sorely needs our aid
> Pray for her: prove your friendship in her need.

Just why did Orderic preserve this epitaph which is so out of harmony with his other remarks about Mabel? Did he have a certain respect for her or did the written words of an epitaph have a kind of sanctity? Under the circumstances, it looks as if Orderic was convinced of the relevance of poison as a political factor and did not hesitate to make accusations of it, particularly by women. That there was much truth in these accusations is very doubtful.

The middle of the twelfth century saw two cases of alleged poisoning within months of each other. William Fitz Herbert, who had been a controversial figure as archbishop of York, was restored to his office in 1154 and died on June 8 of that year as he raised the chalice at mass.[22] Eustace, the son of King Stephen of England, died in 1153 under such suspicious circumstances, so favorable to Henry of Anjou, soon to be King Henry II, that a modern scholar has suspected poison.[23] Actually, the symptoms, sudden seizure at a meal, might suggest among other possibilities acute appendicitis. This possibility will be considered later after reviewing other instances of alleged poisoning in the thirteenth century.

In that century King John was said to have poisoned Mathilda, daughter of Robert Fitzwalter, after an infatuation which failed: she is supposed to have eaten a lethal egg.[24] The king himself fell ill in 1216 in the monastery of Swineshead and died in a few days. One late chronicle said that the king was poisoned there and another chronicler accused a black monk of

Worcester of the deed.[25] The king was buried at Worcester and his reputation was sufficient to cause such stories to rise in the thirteenth century. Other stories of his death connected it with his eating peaches with beer, not a likely poison. These are casual stories and probably have little basis in fact.

The thirteenth century actually saw a case that went to court; that of Walter de Scoteny in 1258–59. The best account is that of Matthew Paris, the great St. Albans chronicler. The conclusion of that case is the last item in his *Chronica Majora*.[26] Even he does not explain why a longtime and apparently trusted seneschal of Earl Richard of Gloucester should have tried to take his master's life as well as that of Richard's brother. Walter was said to have owed William a considerable sum of money.[27] The poisoning, according to one source, took place at the table of Prince Edward, a curious place for such an act. The evidence was apparently that William, as he died, claimed that all the world knew that Walter was guilty.[28] Walter had fled and, after capture in London, was placed in the Tower. Later, he was tried at Winchester, convicted, drawn and hung.[29]

The year 1258 was a turbulent time in England with that country sharply divided between the king, supported by his half brother and others, and a reform group which had seized the government. The judge at Winchester was one of the reformers. Matthew Paris reports at the same time as the Scoteny case the story of William Bussey, an unbelievably arrogant follower of the king's half brother.[30] Perhaps there was bad blood between Scoteny and William, the earl's brother, over money matters which underlay the poison charge when Richard and William fell ill.

If one accepts the reality of poisoning, the problems of what poisons were used and how they were administered still remain. An avid Classical reader, like Orderic, doubtless read of the poisoning of Socrates.[31] However, hemlock was a slow poison, numbing the body with no noticeable effect on the stomach, utterly unlike the "griping of the guts", so quaintly described in the early London bills of mortality. Both laudunum from the opium poppy and aconite were poisons, but they were also classed as medicines.[32] The standard treatise on poisons by Nicanor dealt primarily with noxious plants and animals which would be encountered by "ploughman, herdsman, woodcutter, whenever in the forest or at the plough."[33] There are no hints about concocting poisons and almost an obsession with regard to harmful plants, insects and animals, along with an array of antidotes, some quite fantastic. The Church was much against the use of poison, and the Hippocratic Oath denounced its use. Little poisoning might be expected.

The problem of administering poison was compounded by the lack of privacy at medieval courts. At table there were the common mugs and common bowls of food. Even the events alleged in poison incidents reflect the difficulties. Mabel was said to have prepared a goblet for Arnold, but Gilbert came in first and drank it, forcing Mabel to bribe a servant to poison him, an unlikely story. And why should Adelaide be playing with poisoned apples: too much like Eve. Or the story about Charles the Bad who is alleged to have bribed a troubadour to buy poison from an apothecary and put it in the soups, meat and wine of the French court.[34] Nor could one count on Salernitan doctors, the best in the medieval world, to send both poison and antidote.

Alternatives to explanations of sudden death caused by poisons are open easily in the form of digestive troubles, especially appendicitis. An authority on that disease, after looking over the diagnoses of deaths of English kings, suggested that King Stephen almost certainly died of it: "the iliac passion rather conveys the impression that it was a well known disease."[35] Given the tendency of appendicitis to run in families, not only Eustace, Stephen's son but other members of the Conqueror's family were likely candidates. Henry I was said to have died of eating lampreys which disagreed with him despite his liking for them. His treatment before death is described as a "dose of purgative physic, honestly if overenthusiastically prescibed, careless dispensed and injudiciously administered." William I was said to have had his body ruptured by a sudden thrust against his saddle or by stomach trouble, while both William's father and uncle were thought poisoned, as has been shown.[36]

Something depends upon the chances of death by appendicitis. Today they are small, but this is the result of early diagnosis and effective surgery. The chance of death from appendicitis in the Middle Ages cannot be derived from medieval data. About all that one can do is to assume that certain modern conditions approximate the medieval closely enough to use in an estimate. Probably it can be assumed that persons hospitalized for appendicitis now would have died in the Middle Ages. This would have seemed to have been near five per cent of all deaths, calculating upon an expectation of life of about thirty years.[37] Appendicitis seems to strike more at higher social classes and against those who have a low cellulose content in their diet.[38] Appendicitis must be rated among the most frequent causes of death in the Middle Ages.

Appendicitis was particularly likely to be diagnosed as poisoning then. Unlike food poisoning which would usually make numbers ill, appendicitis struck at individuals. It frequently occurred in time of perfect health, often when the person was asleep.[39] It affects young men oftener than older persons, the very persons, like Eustace, whose lives were important to the feudal ruling class. Thus when a series of persons in the same family died of 'acute stomach trouble' the possibility of appendicitis should be considered. Of course other complaints, especially of the stomach and intestines, might raise such suspicions.

The chance of dying from appendicitis was perhaps as high as five per cent. Lacking modern diagnosis, it, as well as kindred stomach and intestinal ailments, could easily be mistaken for poison. Yet the latter was difficult to arrange, either to get poison or to have it administered by cook or butler in an age of devoted followers. These were devious methods. In a simple age "there must have been more certain and direct means to murder. An axe through the skull or a knife in the back."[40] Ordericus Vitalis is unusual, even as a chronicler, in his obsession with the idea of poison. Unfortunately his extensive writings and authoritative opinions tend to give a venomous cast to this period which it hardly deserves, even though stakes ran high for the violent warbands of Normans in England, southern Italy, or Sicily.

Notes

1. D. C. Douglas, *William the Conqueror* (London, 1964), pp. 408–415.
2. Ordericus Vitalis, *Historia Ecclesiastica*. A new edition and translation into English is being prepared by M. Chibnall, *The Ecclesiastical History of Ordericus* (Oxford, Clarendon Press, 1969–   ). This will be referred to as OVMC. An older edition and translation into French by A. Le Prévost appeared in the series, Société de l'Histoire de France, 5 vols. (1838–1855). This will be referred to as OVLP.
3. For the subject in general, L. P. Stevenson, *The Meaning of Poison* (Lawrence, University of Kansas Press, 1959).
4. E. Dupré et René Charpentier, *Les empoissonneurs* (Lyon, 1909), pp. 9, 13; E.J. Perry, "Poisonings in the Middle Ages," *The Chemist and Druggist*, 128 (1938), 746–748; anonymous, "Poisons and Poisoners from Classical Times to the Renaissance." *Crookes Digest* no. 29 (1957), 19–24.
5. C. J. S. Thompson, *Poison Mysteries in History, Romance and Crime* (London, 1923), pp. 101–104.
6. Thomas Callahan, Jr., "Sinners and Saintly Retribution: the Timely Death of King Stephen's son, Eustace," *Studia Monastica*, 19 (1976), 109–116.
7. OVLP IV, 184.
8. Douglas gives a good summary of their deaths, pp. 408–409. William of Malmesbury, *De gestis regum Anglorum*, ed. W. Stubbs (London, R. S.) I, 211–212; OVMC III, 85; OVLP II, 10, 366; V, 366; William of Jumièges, Migne, *Patrologia Latina*, CXLIX, col. 854.
9. OVMC II, 60; OVLP II, 57.
10. OVMC II, 119, 313; OVLP II, 252, 369.
11. OVMC II, 313; OVLP II, 259.
12. Douglas, *William the Conqueror*, pp. 408–415.
13. OVMC IV, 28-31; OVLP I, 181–183.
14. OVMC II, 29, 78; OVLP II, 28, 72–73; Douglas, 413–414.
15. Douglas, p. 414.
16. L. Delisle in OVLP II, 424; V, xxxii-xxxiv; OVMC III, 151.
17. OVMC II, 55, 88; OVLP II, 52, 81.
18. OVMC II, 50, 56; OVLP II, 47, 53. If this really means that Orderic thought it proper for his abbot to poison Mabel, it is a little hard to say that he is not malicious.
19. OVMC III, 134–137; OVLP II, 410–411.
20. OVMC III, 134-136; OVLP II, 106–110; on Orderic's hindsight, OVMC IV, xx–xxv.
21. OVMC III, 136–139; OVLP, 410–412.
22. Gervase of Canterbury, *The Historical Works*, ed. W. Stubbs (London, R.S. 1879), I, 158.
23. "Sed cum ad mensam, ut in scripto legimus, pransurus sedisset, ad primum edulii gustum insanus effectus miserabiliter interiit," Gervase of Canterbury, I, 155. This occurred about 17 August 1153. Robert of Torigni, in *Chronicles of the Reigns of Stephen, Henry II and Richard I*, ed, R.

Howlett (London, R.S., 1889), IV, 116.

24. Dugdale, *Monasticon Anglicanum*, VI, 147 from a chronicle of Dunmow. In Thompson, *Poison Mysteries*, p. 102, and naturally doubted by S. Painter, *The Reign of King John* (Baltimore, 1949), pp. 234, 261.

25. "Qui nocte illa, de fructu persicorum et novi pomacii potatione nimis repletis, febrilem in se calorem acuit fortiter et ascendit," Roger of Wendover, *Flores Historiarum*, ed. H. C. Hewlett (London, R. S. 1886), II, 196. The story of the poisoning at Swineshead is in the Annals of T. Wykes, *Annales Monastici*, IV, 59, and of the poisoning by a Worcester monk or at Worcester, Annales of Bermundsey. *Annales Monastici*, III, 45.

26. *Chronica Majora*, ed. H. R. Luard (London, R. S. 1880), V, 725–726, 737–738, 747–748. Thompson, *Poison Mysteries*, p. 102.

27. *Chronica Majora*, V, 747–748.

28. Leland, *Collectanea*, I, 243. from a chronicle of Pershore. At Winchester, according to the Annales of Tewkesbury. *Annales Monastici*, I, 167.

29. Annals of T. Wykes, *Annales Monastici*, IV, 120; Annals of Tewkesbury, *Annales Monastici*, I, 167; Annals of Winchester, *Annales Monastici*, II, 98.

30. *Chronica Majora*, V, 726. The judge was Richard, Earl of Clare.

31. Delisle in OVLP V, xxxviii–xxxix.

32. Thompson, *Poison Mysteries*, pp. 29, 33, 70–71; Odell Shepard, *The Lore of the Unicorn* (London, 1930), pp. 123–124 for an antidote in folklore.

33. Nicander, *The Poems and Poetical Fragments*, ed. A. S. F.Gow and A. F. S. Schofield (Cambridge, 1953), p.29. It is, of course, Classical but circulated as one of several *antidotaria* in the Middle Ages.

34. Parry, "Poisonings", p. 750.

35. A. Rendell Short, *The Causation of Appendicitis* (Bristol, 1946), p. 15. "Dimisso autem post colloquium comite, rex subito ille dolore cum veterano emoriodarum fluxu violenter corripitur, et ibidem in curia monachorum decumbens diem clausit extremum octavo kal. Nov." Gervase of Canterbury, I, 159.

36. For hereditary tendencies, F. F. Boyce, *Acute Appendicitis and its Complications* (New York, 1949), pp. 44–45. For the death of Henry I, Henry of Huntingdon, *Historia Anglorum*, ed. T. Arnold (London, R. S. 1879), p.254. For William I, "Sic Guillelmus rex licet nimio ilium dolore angeretur," Stephen of Caen, in J. A. Giles, *Scriptores Rerum Willelmi Conquestoris* (London, 1845) p. 66; William of Jumieges, Migne, *Patrologia Latina* CXLIX, col. 880; William of Malmesbury, *De gestis regum Anglorum*, II, 337; "Sed in ipso reditu viscerum dolor illum apprehendit," Simeon of Durham, II, 213; Florence of Worcester, II, 20.

37. The deathrate of persons from appendicitis in the early part of this century was about eight to fourteen per 100,000 a year. L. I. Dublin and J. A. Lotka, *Twenty-Five Years of Health Progress* (New York, 1937) pp. 388–391, 536, 577. About five per cent of those hospitalized for appendicitis died in Philadelphia, 1928–1932. Matthew Young and W. T. Russell, *Appendicitis, a Statistical Study*, Medical Research Council. Special Report Series, no. 233 (1939), p.57.

38. For upper class mortality, Young and Russell, p. 22. Other conditions, Short, *Causation*, p. 65; Young and Russell, p. 22. As a medieval estimate this may be small, since males and young, those most addicted to appendicitis, were proportionately more numerous in the medieval period than the modern. The standard treatment of appendicitis is: Zachary Cope, *The Early Diagnosis of the Acute Abdomen* (London, 13th ed, 1968). There is no literature on appendicitis in the Middle Ages. J. A. Martínez, "Historia de la Appendicitis," *Revista de la Sociedad Cubana de Historia de la Medicina*, I (1958), 32—41.

39. Boyce, *Acute Appendicitis*, pp. 113, 122, etc.

40. A remark of Professor E. Ashby Hammond on reading the study.

CHAPTER 7

The Date of Henry I's Charter to London

The charter which Henry I gave to London is of importance for a number of reasons. Politically its provisions present
the "sort of type and standard of the amount of municipal
independence and self-government at which the other towns
of the country might be expected to aim."[1] The farm (yearly
tax) of the city designated by the charter is £300 and is so
much less than what London was paying in 1130[2] that it at once
raises the question of cause. Why should as powerful a king as
Henry I, who was also exceedingly fond of money, have
agreed to reduce that great and growing city's tax to half of its
original amount? An explanation of this situation might help
elucidate some of Henry's internal policies which still baffle
one.[3] In addition the date is of interest with respect to the
Historia Britonum of Geoffrey of Monmouth which, it will be
remembered, is the great source of Arthurian romance.

Professor Tatlock has shown that Geoffrey of Monmouth
referred to a number of persons and events of his own day in
his *Historia Britonum*.[4] Among these is an item which reads:

> After Brutus had finished the building of the city
> [London], he made choice of the citizens that were to
> inhabit it, and prescribed them laws for their peaceful
> government.[5]

If "laws" refers to the royal charter, it is apparently the last datable item in the *Historia Britonum* and thus is of great value in determining the period in which the famous book was written. Professor Tatlock was interested in trying to narrow the period of composition of the charter within a closer limit than the 1130-1133 usually agreed upon. He made an intensive study of the lives of the witnesses of the London charter. He amply confirmed the validity of the period 1130-1133 with respect to the witnesses but unfortunately turned up no evidence which would show that any of the witnesses died in the period or even changed status in ways which would enable him to define the period more accurately.[6]

Had Professor Tatlock gone no farther than to have stated that the period of time was 1130-1133, little exception could be taken to his conclusion. However, he went on and asserted as sound conclusions that the charter "might date from the summer of 1130, or more likely from the Easter-time of 1132."[7] Both of these conclusions depend to a large extent upon problems of sampling which were not considered. In addition the last conclusion rests in large part upon the interpretation of charter witnessing while the former involves evidence of the early Pipe Roll of 1130. The results of the study of these aspects are essentially destructive. However, two lines of evidence exist which provide arguments leading to the conclusion that the charter was granted by Henry I shortly before he left England in the late summer of 1133. The first is based upon the pattern of Henry's policies and the second upon another clue in Geoffrey's reference to London which was quoted above. Altogether the topic presents a series of very interesting problems in historical criticism.

Henry I's charter to London was witnessed at Westminster: the assumption is that the king and the charter's witnesses were present in the city at that time.[8] Professor Tatlock's conclusions rest largely upon the "probability in favor of dates when he (Henry I) is known to have been in London, of which there are only three in this period." This reasoning is obviously an example of that very dangerous argument, the argument from silence. It is valid only if silence has meaning: in this case if Henry's activities can be followed closely, day by day if possible. Fortunately, Henry's itinerary has been exam-

ined with care by W. Farrer[9] who tends to date the documents
which illustrate the itinerary by periods of years rather than by
days, weeks, or even months. Despite this editorial caution,
Professor Tatlock writes:

> Now for all the mobility of the Norman court, the 800
> or so items in the Itinerary, and Henry of Huntingdon,
> whose account of the later movements is best, make it
> clear that he seldom was in London.[10]

Can we be certain of this? Let us see what we actually know
about Henry's time.

During the period 1130-1133, the king was in England
only about thirty months, since he was in France parts of those
years. Let us say that he was in England about 900 days.[11]
Undated charters exist which, if only one issues from each day,
would account for about eighty days. That would still leave
nine-tenths of his time about which there is no information at
all. Our knowledge is certainly not accurate enough to justify
an argument from silence.

As has been mentioned, some eighty charters are undated
but give the place of composition. Let us assume, as itineraries
of later kings tend to show, that royal charters issue with some
regularity in time from the Chancery and thus give in their
places of issue a fair sample of the king's movements and
habits of residence. This should be particularly true for the
places in which he stayed any notable length of time.

Of the eighty charters of the period which give the place of
issue, thirteen, five and eight, respectively, come from Winchester, Windsor and Woodstock.[12] These are the places
selected by Professor Tatlock as the residences which the king
preferred and at which he stayed longest. Thirteen came from
London and Westminster,[13] nearly a sixth of the sample. If
these charters illustrate the royal habits of residence, the king
spent about 145 of his 900 days in 1130-1133 at London and
Westminster. This certainly should make one hesitate before
accepting any conclusion based upon the theory that Henry I
"was seldom in London."

One of Professor Tatlock's conclusions was that the charter might more than likely date from the Easter-time of 1132.
This is based upon the theory that the charter would, because

of its great importance, more likely issue from the great council of the kingdom whose one definite meeting in London was near Easter 1132. The problem here is one of the evidence of charter witnesses: does the list of witnesses of the charter of London indicate that a great council was in session?

If the London charter had been drawn up at the time of a general council the fact should appear in the charter witness list. Such councils drew the great men of the kingdom together and placed their names in the witness lists. For instance, a witness list from the time of the council at Northampton includes the names of two archbishops, ten bishops, seven abbots, several earls and many barons.[14] A council of 1132 offers as witnesses in a charter two archbishops, thirteen bishops, the chancellor, five abbots, six earls and sixteen barons.[15] Now, as Professor Tatlock has carefully shown, the witnesses of the London charter include only one bishop, several barons with holdings in Middlesex and adjacent counties, and some none-too-important officials.[16] This very local witness list would thus indicate that no great council was being held at the time and thus would exclude Easter of 1132 as a probable date.

Professor Tatlock's other conclusion was that the charter might date from the summer of 1130. However, the chief difficulty with this conclusion is that no evidence of the charter appears in the Pipe Roll of 1130.[17] It records the Michaelmas rendering of the accounts as the entries latest in point of time. Michaelmas falls on September 29 but the session which bears its name probably began in the two weeks following the feast and ran into November. Henry I left England early in August so that any charters granted by him must have been prepared some weeks before the Pipe Roll accounts were drawn up.[18]

No evidence of the London charter appears in the Pipe Roll. Here we are facing again the argument from silence, but in this case it is very significant. This Pipe Roll contains accounts from London including that city's payments for grants of privileges. It is very difficult to believe that the king granted a charter to London which gave that city such advantages without receiving an appropriate payment which should have appeared on the Pipe Roll. In short the summer of 1130 is a very unlikely time to be considered as a date for the charter.

The two times suggested by Professor Tatlock as "likely" or "more likely" dates seem to be of no more likelihood than any date selected at random. The danger is that since his eminence in the field of literature was so great, his conjectures in the field of history might be given undue weight.

Henry I exhibited two types of strategy which are especially marked. The first was one of constant pressure over a long period of time. From London he had taken large sums of money regularly; the Pipe Roll of 1130 shows that he was exacting more than £500 from London instead of the customary £300. This was only part of that continuous pressure which had filled the treasury so satisfactorily from the royal standpoint. The second pattern of action was a sudden stroke designed to produce a paralyzing effect for a limited period of time, usually upon one side of the Channel when he was ready to cross to the other. "He knew how to wait, to allow circumstances to work for him, to let men work out their own destruction, but he was quick to act when the moment for action came."[19] This pattern appears in his sudden reconciliation with Anselm in 1106, his forcing of fealty to his son before leaving England in 1116 and the marriage of his daughter to Geoffrey of Anjoy before going to England in 1129. Since the grant of the charter was a single act in line with London's advantage, it should fall into the second category of patterns of action.

In the period of his last residence in England, 1131-1133, the obvious time for such a stroke was in the spring or summer of 1133. That he was in the mood for such an action is indicated by certain acts in regard to the Church. After Pentecost, a contemporary chronicler states, the king filled two sees, Ely and Durham, and set up the new bishopric of Carlisle.[20] These actions ended vacancies which had lasted from 1131 and 1128 respectively. They were obviously designed to put the Church in good humor during the king's approaching absence on the continent. The importance of keeping the powerful city of London in the same humor could hardly have been missed by Henry I. Its power was to be indicated by the prominent position which it took in a few years in the succession of Stephen.

The sentence in Geoffrey of Monmouth which Professor Tatlock thought had reference to the charter of London commenced, "After Brutus had finished the building of the city...." While this might be merely a convenient method of introducing the subject, it may also have contemporary connotations. As mentioned earlier, London's financial obligations were sharply reduced by this charter from nearly £ 600 a year to £ 300 a year. This reduction may have been merely a bribe to keep London in line with Henry's plans for the succession of Mathilda. However, it would be well to consider another possibility—that something had happened to London which made such a reduction of farm appropriate. The chronicles do not tell much about London in the years 1130-1133 but to each of those years they do assign a great fire. These statements present an interesting problem in historical criticism since it is not likely that there were so many fires in that period.

A very good contemporary chronicler, John of Worcester, was much interested in fires, reporting them for Gloucester (1122), Rochester (1130), London (1133), Worcester (1133), York (1137), Rochester (1137), Leicester (1137), Hereford (twice in 1138), Oxford (1138), Nottingham (1140) and Winchester (1141).[21] His one report of a London fire reads as follows:

> The greatest part of London, with the principal church of St. Paul the Apostle, in the week of Pentecost which was May 14, was burned by fire.[22]

The account falls between an event of late 1132 and the departure of Henry I in August, 1133, but no year is given. Thus one reading this account might date the fire in 1133 or in any of several preceding years. However, Whitsunday of 1133 did fall on May 14 so that the year is definite enough. It seems unlikely in view of the chronicler's interest in fires that he would have missed an outstanding London fire in those years.

The accounts in the other chronicles read:

> "1131 London was entirely burned." (Annals of Winchester—written about 1200).[23]
>
> "1132 In the same year London was burned in great part." (Roger of Wendover—early XIII Century).[24]
>
> "1131 On April 11 London was almost entirely burned." (*Flores Historiarum*—middle of XIII Century).[25]

> "1130 London was all burned except one ward and a
> half." (Annals of Worcester—early XIV Century).[26]
> "1132 In this year London was almost entirely burned by
> the fire of Gilbert Becket on April 11." (Annals of
> Bermundsey—XIV Century).[27]

The accounts of the fire are all late and, for the most part,
are probably based upon rather vague tradition whose elements were (a) a great fire devastating much of London; (b) in
the early 1130's; and (c) near a spring feast.[28] The reference to
the fire of Gilbert Becket was apparently the result of a tradition arising among the neighbors of the Beckets that at
Thomas' birth a great fire spread from the Becket house to
envelop part of London.[29] Since Thomas Becket was born
before 1120 the tradition throws no light upon a fire a decade
later. This evidence, if actually derived in this fashion, shows
the weakness of single items in the chronicles as evidence of
events.

The evidence then would point to only one great London fire in the years 1130-1133, on May 14, 1133. It was probably responsible for the loss of such things as bells and crosses
by London churches.[30] If, as seems likely, Geoffrey of Monmouth did have the contemporary London scene in mind, the
sequence of events would be (1) London fire of May 14, (2)
some rebuilding of London, (3) grant of charter to London by
Henry I, (4) crossing of Channel by Henry I early in August,
1133, and (5) writing by Geoffrey of Monmouth of that part of
the *Historia Britonum*. If any considerable rebuilding of London
occurred before the granting of the charter, the king cannot
have granted the charter long before he departed. This fits in
nicely with the earlier hypothesis that he granted it just before
he crossed the Channel. Henry's willingness to grant relief to
London casts an unexpectedly favorable light upon his relations with that city although he undoubtedly did leave a problem for his successor who might well wish to exact more
money from a rebuilt London. The evidence would show that
Geoffrey of Monmouth was writing this part of the *Historia* in
the fall of 1133 or later, possibly much later.[31]

Notes

1. William Stubbs, *Select Charters*, etc. (9th ed. revised, Oxford, 1921;) p. 128. For text see also *English Historical Review*, XLII (1927), 80–87.
2. J. H. Round, *Geoffrey de Mandeville* (London, 1892) p. 366.
3. "Did we know as much of Henry's activity in government and administration as we do of the carrying out of his foreign policy, it is more than probable that we should find in it the clear marks of creative statesmanship." G. B. Adams, *The History of England from the Norman Conquest to the Death of John* (1066–1216) (London, 1905), p. 190.
4. J. S. P. Tatlock, "Contemporaneous Matters in Geoffrey of Monmouth," *Speculum*, VI (1931), 206–224; on an even more extensive scale in his *Legendary History of Britain* (Berkeley, 1950), particularly pp. 433–437.
5. The translation is from J. A. Giles' edition, *Six Old English Chronicles* (London, 1896), p. 108.
6. J. S. P. Tatlock, "The Date of Henry I's Charter to London," *Speculum*, XI (1936), 461–469; the list of previous studies on the subject is given at the beginning. The most important is found in J. H. Round, *Geoffrey de Mandeville*, pp. 364–367.
7. Tatlock, in *Speculum*, XI (1936), 469; more recently in his *Legendary History of England*, pp. 435–436.
8. On the relationship of witnesses to charters see my "Attestation of Charters in the Reign of John," *Speculum*, XV (1940), 480–496.
9. W. Farrer, "An Outline Itinerary of King Henry I," *English Historical Review*, XXXIV (1919), 303–382, 505–579.
10. *Speculum*, XI (1936), 469.
11. These places and dates are: 1130, Mar. 30, Woodstock (no. 607); May 4, Canterbury (no. 615); May 8, Rochester (no. 615); May 18, Arundel (no. 616); 1131, Sept. 8, Northampton (no. 654); Dec. 25, Dunstable (no. 666); 1132, Apr. 10, Woodstock (no. 671); Apr. 29, London (no. 672); Dec. 25, Windsor (no. 678); 1133, Feb. 8, London (no. 681); Mar. 26, Oxford (no. 685); and Apr. 30–May 3, Winchester (no. 686).
12. Farrer, *op. cit.*, nos. 597, 611–614, 687–693, 697 for Winchester; nos. 595B, 610, 679–681 for Windsor; nos. 601, 602, 608, 609, 664A–666 for Woodstock.
13. Farrer, *op. cit.*, nos. 616, 661, 670 for London; nos. 660–671, 673, 674, 682–685, 694, 695 for Westminster. I included charters whose dates in years are at least half-covered by the years 1130–1133. The others are nos. 599, 601–607, 615, 617, 654–660, 663, 667–669, 675–677, 686, 696, 696A, 698–705, 707–712.
14. Farrer, pp. 563–564. The shorter lists from Northampton (p. 564) probably indicate that some had not arrived or had already left. None is so purely local as the witness list of the London charter.
15. J. H. Round, *Feudal England* (London, 1895), pp. 482–483.
16. *Speculum*, XI (1936), 462–467.

17. *Magnum Rotulum Scaccarii*, ed. J. Hunter (London, 1833). Cf. also J. H. Round, *Geoffrey de Mandeville*, pp. 365–366 and C. Stephenson, *Borough and Town* (Cambridge, Mass., 1933), p. 181.

18. Apparently he was on shipboard on Aug. 2. Farrer, p. 574 (no. 714).

19. G. B. Adams, *The History of England from the Norman Conquest to the Death of John* (London, 1905), p. 225. Cf. also pp. 143–146, 163–164, and 180–181. This approach to the problem of the date of the London charter and its conclusion was completed before the implications of the London fire were noticed and examined. It thus illustrates the validity of an hypothesis based upon patterns of human action.

20. Henry of Huntingdon, under 1133. Farrer, pp. 570–571, after no. 693.

21. *Florentii Wigorniensis Monachi Chronicon ex Chronicis*, ed. Benjamin Thorpe (London, 1849), II, 77, 92, 93, 94, 98, 106, 107, 128, and 133 respectively. The continuation by John of Worcester commences in 1118 (II, 71).

22. *Ibid.*, II, 93. Maxima pars Lundoniae civitatis, cum principali ecclesia beati Pauli Apostoli, in hebdomada Pentecostes, quod est ii idus Maii igne combusta est.

23. 1131 Londonia tota combusta est. *Annales Monastici*, II, 49.

24. Eodem anno Londonia pro magne parte combusta est. In Matthew Paris, *Historia Anglorum* (Rolls Series) I, 246.

25. 1131 Tertio idus Aprilis Londonia paene tota combusta est. *Flores Historiarum* (Rolls Series) II, 55.

26. 1130 Londonia tota combusta est, exceptam i wardam et dimidiam. *Annales Monastici*, IV, 378.

27. 1132 Hoc anno Londonia tota paene combusta est de igni Gilberti Becket tertio idus Aprilis. *Annales Monastici*, III, 434.

28. Apr. 11, 1132, was Easter Monday. This was pointed out to me by a student, Robert Lohman.

29. "Tradunt propinqui quod die qua ad has mundi natus est tenebras hic noster parvulus, egressus ignis de domo paterna partem plurimam civitatis incendit." *Materials for the History of Thomas Becket*, II, 356.

30. *Victoria County History*, London, I, 81.

31. Since the Brutus reference suggests a rebuilt London, it may indicate a date of writing a year or two later.

CHAPTER 8

Gratian, Irnerius, and the Early Schools of Bologna

In the twelfth century schools of some quality existed in many European countries. Most of them were based upon the reputation and ability of a few brilliant teachers and were personal in appeal rather than institutional. As a result they declined after brief careers of distinction.[1] At Bologna the schools achieved permanence and developed into a great university[2] in answer to the need for more educated persons, particularly in law. The processes of the change from schools to university are not at all clear. In the period, 1100-1150, the gatherings of students and the instruction with few exceptions received little attention from chroniclers and other writers. Thus the origins of the new universities remain rather obscure. Even the development of age and strength produced legends rather than history about their early days.

Bologna, according to accepted opinion, became famous first as a result of the teaching of Irnerius in Roman Law about 1100-1140.[3] Then the appearance of the *Decretum* of Gratian about 1139-1142 stimulated the study of canon law there. Later student gilds emerged and, for reasons which are not at all clear, took over control of the academic structure of the institution. A university developed at Bologna rather than elsewhere because the city was of modest size, maintained neutrality between the pope and the emperor, and was located at a convenient crossroads in the north of Italy.[4] The schools were free from ecclesiastical or other control until 1219 when Honorius III gave the archdeacon of Bologna the right to supervise degrees. All of these are, of course, important factors in understanding the schools in their effect upon the career of the university. Some other factors, such as the geography of the city, the cathedral school and the educational organization of the time have received less attention.

A study of the population of medieval Bologna showed it to be a very large city by medieval standards, and this suggested a modification of the accepted relationship between it and the rising university.[5] Similarly a check on the theoretical length of life of Irnerius' pupils (assuming them to be his) indicated a later date for the career of that great master. Recently scholars have tended to push Gratian forward into the first quarter of the twelfth century. Once commenced, the study of the early schools of Bologna produced a series of interesting possibilities for change in interpretation of their history from about 1088 to 1150. The most startling is that the canon law school probably preceded the school of civil law and was fundamental in the setup at Bologna. The study revealed much information which may be used for a better understanding of these early schools and illustrated their differences even from the institution of the thirteenth century.

I. The Population and Educational Geography of Bologna

The environment of any university has much influence upon the course of its development. Within it the schools have an educational function, first for the city itself and then often for larger areas. Any twelfth century cathedral city normally had as one important task the education of clergy for the diocese. The schools also helped in the education of the business personnel of the city. Although most of that education was such training as a master might give his sons or relatives or even children of friends, the tradition of at least elementary formal education persisted and might be extended to more advanced learning. Furthermore, since educational positions were much like other economic opportunities, the medieval principles of monopoly within geographical areas might be expected to operate. The problem then is largely one of population and of distribution of schools.

The size of the city would have much effect upon the number and wealth of the legal profession. Some estimates have not been very large. "The city of Bologna, with its crooked medieval streets, and its few inns, found its population almost doubled."[6] Since no one assumes that the university had more than ten thousand students,[7] the city's population should have been at most about ten thousand. This can be checked by the area of the city. Medieval cities usually held about 100-125 persons to the hectare (2.5 acres) unless they were either very crowded or quite sparsely inhabited.[8] Tenth century Bologna covered 115 hectares and thus should have numbered about 12,000 persons.[9] However, it grew rapidly. The early thirteenth century walls enclosed about 208 hectares, and the city thus had a population of more than 20,000. By the middle of the thirteenth century it had reached about 70,000 and was among the great cities of Italy.[10] This city, even in the twelfth century, had learned and wealthy lawyers, among whom were doubtless Irnerius and the Four Doctors.

Such wealthy and busy lawyers might well not be interested in organizing a school of law. However, they might be willing to teach, if the students would accept responsibility for organizing the classes, and they could be certain that teaching duties would not interfere with their legal activities. Thus the hours assigned for Civil Law lectures were before nine in the morning and in the afternoon. These were probably designed not to conflict with the hours of the law courts in which both the professors and the students were interested. Their classes would be normally held in their houses as a matter of convenience to the professors. Under these circumstances one can understand why the Civil Law School was organized by students.

Only casual items remain by which the academic geography of twelfth century Bologna can be reconstructed and some of these are derived from later periods. About 1230 the Civil Law Professor Azo is alleged to have refused to lecture in the square of San Stefano because it lay outside of the bounds of the old royal city.[11] He felt that education in Civil Law should be carried on within the jurisdiction of the Emperor, Frederick II. The significance of areas within the city is indicated by this item although it is probably more important in theory than it was in practice. Azo thought that Civil Law should be taught only west of the Aposa, that is, approximately along the line of the old east wall of the city. In general, as can be seen from the map, the school areas were in the suburbs adjoining the southern part of the city. The central part and even some of the suburbs were studded with those high and formidable towers of which only two examples remain today.[12]

The situation at Bologna was probably much like that at London[13] when Henry of Blois, acting bishop of London about 1138, ordered the cathedral chapter of St. Paul and the archdeacon of London, William, to excommunicate anyone who presumed to teach in the city of London without the license of Henry, Master of the Schools.[14] The exceptions were the masters in the schools of St. Mary le Bow and St. Martin le Grand. This illustrates several features of the current academic situation. The first was the power of the master of the schools at the cathedral to license anyone, not merely in his own schools of St. Paul but anywhere else in the city, except in churches already privileged to have schools. The second is the idea of educational monopoly reserved to certain churches within the city. The third is that nothing is said about subject matter. In Paris the rights of teaching were held by St. Genevieve and St. Victor as well as by the cathedral.[15]

Before A. D. 906 the cathedral had apparently been the Church of St. Peter and St. Paul, one of the complex of churches usually known by the name of San Stefano outside of the Porta Ravegnana. In 906 the new cathedral church of St. Peter within the old walls was finished.[16] Since by that time cathedrals were supposed to have schools, the old cathedral should have had one and, in accordance with principles of academic monopoly, would have kept it even though the bishop moved into the city. This is apparently what happened. Irncrius, who taught arts before law, was alleged to have lectured in the corner of the great square of San Stefano.[17] In

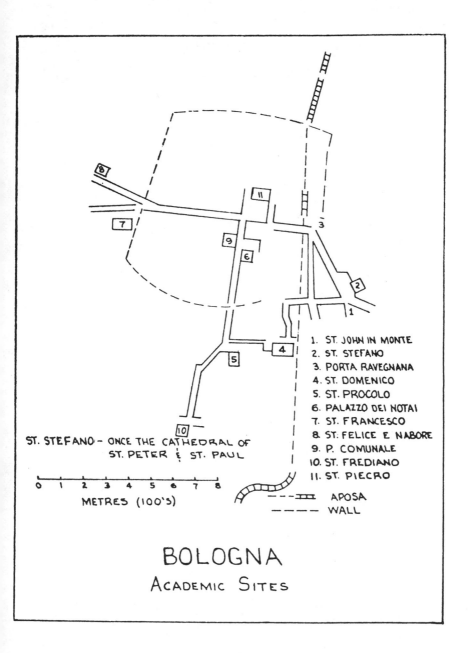

1. ST. JOHN IN MONTE
2. ST. STEFANO
3. PORTA RAVEGNANA
4. ST. DOMENICO
5. ST. PROCOLO
6. PALAZZO DEI NOTAI
7. ST. FRANCESCO
8. ST. FELICE E NABORE
9. P. COMUNALE
10. ST. FREDIANO
11. ST. PIECRO

ST. STEFANO - ONCE THE CATHEDRAL OF
ST. PETER & ST. PAUL

0 1 2 3 4 5 6 7 8
METRES (100'S)

⊶⊢⊡⊢ APOSA
------- WALL

BOLOGNA
ACADEMIC SITES

the early thirteenth century Buoncompagno read his treatise *Rhetoria Antica* before the university of professors of canon and civil law at St. John on the Mount in the place called Paradise, a site very near San Stefano.[18] His subject was one taught in the canons' school.

A second school area in the thirteenth century in Bologna was near the Church of San Francesco.[19] At that time it was the center for the study of arts and certain professional subjects. Its earlier history is unknown. Nearby was the Church of San Felice and San Nabore where Gratian is said to have lived in the first half of the twelfth century.[20] An easy conjecture is that Gratian taught in the school there, but if he did, no trace remained of a canon law tradition there.

The center of legal education, both of canon and civil law, by the thirteenth century was near the Church of San Procolo in the southern part of the city. In that century San Domenico was built and shared the attention of the student group. One clue to the location of the students at San Procolo is the burial of two of the Four Doctors, Bulgarus and Martinus, in that church.[21] Since the professors usually taught in their homes,[22] their schools should have been near the church. Possibly the prestige of these great doctors led to the migration of the students to this quarter of the city, assuming that till then they had listened to Irnerius near San Stefano and just possibly to Gratian near San Felice.[23]

The close association of even the law schools with the bishop and archdeacon is clear in a number of ways. The rector, if the Paduan custom illustrates a custom taken from Bologna as most of its customs were, was installed in the cathedral.[24] An examination by ancient doctors was held at St. Peter's as early as 1179.[25] Later examinations are known to have been held there in the presence of the bishop, the archdeacon or a deputy.[26] The friendly relations with the cathedral personnel as well as with other churches of the city would seem to suggest that the university and professors acted with the approval of the bishop and the archdeacon, who was master of schools there, from the beginning of the schools. Thus the letter of Honorius III of 1219 would seem to be the usual medieval approval of existing custom rather than an ecclesiastical invasion in a field previously open to any who wished to teach.[27]

The geographical distribution of the schools and a few other facts about them set up another uncertain chronological hypothesis. The earliest schools should have been at San Stefano with a second possibly at San Felice. For a time Irnerius taught logic and then civil law at the first,[28] and Gratian may have taught canon law at the other. Yet, the law students moved to San Procolo. Then, apparently the arts group shifted in large part to the San Felice-San Francesco district. Why did they move? There are obvious disadvantages of a student group in a center of religious worship. The presence of large numbers of men and boys was hardly compatible with the quiet and dignity of such an area as San Stefano, since medieval students were often riotous.[29] Against the background of these three student areas in a city which, for the twelfth century, had a very large and prosperous population, the history of the early schools must be seen.

II. Gratian

In the field of canon law Gratian occupies a position of significance somewhat similar to that of Irnerius in civil law.[30] He wrote the basic text, the *Concordia Discordantium Canonum* usually called the *Decretum* or *Decreta*, which became the text of the study of canon law. This has been the subject of many studies lately in which naturally Gratian and the *Decretum* have been important topics.[31] If this text should be pushed forward in time much before the date usually assigned to it, 1140, the chronological priority of civil law would be imperilled.

Contemporary evidence about Gratian, like that about Irnerius, is scant. He seems to appear in the report of a canonical case in 1143 as a consultant judge.[32] The other date is that of his *Decretum* which, since manuscripts of it contain items from the Second Lateran Council of 1139, is usually given as shortly after that council. There is a tendency recently to feel that these items are additions[33] and that the composition was somewhat earlier.

The arguments for an earlier date of composition are several. Paucapalea, usually considered the pupil of Gratian and a commentator on his work, completed his commentary in 1148. However, at least two writers on the decretals had preceded him.[34] Since the decretalist technique was developing slowly, this took time. Gratian carefully omitted all direct references to Roman Law: he would hardly have done this if Irnerius and his school had been important at the time.[35] No references to popes appear later than those to Paschal II (1099-1118),[36] and the only date given in the documents appears for 1105.[37] The period following the Concordat of Sutri of 1111 seems about the proper time for the book to have been composed.[38] Even the idea that the *Decretum* was composed at Bologna is doubted:[39] perhaps Rome was the place. A defense of the traditional date still would admit a long period of composition ending with the addition of the canons of 1139.[40]

Later writers add a variety of items. A Tibur (near Rome) chronicle states that Gratian wrote the *Decretum* in the time of Pope Calixtus II (1119-1124).[41] Burchard of Erspurg (early 13th century) claims that Gratian wrote about the period of Lothair (1125-1138), telling of him just before he wrote of Irnerius.[42] Under the year 1130, the best informed chronicle on intellectual history of the twelfth century mentioned his writing and called him Bishop of Chiusi:[43] he had evidently been born near there at least. Finally the poem called the *Norman Standard* seems to indicate that Gratian was with Pope Innocent II at the synod or Council of Reims in 1131.[44] He was known as a monk of San Felice in Bologna. Even to the next generation he was evidently a shadowy person about whom little was known.

This evidence would seem to indicate that Gratian wrote first and only later became a legal authority. Pope Alexander III may well have been his pupil in the 1120's, since he died at a great age in 1181 and can have hardly been less than eighty then.[45] Peter Lombard who came to Paris from Bologna about 1135 seems to have been familiar with the *Decretum* at the time, for he used it in his works. It is also possible that Gratian taught at San Felice.[46] Within a generation after 1120, monks were forbidden to participate in formal legal business; but many apparently did participate earlier.[47]

The problem here is whether Gratian began a school of canon law at Bologna or merely continued or perhaps augmented it. Such a school might be identified by outstanding students or earlier texts. It is thus interesting that an archdeacon of Bologna, Lambert de Fagnano Scannabecchi, not only became pope as Honorius II in 1124 but actually raised five canons of Bologna to be cardinals during 1125 and 1126. These men were Gherardo Caccianemici (to be elected pope later as Lucius II (1144-45), John, Peter Cariaceno de Carisendo, Ugo Geremei, and Sigizzo Bianchetti.[48] This Ugo, or Hugh, may possibly be the author of a treatise on the *ars dictandi* written at about this time.[49] It seems reasonable to suppose that these men were elevated in part for their knowledge as well as because of the pope's acquaintance with them. What these promotions did for Bologna can well be imagined.

In the great debate between papal and imperial partisans in the eleventh century two types of legal literature appeared. One was by well known ecclesiastics, usually associated with the Papal Curia, such as those of the cardinals, Atto, Deusdedit and Gregory, and bishops Anselm of Lucca and Bonizo.[50] The second was a long series of anonymous writings in Italy, attempting to organize the content of canon law.[51] With one exception, this series seems to come to an end at about 1125.[52] One would expect, as did the authors of the history of the collections, that this series ended because of the widespread acceptance of the text of the *Decretum*.[53] It adds to the evidence that Gratian published his work at least as early as 1125. The locale of the series is in some cases, Rome,[54] but one wonders if many of these were not also the result of a school at Bologna.

The evidence presents a suggestion rather than a conclusive argument. Gratian was writing and possibly teaching at San Felice between 1115-1125: he may have moved to Rome with the cardinals in 1125-6 or later. The composition of the many other canon law treatises somewhat earlier as well as in this period shows an original interest in this subject, possibly at Bologna. The cardinals could have been chosen for favoritism or for political reasons, but Bologna's reputation for learning then makes a case for believing that they were selected because of their wisdom. All of this, amorphous as it is, would indicate a very considerable interest in canon law at Bologna early in the twelfth century. The fact that the rector of the Law School was always a clerk suggests that the canonists had been organized before the civilians.[55] It is interesting that Ralph Niger, writing about 1179-89,[56] said that an interest in Roman Law had been propagated by none other than Irnerius, whence it had spread to Rome and from there over the earth. This suggests that Irnerius had appealed largely to canon law students.

III. Irnerius (Gernerius, Guarnerius, Warnerius, etc.)

Writing of Irnerius, Rashdall commented, "Unquestionably it was his lectures that first raised Bologna to European fame."[57] The brilliance of his successors who, indeed, spread his reputation and the later prominence of Roman Law have tended to enhance this impression. The splendid tombs of thirteenth century law professors, tombs such as mere professors have attained nowhere else, have encouraged this tradition. A recent account of Irnerius' life runs as follows:[58] birth about 1055-60; study at Bologna under the doctor of law, Pepo; teaching of arts before 1100 and then the law until after 1130; legal activity first with the great countess, Mathilda of Tuscany, and then with the emperor, Henry V; and death, perhaps about 1130-40. He had, according to tradition, four great students, of whom he is alleged to have said:[59]

> Bulgarus has the golden tongue, Martin, fulness of knowledge, Hugo, understanding of the law, James is myself.

These men appear in a series of legal documents which indicate that they were active in the period from 1151 to their deaths in the years 1166-78. All of this sets up a tradition of teaching of civil law going back a century, since Pepo appeared in a document of 1076.[60]

Actually there is no evidence showing that Irnerius either studied with Pepo or even lived near his time. The Wernerius, *missus domini imperialis*, of 1100 is almost certainly another person.[61] On January 28, 1112 Irnerius was listed first among

several barristers *(causidici)* in the report of a case near Ferrara.[62] The following year he appeared in a document of Tuscany's Countess Mathilda. Since the emperor, Henry V, inherited some of her rights, it is not surprising that Irnerius next
appears in a series of imperial documents chiefly in 1116-8, but
with one later instance in 1125.[63] In some of these he appears
as a judge. Contemporary chroniclers tell nothing of his activities or even of his death. His reputation would seem to
derive from a later date. Thus it may be doubted if "his lectures
first raised Bologna to European fame." Indeed, the sudden
end of his judicial activities in 1118 suggests that he turned his
attention to teaching at that time.

     Later chronicles give other items of information. As Mas-
ter Guarnerius of Bologna, he, with other wise men of the law
(legisperiti), participated in the election of an anti-pope at Rome
in 1118.[64] A thirteenth century writer, perhaps copying from a
twelfth century chronicler, alleged that Irnerius was instigated
to read Roman Law by the Countess Mathilda (who died in
1115) in the time of the Emperor Lothair (1125-1138).[65] The best
informed chronicle upon the intellectual history of the time,
that of Mont-Saint-Michel, discusses Irnerius under the year
1032![66] This information, together with the actual dates of his
activity, raises the question whether he taught at Bologna as
early as 1100. Other evidence about the time of his teaching
relates to his students. His writings, all glosses, give no
chronological information.[67]

     In contrast to Irnerius, who had little contemporary pub-
licity, the Four Doctors merited a good deal. Two chroniclers
mention their presence at Roncaglia and one of them says that
the Doctors were students of Irnerius.[68] They appear together
in a document of 1154[69] and, in 1162, are mentioned as the four
outstanding teachers of Bologna.[70] They appear singly in documents after 1151 and died during the years 1166-78, three
probably in the first three years of this period.[71] Two of them,
Bulgarus and Martin, wrote treatises which can apparently be
dated as early as 1140[72] and in that year Jacopus is alleged to
have been teaching in the city.[73] Under these circumstances
they seem to have been students of Irnerius of about the same
age.[74]

Irnerius' students died, on the average, about 1169. Some estimate of the time when they studied law with Irnerius may be made if we start with certain assumptions: (a) that they were of a certain age when they studied law, (b) that they did not appear before 1140 or were well known before 1151, and (c) that they enjoyed the usual medieval longevity. They probably studied law when they were about 18-23 years of age. Since all of the four became famous, which they could hardly have done before they were forty, they may well have had the expectation of thirteenth century Englishmen, of eighteen years at that age, and have lived to about fifty-eight.[75] That is, they should have lived about thirty-five years after finishing their law course. Thus if they died about 1169, they should have finished their law study about 1134, after studying with Irnerius from about 1129. Since the expectation of thirteenth century Englishmen was a very favorable one, and the Four Doctors could hardly have studied law earlier in life, their association with Irnerius can scarcely be pushed farther back than 1130.[76]

The date of Irnerius' teaching can be approached in another way. Odofredus, a thirteenth century professor of law, gives a line of succession of masters from Irnerius to himself: Irnerius, Bulgarus, John Bassianus, Azo, James Balduini, and Odofredus.[77] There are five generations to be considered. Assuming that since they were famous men, they had an expectation of life of fifty-eight and a teaching career of thirty five years. We can then estimate as follows. Since the students might study with their professors at any time in their career, a generation would be about half a teaching career or about eighteen years. If Odofredus finished studying with James Balduini about 1230,[78] Bulgarus should have completed his study with Irnerius about ninety years earlier or about 1140. However, professors probably had more students later in their careers as their reputations grew. This should increase the length of the generation and push back Bulgarus' study with Irnerius (on a theoretical average) toward 1130.

Irnerius' career as a teacher, at least of distinguished students of civil law, seems to fall in the 1130's and thus well after the death of Henry V in 1125. From 1112 to 1118 he engaged in successful legal ventures, apparently on the side of Henry V. This phase of his career suddenly ceased in 1118, a cessation which raises an interesting question. Did he change over to the side of the Papacy? Ralph Niger's suggestion that Irnerius was the source of Papal interest in Civil Law might indicate that this was so. His teaching of ecclesiastics at Bologna in the subject of civil law in the years following 1118 would then have preceded his appeal to laymen or at least distinguished lay students there. The impetus which he gave to the study of civil law as a distinct subject thus came in the second quarter of the twelfth century, more nearly about 1130 than 1110. The chances that the law school was well organized or well known before the middle of the century are few unless it can be shown that Irnerius had important predecessors. Only Pepo has been suggested and his influence was not great.

IV. The Canons' Schools

From the standpoint of history the canons' schools should be the best known of the early schools of Bologna. Documents show the establishment of endowments by two eleventh century bishops of that city, and items in two saints' lives give clues to the type of study of the schools. These are very well known. The fortunate preservation of letters written by masters and students regarding studies in treatises on the *ars dictandi* give interesting information about phases of life there early in the twelfth century. Eventually in the thirteenth century the members of schools there were recognized or perhaps reorganized as another university.[79] The subjects taught there tell something of its earlier history. The picture of these schools presented by all of these data is not only informative but also quite consistent.

The schools of Bologna advanced slowly in the eleventh century. Bishop Adalfredo in 1054 set up a large endowment in favor of the canons of the cathedral that they might learn, teach and spread knowledge.[80] In 1065 Bishop Lambert added to it.[81] This should have meant that the canons' school was of some size and was larger than the usual one room school which opened the way to rather elementary ecclesiastical

knowledge. Probably even before this a future bishop of Ac-
qui, Guido (1035-70), came from some distance and studied
the liberal arts.[82] After the endowment Bruno, later Bishop of
Segni, studied not only the arts but something regarded as a
part of sacred studies.[83] In the ill defined state of studies then
this might refer to almost anything associated with ecclesiastical practice, even the writing of letters, known as the *ars
dictandi*. In any case it shows that Bologna had a reputation in
northern Italy in that century.

The teaching of the *ars dictandi* at Bologna is apparent in a
series of treatises in that subject in the twelfth century. The
earliest identified by Haskins as associated with that city was
by Albertus of a mysterious Samaria, a relative of an archpriest
of Bondeno near Ferrara, who wrote about 1111-1118.[84]
Shortly thereafter Hugh, canon and master, produced his
Rationes Dictandi Prosaici. An anonymous *Rationes Dictandi* appeared about 1135,[85] while Bernard of Bologna wrote about
1145 and a Guido about 1160.[86] Two of these, Hugh and
Guido, were canons and teachers at Bologna. This suggests
that the *ars dictandi* was taught at the cathedral school. This
subject included the writing of ecclesiastical letters and thus
prepared one for ecclesiastical as well as lay careers. Indeed the
union of the two may have been the precedent for the later
joint curriculum of canon and civil law. The great age of the *ars
dictandi* at Bologna seems to have been about 1160.[87]

Hugh's treatise of about 1123 states that Bologna is already
known for the *ars dictandi*, philosophy and medicine.[88] He
does not mention law although it was, of course, well known
there then. He thus seems to be listing the subjects taught in
canons' school. The rather unlikely suggestion that medicine
was taught in such a school, however, is brought up again
when medicine occurs in the subjects taught in the canons'
school at the time it became another university in the thirteenth century.[89] Probably the great numbers of students, who
in the thirteenth century congregated near the Church of San
Francesco, overtaxed the endowment of Bishop Adalfredo.[90]
The library of the chapter, which may represent the interests of
the original canons' school, again shows little law but much of
the other subjects taught there.[91]

A most intriguing letter in Hugh's collection is addressed to a famous teacher whose initial is G. He was, according to the letter, endowed with divine and human wisdom, and his fame was widespread.[92] G., of course, could indicate a number of common names such as Guillelmus and Guido, but it could also stand for Gratianus and Gernerius (Irnerius). The form of address and references to G.'s learning offer some interesting suggestions. Even the use of an initial suggests that contemporaries knew him well.

The correspondent places G.'s name in the address ahead of his own, that of a priest. Since another well known writer, Albertus of Samaria, placed his name after that of a priest, just being an outstanding teacher was not sufficient to outrank a priest. It is doubtful if a monk (not a priest) would outrank a priest either and relatively few monks were priests. Thus Gratian, as a monk, is probably to be excluded. Assuming Irnerius was the G. and the letter written long before 1123, he had already served as a judge and thus would have held very high prestige.

This G. had a reputation for *prudentia, probitas* and *nobilitas,* characteristics which point to law. He was a master and dominus, thus a man of great eminence. The most striking attribution is that G. was a doctor, a term used for distinguished lawyers at the time[93] and seldom of others except theologians. The term divine and human wisdom might certainly have been applied to Roman Law in the thirteenth century.[94] The largest division of Roman Law, *res* (property) was divided into divine and human property. Law thus cannot be excluded from consideration as divine and human wisdom, although the expression might have a more general connotation, indicating philosophy.[95] Irnerius was said to have taught the liberal arts (particularly logic) before he turned to law.[96] In any case the letter indicates that a quite famous man was teaching at Bologna.

The letters show, as Professor Haskins noticed, a great flexibility of organization of study. The masters seem to have felt free to teach or not as they pleased. Obviously if some were canons, as we know that Hugh and Guido were, their income as canons was probably much greater than what they earned as teachers, so that they could be very independent in regard to their teaching. Much depended upon the students as to whether classes were set up or not. Nothing is said about school organization, although in one case a writer, apparently Canon Hugh, seems to be indicating the range of intellectual interest of the schools and of the teachers there. The schools, even under the auspices of the canons, were still very much groups of masters and students.

V. Steps in the Schools' Early Development

The definition of the types of schools of Bologna shows a considerable group of masters and students there in the early twelfth century. The city was a populous, energetic and vigorous place. Its citizens probably regarded the students as one element of its busy life, still so few that they made little difference there. In certain limited clerical circles its teachers had by 1100 a reputation sufficient to attract students from northern Italy. The early twelfth century was to see an increase both in the size of the city and the fame of its schools.

Yet well past the middle of the century there is no evidence of institutional organization. The emperor, Frederick Barbarossa, in his edict *Habita* speaks only of teachers and students, not of faculties or even of specific groups.[97] The relationship was such that a student might be tried before the bishop of his professor. Also in announcing his election as pope in 1159 Alexander III addressed the bishop, the canons and the professors and masters of Bologna.[98] Since the bishop was the theoretical head of the schools and some of the canons were teachers, this was an address to the academic system. There is no consciousness of institutionalization although there is evidence of the acknowledgement of Bologna as an outstanding intellectual and teaching center.[99] The advance achieved was primarily in developing schools based upon authoritative professors.

As late as 1096 Pope Urban II sent a letter to the clergy and people of Bologna commending them for remaining steadfastly loyal to him without referring to either the teachers or the teaching of that city.[100] This is worth noticing even if it is not particularly significant. Well known evidence already mentioned shows that students from some distance had come to study at Bologna by 1100. The letters in Canon Hugh's collection of about 1124 indicate that the canons' school was widely known and had at least one famous teacher, that G. who might have been Irnerius (Gernerius). Here were taught the arts, the *ars dictandi*, presumably some medicine and possibly some theology. Yet the limits of its reputation probably were still within northern Italy.

Canon law became important certainly in the 1120's and probably earlier. The election of Honorius II as Pope and his appointment of several canons of Bologna as cardinals must have enhanced that city's academic prestige. Then the publication of the *Decretum*, assuming that it was published by 1125, added greatly to the study of the subject. "The numerous commentators who, at Bologna and elsewhere, succeeded each other to the number of more than a dozen in less than forty years of whom many became bishops and cardinals indicate the great importance which attached to the study of the *Decretum* and the high esteem which it enjoyed in ecclesiastical circles."[101] The persons listed, however, are with one exception Italians. It seems to show that study at Bologna now appealed to all Italy but not too much to countries beyond the Alps for a time. The popularity of canon law and its professors doubtless tended to strip the school of its teachers and explains why the doctors were required to teach at Bologna for a year or two following the completion of their study. When Lucius II appointed four more Bologna clerks as cardinals in 1144-1145,[102] and Eugenius III added another a few years later, the popularity of the city among canon law students must have reached a very high level.[103]

Roman law was taught by Irnerius probably within the period 1118-1140 and had a strong influence, probably in the early part of the period, upon the Roman Curia. Great impetus was given by attention paid to it by the emperor Frederick Barbarossa in the late 50's and its leaders, the Four Doctors. The Authentic *Habita* apparently gave to the Civil Law and other students the same right of having a professor as judge as the canon law students had enjoyed earlier in having the bishop or archdeacon as their judge.[104] This again tends to indicate that the Canon Law students came earlier and in greater numbers than the Civil Law students and thus they secured the leadership when the University organized. Little resistance would be put up against this leadership because the Canon Law Professors were called away so quickly to responsible positions and the Civil Lawyers were busy with the legal practice of a great city.

Notes

1. On this among other works see H. Denifle, *Die Entstehung der Universitäten des Mittelalters bis 1400* (Berlin, 1885) and a recent article by H. Grundmann, "Vom Ursprung der Universitat im Mittelalter," *Berichte über die Verhandlungen der Sachsischen Akademie der Wissenschaften zu Leipzig*, phil-hist. KI., CIII (1957), 1–66.

2. For the background of this period see, among others, C. H. Haskins. *The Renaissance of the Twelfth Century* (Cambridge, 1927) especially ch. VII, and his lectures, *The Rise of Universities* (New York, 1923), recently re-edited by T. E. Mommsen. On Bologna see H. Rashdall, *The Universities of Europe in the Middle Ages*, revised by F. M. Powicke and A. B. Emden (Oxford, 1936), I. and A. Sorbelli, *Storia della Universita di Bologna, I Il medievo* (Bologna, 1944). The collection of information in M. Sarti et M. Fattorini, *De Claris Archigymnasii Bononiensis Professoribus* (2nd. ed. Bologna, 1888) is still basic.

3. Perhaps even as early as 1088 (the date officially set for the founding of the University). Quirinus Breen, "The Twelfth-Century Revival of the Roman Law," *Oregon Law Review*, XXIV (1944–5), 266. This is a very good introduction to this revival.

4. Bologna was a center of Celtic settlement, a group which has always had intellectual interests.

5. See my *Late Ancient and Medieval Population*, Vol. XLVIII, pt. 3 of the *Transactions of the American Philosophical Society* (Philadelphia, 1958), p. 111, n. 78. Hereafter cited as LAMP. Notably the idea that in such a large city important lawyers might perfer to leave details of lecturing and administration to the students since they would be busy with legal activities which paid much better. After all, this is still true of many law professors in the Mediterranean region.

6. N. Schachner, *The Medieval Universities* (London, 1938), p. 157.

7. The small number of professors identified as teaching at Bologna in the twelfth century suggests a student body closer to one thousand than ten thousand.

8. Russell, LAMP, p. 63.

9. *Ibid.*, p. 111.

10. *Ibid.* Even Sorbelli speaks of the change the number and wealth of the

students brought to the city. Cf. Sorbelli, p. 211.

11. Rashdall, I, 217, n. 4. Sarti et Fattorini, I, i, 86. From Odofredus, L. S. Si duas Dig. De excusat.

12. A. Finelli, *Bologna ai tempi che vi soggorno Dante* (Bologna, 1929).

13. As was believed strongly by G. Manacorda, *Storia della scuola in Italia* (Milan, 1914), I, i, 186–216 but not by Rashdall, I, 20–22, 231 or Gaines Post, "Review: *The Universities of Europe in the Middle Ages* by Hastings Rashdall," *Speculum*, XII (1937), 131–3.

14. "H. Del gratia Wintoniensis ecclesie minister capitulo Sancti Pauli et Willelmo archidiacono et ministris suis salutem. Precipio vobis pro obedientia ut trina vocatione sententiam anatematis eos proferatis qui sine licentia Henrici Magistri Scolarum in tota civitate Lundon legere presumpserint preter eos qui scolas Sancte Marie de Archa et Sancti Martini Magni regunt. Teste Magistro Ilario apud Wintoniam." Endorsed "De cancellario." *Historical Manuscripts Commission*, 9th Report, i, 45b. For explanation of situation see K. Edwards, *The English Secular Cathedrals in the Middle Ages* (Manchester, 1949), pp. 190–191.

15. Gaines Post, "Alexander III, the Licentia Docendi, and the Rise of the Universities," *Anniversary Essays in Medieval History by the Students of C. H. Haskins* (Boston and New York, 1929), p. 256, n. 6: Rashdall, I, 276.

16. "Bologna," *Catholic Encyclopedia* (New York, 1907), II, 640.

17. Sarti et Fattorini, I, 16; Rashdall, I, 217; also I, 113, note I.

18. L. Rockinger, *Briefsteller und Formelbucher des elften bis vierzehnten Jahrhunderts in Quellen un Erorterungen zur bayerischen und deutschen Geschichte* (Munich, 1863), IX, 1, p. 135. See also Rashdall, I, 146.

19. G. Zaccagnini, *La vita dei maestri e degli scolari nello studio di Bologna nei secoli xiii e xiv* (Geneva, 1926), pp. 33–34.

20. Sarti et Fattorini, I, 331.

21. Sarti et Fattorini, I, 42.

22. Zaccagnini, pp. 33–34, 70–72; H. Koeppler, "Frederick Barbarossa and the Schools of Bologna. Some Remarks on the 'Authentica Habita'," *English Historical Review*, LIV (1939) 392–3.

23. The burial places of Irnerius and of his alleged successor, Jacobus, are unknown. Possibly they were in the San Stefano district.

24. Rashdall, I, 184–185.

25. Rashdall, I, 232.

26. Zaccagnini, p. 80.

27. Rashdall, I, 20–22, 231.

28. See below n. 98.

29. G. Pare, *La renaissance du XIIe siècle* (Ottawa, 1933), p. 78. Other problems may have been the danger of losing jurisdiction over the schools to pope or emperor and the matter of fees from students. See my "The Early Schools of Oxford and Cambridge," *The Historian*, V (1943), 68–69.

30. S. Kuttner, "The Father of the Science of Canon Law," *Jurist*, I (1941), 2–19.

31. S. Kuttner, "Institute of Research and Study in Medieval Canon Law. Bulletin for 1955," *Traditio*, XI (1955), 429–448; "Institute of Research and Study in Medieval Canon Law. Bulletin for 1956," *Ibid.*, XII (1956), 557–662.

32. Kuttner, "The Father of the Science of Canon Law," *Jurist*, I (1941), p. 3.

33. A. Vetulani, "Nouvelles vuse sur le Décret de Gratien," *La Pologne au Xe Congrès International des Sciences Historiques à Rome* (Warszawa, 1955), pp. 94–95.

34. Vetulani, p. 93. See also the French summary of his *Dekret Gracjana I Pierwsi Dekretysci w Swietle Nowego troda* (Krakow, 1955), pp. 157–160.

35. Vetulani, pp. 97–98, 100.

36. *Ibid.*, p. 96.

37. *Ibid.*, pp. 94–95.

38. *Ibid.*, p. 101.

39. *Ibid.*, pp. 102–3.

40. G. Fransen, "La Date du Décret de Gratien," *Revue d'Histoire Ecclésiastique*, LI (1956), 530–1.

41. *Monumenta Germaniae Historica, Scriptores* (Berlin, 1826–96), XXII, 361, 1. 30. Hereafter cited as *M. G. H., SS*. "Nota; hoc tempore Gratianus compilavit corpus canonum." This evidence is thought to have come from Monte Cassino.

42. "Huius (Lotarii primi imperatoris) temporibus magister Gratianus canones et decreta, quae variis libris erant dispersa, in unum opus compilavit, adiungensque eis interdum auctoritates sanctorum patrum secundum convenientes sententias, opus suum satis rationalabiliter distinxit," E. Besta, *L'opera d'Irnerius contributo alla storia del diritto romano* (Turin, 1896), p. 55; M. G. H., SS, XXIII, 342.

43. Of Robert de Monte, see R. Howlett, ed., *Chronicles of the Reigns of Stephen, Henry II and Richard I* (London, 1889, Rolls Series), IV, 118. "Gratianus, episcopus Clusinus, coadunavit decreta valde utilia ex decretis, canonibus, etc." Ughelli gives a bishop Peter in 1126 and 1139 and a bishop Martin in 1146. There is room for Gratian. Cf. F. Ughelli, *Italia sacra* (Rome, 1644–62), III, 631–633.

44. "Draco Normannicus" by Etienne of Rouen, a monk of Bec, writing about 1168–70, but who had entered Bec about 1143. *Chronicles of the Reigns of Stephen, Henry II, and Richard I* (London, 1885, Rolls Series), II, xiii, xiv, xvi, 650; M. G. H., SS, XVIII, 163.

45. M. Pacaut, *Alexandre III* (Paris, 1956), p. 58.

46. On an interesting possibility that monks moved from Ravenna to Bologna about 1118, see A. Gaudenzi, *Lo svolgimento parallelo del diritto longobardo e del diritto romano a Ravenna, Memorie—alla classe di scienza morale della R. Accademia delle scienze dell istituto di Bologna* (Bologna, 1908), pp. 26–30, 36–37, 95.

47. Some even later. Cf. S. Kuttner and E. Rathbone, "Anglo-Norman Canonists of the Twelfth Century: an Introductory Study," *Traditio, VII* (1949–51), 281.

48. G. Moroni, *Dizionario di erudizione storico-ecclesiastica* ...V (Venice, 1840), pp. 308–309 (under Bologna).
49. See below, note 85.
50. P. Fournier et G. Le Bras, *Histoire des collections canoniques en Occident depuis les Fausses Décrétales jusqu' au le dècret de Gratien* (Paris, 1931). II, 21 for Atto, cardinal of St. Marks; II, 25–26 for Anselm of Lucca; II, 41 for Deusdedit; II, 146 for Bonizo; II, 170 for Gregory, and II, 82–87 for Ivo of Chartres, not at the Curia.
51. Fournier et Le Bras, II, 127, 138, 146, 151, 154, 162, 167, 169, 170, 181, 191, 195, 197, 202, 210, 221 and 224.
52. The exception is A.D. 1133–37. Fournier et Le Bras, II, 225.
53. Fournier et Le Bras I, viii, II, 221. By choosing to include this last and somewhat isolated item, the editors accept the conventional date of the *Decretum*.
54. Fournier et Le Bras, II, 146, 162, 181 and 202.
55. Zaccagnini, p. 9; Kibre, pp. 46–47; Rashdall, I, 184.
56. "Cum igitur a magistro Peppone velut aurora surgentis iuris civilis renasceretur initium et postmodum propagante magistro Warnerio iuris disciplina (ed. disciplinam) religioso (s) cemate traheretur ad curiam Romanam et in aliquibus partibus terrarum expanderetur in multa veneratione et munditia ceperunt leges esse in honore simul et desiderio...." H. Kantorowicz and B. Smalley, "An English Theologian's View of Roman Law," *Mediaeval and Renaissance Studies*, I (1943) 250.
57. Rashdall, I, 114.
58. Sorbelli, pp. 36–38.
59. From Otto Morena in F. Guterbock, *Das Geschichtswerk des Otto Morena* (Berlin, 1930). See also *M. G. H., SS*, New Series, VII and Old Series, XVIII, 607. The translation is from Haskins, *Renaissance*, p. 200. The Latin is: "Bulgarus os aureum, Martinus copia legum, Mens legum est Ugo, Jacopus id quod ego."
60. Rashdall, I, 112; H. H. Fitting, *Die Anfange der Reschtsschul zu Bologna* (Berlin and Leipzig, 1888), 1, 24.
61. For Pepo see Kantorowicz and Smalley, p. 250; for Wernherius, Besta, pp. 62–64.
62. L. Simeoni, "Un nuovo documento su Irnerio in 1112," *Atti e memorie della R. Deputazione di storia patria per l'Emilia e la Romagna*, IV (1939), 55–60. He is called 'Guarnerius Bononiensis.' See also his "Bologna e la politica di Enrico V," *Ibid.*, (1936–37), 141–163; "La lotta dell' investitura a Bologna e la sua azione sulla citta e sullo studio," *Memorie della R. Accad. delle scienze dell'Istituto di Bologna*, class mor. ser. IV, III (1941).
63. E. Besta, *L'Opera d'Irnerio* (Torino, 1896), pp. 68–74. In March, April and May of 1116 at Padua, Reggio and Governolo; on 15 May 1117 at Governolo; on 21 June 1118 at Bombiana and 18 August at Treviso; on 10 December 1125 at Treviso.
64. Landolfo di San Paolo. *Hist. Med., M.G.H.*, SS, XX, 40. Besta, pp. 66–72.

65. Burchard of Ersperg who died in 1226. He is supposed to have copied from John of Cremona. After mentioning the work of Gratian, he continues, "Eisdem quoque temporibus dominus Wernerius libros legum qui dudum neglecti fuerant nec quisquam in eis studuerat, ad petitionem Mathildae comitissae renovavit et secundum quod olim a divae recordationis imperatore Iustiniano compilati fuerant, paucis forte verbis alicubi interpositis, eos distinxit in quibus continentur instituta." *M.G.H.,* SS, XXIII, 342.
66. The author was Robert de Monte. *Chronicles of the Reigns of Stephen, Henry II and Richard I, IV,* p. 25.
67. H. Kantorowicz and W. W. Buckland, *Studies in the Glossators of the Roman Law* (Cambridge, 1938), pp. 36−37.
68. "1158—habensque quatuor iudices, videlicet Bulgarum, Martinum, Iscobum, Hugonem, viros disertos, relligiosos et in lege doctissimos legumque in civitate Bononiensi doctores. Rahewini Gesta Friderici Imp. lib. iv. Istorum autem quatuor doctorum et complurimorum aliorum fuit magister Guernerius, antiquus doctor."—Otto Morena, *M.G.H., SS.,* XVIII, 607. Besta, p. 73.
69. *Chartularium Studii Bononiensis,* Imola, 1907, III, 103.
70. "1162 Pollebat equidem tunc Bononia in litteralibus studiis pre cunctis Ytalie civitatibus quatuor legum columpnis inter ceteros magnifice radiantibus." E. Monaci, ed. *Gesta di Federico I in Italia* (Roma, 1887), p. 20.
71. This information is available in Kantorowicz and Buckland under each of the doctors. Possibly Martin died earlier.
72. Kantorowicz and Buckland, pp. 44, 68−69 and 86.
73. Reported by Huguccio, c.31, c.2 q.6; Pacaut, p. 59.
74. This is denied by Kantorowicz and Buckland, p. 104.
75. J. C. Russell, *British Medieval Population* (Albuquerque, 1948), pp. 181, 183. Table 8.3.
76. Besta had his doubts about the date of Irnerius' teaching. Cf. Besta, pp. 75−6.
77. Sorbelli, p. 31.
78. Sarti et Fattorini, *De Claris Archigymnasii Bononiensis Professoribus.* 165. Although not yet a doctor, Odofredus was married in 1228 and probably finished his law career in the next year or so.
79. P. Kibre, *The Nations in the Mediaeval Universities,* (Cambridge, 1938), pp.12−13; Rashdall, I, 238. Notice the similarity of the subjects noticed below to those of the thirteenth century university. It is these which make it clear that the second 'university' was merely the canons' schools reorganized in imitation of the law schools.
80. Sorbelli, p. 16.
81. "Idcirco nostros canonicos in studiis intentos esse decrevimus." Sarti et Fattorini, I, 6, 48. Rashdall, I, 130.
82. "Ubi aliquot annis non minus sanctis moribus quam litterarum disciplinis incumbens socios et aemulatores sui in utroque studii honore devicit." *Acta Sanctorum,* June, I, 229. Rashdall, I, 108.

83. "Divinae paginae propensius operam dedit." *Acta Sanctorum*, July, IV, 479. Rashdall, I, 108.
84. C. H. Haskins, *Studies in Medieval Culture* (New York, 1929), pp. 173—176. He is called Master Albertus Samaritanus by Hugh Rockinger, pp. 183—184.
85. Haskins, *Medieval Culture*, pp. 180—181. He may have been the cardinal of the name promoted in 1125.
86. Haskins, pp. 182, 183—184. On June 3, 1154 a Guido presbyter appeared as a witness of Bishop Gerard's charter, "Actum per manum Guidonis in camera qui est super Scalam." L. V. Savioli, *Annali Bolognese* (Bassano, 1784), I, ii, 237, Guido canon of Bologna appears on April 13, 1129. *Ibid.*, p. 176.
87. Haskins, *Medieval Culture*, p. 188.
88. Besides the *ars dictandi*, the statement, "vel philosophie gradus ascendere vel scientiam iugiter proficere vel Ypocratis prudentiam et Tullianum eloquentiam." Rockinger, Briefsteller, p. 63.
89. Rashdall says the subjects were medicine, surgery, notaria, philosophy, astrology, logic, rhetoric and grammar. Rashdall, I, 241—242. For medical education in the thirteenth century and later see V. L. Bullough, "Medieval Bologna and development of medical education," *Bulletin of the History of Medicine*, XXXII (1958), 201—15.
90. Rashdall, I, 188.
91. A. Sorbelli, *La Biblioteca Capitolare delia Cattedrale di Bologna net secolo xv* (Bologna, 1904, Notizie e catalogi 1451), pp. 84—140.
92. "G. doctorum precipuo, morum probitate conspicuo, divina et humana sapientia predito, A. solo nomine presbiter quicquid utriusque vite felicius." Rockinger, Briefsteller, p. 82.
    "Vestre prudentie et probitatis atque nobilitatis fama, reverentissime magister et domine, longe lateque diffusa a non nullis veridicis mihi relata de longissima regione ad vestre doctrine studium venire vehementer persuasit. Etenim sic ad aures nostras pervenit, sic verum esse nostra cognitio inventi, vos nobili genere natum sapientia illustratum, morum probitate condecoratum." *Ibid.*
93. Rashdall, I, 112, particularly note 5.
94. G. Post, "Philosophantes and philosophi in Roman and Canon Law," *Archives d'histoire doctrinale et littéraire du moyen âge*, XXI (1954), 135—38
95. Philosophy was described as divine and human *scientia* or *cognitio* by a widely used text, Isidore's *Etymologies*, II, xxiv, i, 9; VIII, vi, 1.
96. Rashdall, I, 111.
97. H. Koeppler, "Frederick Barbarossa and the Schools of Bologna. Some remarks on the Authentica Habita'," *English Historical Review*, LIV (1939), 577—607.
98. "Ad Gerardum episcopum, canonicos et legis doctores caeterosque magistros Bononiae commorantes." Koeppler, p. 593.
99. See note 19.

100. "Urbanus Episcopus, Servus Servorum Dei dilectis filiis cattholicis in clero, populo Bononiensi salutem et apostolicam benedictionem. Bonitati vestrae gratias agimus quod inter schismaticos et hereticos constituti, quidem semper in fide catholica permanistis, quidam vero per Dei gratiam veritate comperta et errorum devia dimisistis, et jam que catholice fides sunt sapitis. Hortamur ergo in Domino dilectissimi, ut in veritatis via viriliter incidatis et bonis initiis meliores eventus adire procuretis." J. P. Migne, ed. *Patrologiae Cursus Completus. Series latina* (Paris, 1844–64), CL, 500.

101. J. de Ghellinck, *Le mouvement theologique du XIIe siécle* (Burges, 1918), pp. 211–212, 238.

102. Moroni, *Dizionario, di erudizione storico-ecclesiastica*...V, pp. 308–309 (under Bologna). By Lucius II: Ubaldo Caccianemici, S. Guarino Fuscari, Ranieri Mariscotti and Hugh Misani and by Eugene III: Ildebrando Grassi.

103. See the words of Eugenius III about the fame of Bologna. Sarti et Fattorini, p. xvi.

104. Koeppler, pp. 588–606. On the role of the Four Doctors at Roncaglia see *Ibid.*, pp. 586–88.

CHAPTER 9

Ranulf de Glanville

In some respects history has been kind to Ranulf de Glanville.[1] An eyewitness vividly recounted Glanville's share in the spectacular capture of King William the Lion of Scotland in 1174. Chroniclers reported his successes as Justiciar of England from 1180 to 1189, while historians have praised the great advance in the development of the common law during that decade. Contemporary documents show him Sheriff of Yorkshire from 1163 and founder of three religious houses in East Anglia. In the *Dictionary of National Biography*, none other than the highly respected Frederick William Maitland wrote of him:

> The picture we get of him is that of an active, versatile man, ready at short notice to lead an army, negotiate a peace, hold a council, debate a cause; above all faithful to his master.

And there is more about Glanville's contribution to the common law.[2]

But if Maitland gave generously, he could also take away. He questioned Glanville's authorship of the *De Legibus Anglie*, the first great treatise on English law, in spite of the fact that "ever since the book was printed, it was known as Glanville." It might be amended "almost since it was written." Maitland proceeded:

> The book looks more like the work of one of the clerks of the royal court than that of the great justiciar, who during

126

the last years of Henry's reign, can have had little time for writing a legal treatise.

He suggested as author Glanville's relative and clerk, Hubert Walter. Since Maitland's guesses were usually regarded as brilliant conjectures, doubt was cast upon Glanville's claim, almost universally granted until then.

The opinion of Maitland was followed by Bishop Stubbs and, oddly enough, by one of the bishop's chief detractors, Professor Sayles.[3] It apparently caused others to hesitate between outright attribution of the treatise to Glanville and a reservation about such an attribution. Lady Stenton added another candidate for its authorship, Geoffrey Fitz Peter.[4] However, both Hubert Walter and Geoffrey Fitz Peter were more interested in administration than in law. Moreover, neither of them has ever been suggested as the author of anything else, while there is good reason to believe that Ranulf wrote both the remarkable crusading chronicle, *The Conquest of Lisbon* and the short but interesting account of an East Anglian shiremoot a few years later.[5] Out of fairness to Maitland, it should be added that later he was willing to admit that the author of *De Legibus Anglie* might have been either Glanville or his nephew, but he buried this admission where some scholars are sometimes too supercilious to look, in the *Encyclopaedia Britannica*.[6] Probably then we may agree with Professor Hollister that it "was written under the direction of Henry II's able justiciar"—the author was Glanville or his ghost writer.[7]

An immediate objection to these attributions is that Ranulf, who died on the Third Crusade in 1190, could not have been old enough in 1147 to have written an account of the one great success of the Second Crusade. Do not the library cards give 1130-90 as the limits of his life, a suggestion apparently of an early biographer?[8] However, two contemporary chroniclers, William of Newburgh and "Benedict" say that Glanville resigned as justiciar in 1189 because he was very old (*grandevus*) and worn out by old age and toil.[9] *Grandevus* ought to mean (this is my one appeal to demography) that Glanville was at least in his seventies at his death. Data from his social class in the thirteenth century show that a tenth of the men at thirty years of age lived on past seventy.[10] The frequency with which men served vigorously in their sixties marks that time of life as less than a great age. Corroborative evidence of Glanville's great age appears in a document which shows him in 1185 in custody of a *niece* said to be over sixty years of age.[11] If Glanville was more than seventy in 1190, he was more than twenty seven years of age in 1147, quite mature enough to have been the author of the account of the conquest of Lisbon.

The treatise, *De Legibus Anglie*, bears no statement of authorship: a later hand states that it comes from the time of Glanville.[12] Its latest editor defines it as probably a draft which the author allowed to circulate and whose composition was interrupted in 1189.[13] Thus, it was a working collection prepared with some care by the author. Parts were unfinished: the last chapter on criminal law notably so. Two documents of 1187 are inserted although not reduced to the normal form of other documents in the treatise.[14] One may assume that composition actually had continued over a period of time, probably developing from those rolls of Ranulf de Glanville, mentioned after his death as the source of some legal information.[15]

The writs used as illustrations are obviously real ones. While the names of several officials of the reign of Henry II appear, that of Glanville appears most often, including those latest in time. The editor has shown that "at least some of the writs [the author] had as models were probably justiciar writs."[16] Most of the opinions given in the treatise come from Glanville and his close associates. Two were his own, four came from his nephew, Hubert Walter, two from Osbert Fitz Hervey, possibly another relative, and one from the preceding justiciar. Thus of the twelve opinions cited in the book, nine probably come from Ranulf, his family, and close friends.[17]

While the treatise is, for the most part, a straight forward business-like discussion of the writs and law of the time, in one section the author waxes eloquent over a new assize, apparently of Windsor, which allowed a plaintiff to secure a writ placing himself upon the county rather than upon a judicial duel.[18] The statement is "full of sentiment" and shows the author excited over the improvement of procedure from an unpredictable and illogical judicial duel to dependence upon the intelligence of a panel of legal men in the county. A second passage gives the reasons for his writing the treatise. He praises Henry II first for his military skill and then turns to the king's prudence, the impartiality of his court to rich and poor and the excellence of the judges in their administration of the law. He feels that although law remains unwritten, it would be well to write out many of the principles and practices of the courts.[19]

The treatise, even if unfinished, still bears the imprint of the author's personality and style: the imprint of a strong, original mind. He defines his purpose and proceeds in a well-organized exposition of the subject. He likes to include documents, even of some length. He has a hero, Henry II, and cherishes the opinions of his own family. He shows great enthusiasm for judicial excellence. These characteristics and interests occur in the other writings, already mentioned, and seem to indicate that Ranulf was also their author.

Professor Helen Cam edited the East Anglian Shire-Moot of Stephen's reign. It is "of considerable interest—for the light which it throws on central and local administration and justice in the reign of Stephen."[20] In the presence of King Stephen, Abbot Ording of Bury St Edmunds presented his claim to retain certain legal jurisdiction in the abbey's court. In place of documents, the author reports remarks by abbot and king and a long speech by a Hervey de Glanville (possibly Ranulf's father) bringing knowledge from his fifty years' experience in the local courts. The abbot and Hervey are the heroes and the Glanville family is present, not merely in the elderly Hervey but in a Robert de Glanville and probably in a Hervey Fitz Hervey. The concluding sentence is both a statement of purpose of writing and a tribute to excellence:

> These things, indeed, are written lest it escape people later how vigorously both prelates and wise men who were in the Church [i.e., of Bury St Edmunds] labored to maintain and preserve the same liberty.

The final step came "after a few days when the king came to St Edmunds where the Abbot—with advice of the barons of the Church and with the aid of the barons of the king" brought the case to an end.

Why should Ranulf, if he was the author, have been so interested in Bury St Edmunds at that date, which must have been between 1148 and 1153?[21] Many years later, in 1182, Glanville seems to have been a member of the abbot's council, mentioned in the shire-moot account, that group of "magnates, as well law as literate, without whose counsel and aid the abbey could hardly run." And when a messenger went to Glanville near that time, the latter told him that he well knew that forty pounds ought to be paid by the village (of Bury St Edmunds) annually to cover the cost of the church's lights.[22] Since position on the abbot's council normally went to local men of wealth and influence, probably Ranulf or other members of his family were members of the council at the time of the shire-moot.

The third work thought to be Glanville's is the *Conquest of Lisbon*. Unlike the others, it is cast in the form of a letter which probably begins, "To Osbert of Bawdsey, R. sends greetings." Its purpose is then stated:

> We confidently believe that you will have a great longing to know how it goes with us, and you may rest assured that a like yearning is felt by us concerning you. Accordingly we will set forth in writing all the events of our voyage which have been worth telling, whether fortunate or adverse, and all that was done or said or seen or heard in its course.[23]

The recipient then should have been a close, even intimate friend of the writer. The lack of a more formal or florid salutation indicates that it was not designed for the patronage of a very distinguished person. The length and detail of the report suggest that the author was accustomed to writing and took the task in stride.

The name, Osbert of Bawdsey, Professor David found in the witness list of the charter by which Ranulf de Glanville founded and endowed Butley Priory in 1171.[24] That witness list is arranged by order rather than by dignity, that is, all of the clergy first and then all of the laity.[25] The scene is clear. The charter is read in the presence of Bishop William of Norwich and of his *familia*, a long list of masters among whom is the

bishop's writer. Other clergy and a sizable list of laymen follow, among whom is an Osbert de Glanville. The charter, or at
least its *tenor,* had probably been prepared beforehand by the
Glanville clerk, whose name would normally appear at the end
of the list of clerks, in this case, Osbert, Clerk of Bawdsey.[26]
Thus it seems likely that Osbert was a member of the household of the Glanvilles. This assumes, of course, that this is the
Osbert of the crusading chronicle, now twenty-four years
older. Since R. the author-crusader, was in the Glanville tent
at Lisbon, it is not surprising that Osbert proves a friend so
intimate that he deserved such a letter.[27]

One-fifth of the chronicle consists of sermons, speeches,
and letters.[28] The author secured an Arabic letter from an
interpreter. The long sermons are so detailed that they probably were copied from borrowed manuscripts. Indeed, an odd
expression in one long sermon reads as if it had been a margin-
al note (to the speaker from the speaker) which had been
drawn into the text by a copyist's mistake.[29]

The author obviously had some acquaintance with the
Bible and with Solinus's *De Mirabilibus.* He has been thought to
be a priest, probably the author of the longest sermon in the
text. However, he records actions and includes documents
frequently without naming the authors or writers and never
says that he is either a priest or participant in the religious
services of the expedition. On the basis of his apparent interests, it is as easy to feel that he was one of the judges. He
devotes a section to the legal organization of the crusade:[30]

> They constituted for every thousand of the forces two
> elected members who were to be called judges or *con-*
> *iurati,* through whom the cases of the constables were to
> be settled in accordance with the proclamation and by
> whom the distribution of moneys was to be carried out.

But the author was deeply interested in many phases of the
crusade, including the strategy and details of the fighting.
According to Professor Constable, "His remarkable and vivid
narrative is perhaps the most detailed record of any military
expedition of the twelfth century."[31]

The author's hero was another Hervey de Glanville, both

for his military leadership and for his oratory in council meetings. A stirring purple patch reads:[32]

> Each of us ought to do his utmost in order that in the
> future no stain of disgrace shall adhere to us who are
> members of the same stock and blood. Nay, more, recall-
> ing the virtues of our ancestors, we ought to strive to
> increase the honor and glory of our race rather than cover
> tarnished glory with the rages of malice. For the glorious
> deeds of the ancients kept in memory of posterity are the
> marks of both affection and honor. If you show your-
> selves worthy emulators of the ancients, honor and glory
> will be yours, but if unworthy, disgraceful reproaches.
> Who does not know that the race of the Normans declines
> no labor in the practice of continuous valor? The Nor-
> mans, that is to say, whose military spirit, ever tempered
> by experience of the greatest hardships, is not quickly
> subverted in adversity, and in prosperity which is beset
> by so many difficulties, cannot be overcome by slothful
> idleness.

Like the other two works, the *Conquest of Lisbon* is unique
in its field in the twelfth century. All three have an obviously
close association with the Glanville family: Herveys de Glanville are heroes of two of them and other Glanvilles are present; Ranulf and his relatives furnish a high proportion of
opinions in *De Legibus Anglie.* All three include documents and
speeches or opinions, a rather unusual trait in that period. All
definitely define the purpose of writing and all offer enthusiastic statements of policies and actions. All have a slightly disor-
ganized appearance, as if the author had not given them a
thorough revision. None has a direct statement of authorship,
but *De Legibus* was known as Glanville from an early date and
the chronicler's initial letter was "R". The difference in time of
composition would indicate a continuous interest and experience in writing which one might expect: most writers in their
later years are merely continuing a habit which they acquired
early in life. From this point we are assuming that the three are
the work of one man and that author, Ranulf de Glanville. One
is welcome to doubt on the subject: it is almost too good to be
true, a hitherto unknown chapter in the life of England's great

justiciar. Belief in his authorship is enhanced if the writings seem to fit into the rest of Glanville's career.

These writings are not literature for its own sake. As Professor Haskins has written of the patronage of Henry II:[33]

> Still more significant are those unique works, Glanville and the Dialogus, which could have been written only at the court whose procedure they so minutely describe. In this sense the most characteristic works of Henry's court are those with the least literary pretension.

The result is rather the production of a written memory—much as the charter recorded an action—often livery of seisin—which was seen and attested by witnesses. Again, this is what one might expect of Glanville, trained in the work of the local courts. Only these writings recorded great actions: the preservation of the liberties of Bury St Edmunds, the very successful capture of Lisbon, and the production of a fine law and procedure in England.

The well-known parts of Glanville's career fall easily into two periods of about thirteen years apiece—from 1163 to 1176 and from that year until 1189. In the first period he served mostly as a sheriff and in the second as an itinerant justice and justiciar. The charter witness lists of 1176-80 show him among the top ranking clerks of the court (although not a clerk himself) and as justiciar he ranked after the earls but before the barons.[34] In dignity he rated very high throughout the latter period. In those years also he associated with the writers of the period, who report a series of interesting and illuminating conversations and remarks—words which suggest possible mutual interest in literature and writing. For instance, to Walter Map he commented critically upon the failure of noble families to educate their children, indicating a deep concern for literacy. This remark also shows his willingness to criticize the Norman ruling families. Yet he defended them when Gerald of Wales asked him why the Normans were putting up less resistance to the French than they had originally done. Ranulf, proud of his ancestors, mentioned terrible losses in battles in the time of Louis the Pious and Raymond of Cambrai. Gerald, himself a gentle exponent of Welsh Power, offered another reason, the cruelty of the Norman Conquerors.[35]

Some of the conversations centered about administrative and legal procedure. The monk, Joscelin of Brakelonde, tells how the justiciar was the first to suspect that Bury St Edmunds' newly elected abbot, Sampson, might rule with less advice than was proper.[36] At Canterbury, Gervase the Chronicler tells how *Ranulfus, prefectus Anglie,* stressed the advisability of a middle course between bishops and monks over rights of election to the archbishopric and advised no appeal to Rome. "If you seek out Rome, Rome will only destroy you," advice which suggests the bias of one who had been on the other side from Thomas Becket.[37] Roger of Hoveden, chronicler and probably an itinerant justice, credited Glanville with a base of written laws which included a group of laws professedly by the Conqueror, the collection known as the *Leges Edwardi Confessoris,* Glanville's *De Legibus Anglie* and certain ordinances of Henry II.[38] As is mentioned in the preface, the author of *De Legibus* says:

> But there are certain general rules frequently observed in court which it does not seem to me presumptious to commit to writing, but rather very useful to people and highly necessary to aid the memory. I have decided to put into writing at least a small part of these general rules, adopting intentionally a commonplace style and words used in court to provide knowledge of them for those who are not versed in this kind of inelegant language.

He thus hints that he could write elegantly if he wished.[39]

To Glanville "time was of the essence" in legal procedure. He was proud of the rapid justice of the English courts. In a conversation with Walter Map, that witty courtier attributed the speed of English justice to the nearness of the king. "It is true (that cases are decided faster in royal than ecclesiastical courts) but if your king were as far from you, as the pope is from the bishops, you, I believe would be equally slow." Glanville laughed but did not deny it, although he might have claimed partial credit for judicial promptness then.[40] Peter of Blois, a widely traveled writer, wrote, "If cases are tried in your presence, all things proceed according to the rules of judgment and justice."[41] The chronicler of Abingdon gives an intimate picture of Ranulf with the bishops and justices at the Exchequer examining the privileges of the abbey and sternly requiring the king's officers to observe them.[42] Another chronicler, Richard of Devizes, called him the "eye" of the king,[43] and a very good chronicler, William of Newburgh, called him a man of exceptional prudence.[44] Gerald of Wales wrote more than the others and naturally had more to say of Glanville. The justiciar was a *vir magnificus sapiens ut erat simul eloquens*.[45]

Such favorable opinions were not quite unanimous: the exception is called "a very bad story from a good source."[46] Glanville is alleged to have condemned to death Gilbert de Plimpton, a young man of a very prominent family, because Gilbert eloped with an heiress, whom Ranulf wished to give in marriage to his friend, Reiner. The young man was saved by the intervention of Bishop Baldwin of Worcester. At first sight the story reads like a romance of love triumphing over money. All Gilbert had done was to smash six doors of the heiress's home, steal some valuable goods from her father and kidnap the girl. To Glanville this seemed like a serious breach of the peace: had a peasant done these he would have been hanged forthwith. That Ranulf did not let the high social position of Gilbert deter him from giving Gilbert what a man of little status would have received seems rather to his credit. Although Henry II canceled the sentence of death, he still kept Gilbert in prison the rest of his reign. It was the kind of justice that *De Legibus Anglie* claimed for England then.

The earlier period, 1163-76, seldom saw Glanville's name in charter witness lists, presumably because he spent most of his time in Yorkshire as its sheriff. There he celebrated his greatest military feat: the capture of King William of Scotland. He is singled out by Gerald of Wales as the commander in that incident near Alnwick Castle in 1174.[47] "Benedict" names other captains as well, and speaks of the English finding William playing with his knights, thinking that the approaching army was that of his subordinate, Duncan.[48] The lyrical description of the eyewitness, Jordan Fantosme, is more detailed.[49] Ranulf counseled, "Let us act prudently. Let us send spies to estimate (the number) of their followers." The spies report. "Thanks be to God. Now take your arms, wrongly would you be discouraged." The attack was prudently planned by the English, and the Scottish king fittingly surrendered to Glanville, who at once sent his man Brian south with the news. Late at night Brian found the court, demanded to be heard and was received when the king heard the noise and wanted to know the reason for it. But the king asked first about Ranulf which indicates something of his great respect and affection for Glanville. The story was sensational: a sheriff with neighboring lords and local levies had captured William the Lion, a victory on the very day on which Henry II had done penance for the death of Becket. Ranulf de Glanville was responsible—or was it Thomas Becket—or God?

If his military and diplomatic actions were obscured by anonymity before 1174, they stand out after the publicity of that year. He went as ambassador to the court of Flanders in 1177, led an army into Wales in 1183, journeyed as a diplomat to Norway in the same year, and in 1186 both crossed to France on royal business and made peace in Wales. Even at the very end of the reign he was busy: in 1188 he led an army to the support of the hard pressed king. At the coronation of Richard he led a group to quiet a demonstration against the Jews. And in his last days he was a "leader in the successful crusading division which preceded the main force of Richard I."[50] So Glanville shared in the activity of a court which "was an important center of international relations, both intellectual and political."[51] To Glanville warfare and diplomacy were instruments of policy to maintain peace and protect law. He, it should be noticed, did not give William the Lion time to arm nor to set up tournament conditions. Like any sheriff he had to round up breakers of the peace: that those breakers happened to be a king and members of a royal court was a matter of chance. It obviously was not an age of chivalry, nor was Glanville the chivalrous knight. A knight, yes—*politicus, literatus, prudens etiam sorridens.*

This leaves the problem of Glanville's early career, before 1163, probably at least the first forty years of his life.[52] Two actions of that year throw light upon those years. For an even earlier period the two writings about the East Anglian Shire-Moot and the capture of Lisbon supplement this information.

On 25 January 1163 Henry II returned from the continent after an absence from England of several years. During that time Richard de Anstey had pursued his famous legal battle to secure some family holdings through episcopal, papal, and royal courts, but still needed further royal action to complete it, since "Justice in the king's court at the beginning of Henry II's reign was uncertain and entirely dependent upon the king's pleasure."[53] In his need to ascertain the king's pleasure, Anstey sought the advice of Glanville.[54] This suggests that Ranulf had advice to offer about the king's court which he had probably acquired through participation in the court in the preceding months on the continent.

The second action of 1163 was Henry II's appointment of Glanville as sheriff of Yorkshire, a position he would hold for many years. The sheriff, with headquarters at Richmond, had a key position in the defense of England against Scotland. By this appointment the king showed his high regard for Ranulf's administrative and military ability: he should have had some rather concrete evidences of this before making such an important appointment.

The two treatises attributed to Glanville provide clues to reasons why he was regarded highly by the king. The shire-moot account shows King Stephen and his court listening with obvious respect to the elderly Hervey de Glanville as he recounted his half-century knowledge of Bury's rights. In that assembly were several Glanville crusaders. Hervey Fitz Hervey was probably the leader of the East Anglian contingent of the expedition which had captured Lisbon just a few years earlier. Ranulf was probably there as well as others who had been in the Glanville tent before Lisbon. Crusaders rated high in twelfth-century England: even a king would listen respectfully to a Glanville.

The Conquest of Lisbon, the other treatise, pictures the careful organization of the crusading fleet, the smooth cooperation between the crusaders and the Portuguese, and the success of the well planned siege of Lisbon. Yet this success was accomplished by only knights and lesser people, the lower of the "Two Levels of Feudalism," as defined by Professor Strayer.[55] This orderly achievement contrasted sharply with the chaos and failure of the upper level of feudalism in those years: the civil war and weak administration in England, the political disorder in France and the awful failure of armies led by top feudal sovereigns of Europe in the Second Crusade. No wonder Henry II saw future leaders in the men who served at Lisbon. And men trained in the lesser courts of England might bring with them into the central government such ideas as equality before the law and award of proof based on apparent guilt of the accused.[56]

In this study three aspects of Glanville's career are emphasized: the rest is very well known. The first is his association with Bury St Edmunds, a notable intellectual and religous center which may well have been responsible for those interests in his life. The second is the length of his career, embracing both the Second and Third Crusades, and that his participation in the conquest of Lisbon probably started him on his magnificent career in law, politics and warfare. The third is his association with the authors of his time, his own writings, and his great interest in documents, literacy, and literature. This intellectual activity constitutes a fine chapter in the history of twelfth-century England, one which deserves more attention than it has received.

Earlier in this study eulogies of Glanville, mostly of the end of his career, have been given. He fulfilled the promise offered at the beginning of his career, as defined in Professor David's description of the crusader-chronicler: "a singularly appealing figure, an enthusiastic traveler, an absorbed observer of the lands which he visited, of sturdy moral principles, thoroughly loyal to his own cause and his own religion."[57]

Appendix: Further Notes on the Authorship Problem

Maitland (D. N. B.) gives as a reason for suggesting Hubert Walter as the author that Bracton coupled his own name with that of Hubert Walter as examples "in order to show how fatal it was for a pleader to make mistakes in them." If these names were random choices this might be important. It is as easy to suggest that the names are samples of two easy types of mistakes, forgetting to put a "de" in Bracton's name and adding a "filius" to that of Hubert Walter.

It has been suggested that a computer be put to work on the problem. This has its limitations since a computer is just a machine. It should do the same type of work that is done directly in this study by showing great similarities in point of view or style or in some other way. For instance the author of *De Legibus* says that he is using an inelegant style of writing. Would not the percentage of words used in this treatise tend then to be like other legal documents or treatises? And if it is a matter of types of words and their use, could Glanville not have altered these over a period of several decades following the fashions of the times in writing? Are not the most permanent, continuing characteristics those of motivation, interests, and general literary habits? This is not to deny the value of computer use, which I have used quite satisfactorily.

Notes

1. A recent excellent sketch is in Francis West, *The Justiciarship in England, 1066–1232* (Cambridge, 1966), pp. 54–63. Both names show variants: Rannulfus, Randulfus, Glamvilla.
2. *Dictionary of National Biography,* under Glanville. Also see appendix.
3. William Stubbs, *Select Charters,* etc. (Oxford, 6th ed., 1921), p. 190; George O. Sayles, *Medieval Foundations of England* (London, 1948), p. 286.
4. D. M. Stenton, *Pleas before the King or his Justices 1198–1202,* vol. I (Selden Society, 1953), 9–10. The treatise has recently been edited by G. D. G. Hall, *The Treatise on the Laws and Customs of the Realm of England* commonly called Glanville (London, 1965, Thomas Nelson). The attribution question is discussed on pp. xxix–xxxiv. Also see appendix to this study.
5. Charles W. David, ed., *De Expugnatione Lyxbonensi* (New York, 1936, Columbia University Records of Civilization); Helen M. Cam, "An East Anglian Shire-Moot of Stephen's Reign, 1148–53," *English Historical Review,* XXXIX (1924), 568–571. It is edited on pp. 569–71.
6. Under "English Law, History of" (14th ed., 1929).
7. C. Warren Hollister, *Making of England* (Boston, 1966, Heath), p. 131.
8. By J. H. Beale, in John Beames, *A Translation of Glanville* (Washington, 1900), p. lx.
9. R. Hewlett, ed., *Chronicles of the Reigns of Stephen, Henry II and Richard I* (Rolls Series, 1885–86), I, 302; William Stubbs, ed. *The Chronicles of the Reigns of Henry II and Richard I known commonly under the Name of Benedict of Peterborough.* II (Rolls Series, 1867), 87.

10. J. C. Russell, *British Medieval Population* (Albuquerque, 1948), pp. 180–181.

11. *Rotuli de Dominabus* (Pipe Roll Society no. 35, 1913), p. 80. The complicated problem of Glanville's family needs the care of an expert genealogist.

12. "Incipit tractatus de legibus et consuetudinibus regni Anglie tempore regis Henrici Secundi compositus, iusticie gubernacula tenente illustri viro Rannulfo de Glanvilla iuris regis et antiquarum consuetudinum eo tempore peritissimo." Hall, p. 1.

13. Hall, p. xxxiii.

14. Hall, p. xxxiii. *De Legibus* viii, 2, 3.

15. *Memoranda Roll, 1194–1200* (Pipe Roll Society no. 59, 1943), p. 86.

16. Hall, p. xxxiv.

17. Hall, p. xlv.

18. Hall, pp. 28–37. *De Legibus*, ii, 7.

19. Hall, pp. 1–2. Ranulf's charter setting up the Abbey of Leiston reads that it was for the soul of Henry II as well as for those of himself and his wife. Dugdale, *Monasticon Anglicanum*, VI, 881.

20. Cam, pp. 568–571.

21. Charles W. David, SPECULUM, VII (1932), 54, note 6.

22. Joscelin of Brakelond in T. Arnold, ed., *Memorials of St. Edmund's Abbey* I (Rolls Series, 1890), 232, 276 respectively.

23. David, *De Expugnatione Lyxbonensi*, p. 53. At one time Robert, Dean of Lisbon, seemed a possibility as author, on the chance that he, like the new bishop, Gilbert of Hastings, and canons, Gilbert of Kent and Martin of Romney (Rumenal), was English. For documents, David, pp. 178–180, n.5.

24. Charles W. David, "The Authorship of the *De Expugnatione Lyxbonensi*," SPECULUM, VII (1932), 50–58, esp. p. 56.

25. This was normal then, but in England changed to arrangement by dignity. For this see my "The Triumph of Dignity over Order in England," *The Historian*, IX (1947), 137–150.

26. Discussed many years ago in my "The Significance of Charter Witness Lists in Thirteenth Century England," *New Mexico Normal University Bulletin* (now New Mexico Highlands University), supplement to no. 99 (1930), pp. 11–14.

27. David, *De Expugnatione Lysboniensi*, p 42.

28. David, pp. 68, 71–85, 99, 105–111, 111–113, 115–119, 120, 123, 137, 139, 147–159.

29. David, p. 77.

30. David, p. 45 for Bible and Solinus; for association with council, pp. 101, 105, 167, 171; for legal organization, p. 57.

31. Giles Constable, "The Second Crusade as seen by Contemporaries," *Traditio*, IX (1953), 221.

32. David, p. 105. Other references to him appear on pp. 54–55, 56–57, 96–97, 104–105, 164–165 and 168–169.

33. C. H. Haskins, "Henry II as a Patron of Literature," *Essays in Medieval*

History presented to Thomas Frederick Tout (Manchester, 1925), p. 77. On the purpose and structure of the charter, see my "Attestation of Charters in the Reign of John," SPECULUM, XV (1940), 480–496, esp. pp. 491–98.

34. He first appears in 1171–73; Léopold Delisle, *Recueil des Actes de Henri II* (Paris, 1896), I, 579; in 1175: *Cartae Antiquae* (Pipe Roll Society vols. 55, 71, 1939, 1957), nos. 184, 576, 603; 1176–1180, nos. 577, 156, 79, 525 respectively by time; as examples in 1180–89, nos. 607, 616, 358.

35. Walter Map, *De Nugis Curialium*, i, 10: Giraldi Cambrensis Opera (Rolls Series), VIII, 258: from the "De instructione principum:"

36. *Memorials of St. Edmunds*, I, 232.

37. William Stubbs, ed., *The Historical Works of Gervase of Canterbury* I (Rolls Series, 1879), 447–48. Other references to this controversy appear in I, 309, 317, 318, 398, 439, 441, 447, 455.

38. William Stubbs, ed., *Chronica Magistri Rogeri de Hoveden*, II (Rolls Series, 1859), 215.

39. Hall, p. 1.

40. *De Nugis Curialium*, v, 7.

41. Quoted by W.U.S. Glanville-Richards, *Records of the Anglo Norman House of Glanville* (London, 1882), p. 29: specific source not given.

42. J. A. Stevenson, ed., *Chronica Monasterii de Abingdon*, II (Rolls Series, 1858), 297.

43. Devizes: *Chronicles of the Reigns of Stephen, Henry II and Richard I*, III, 385.

44. Newburgh: *ibid.*, I, 302.

45. *Giraldi Cambrensis Opera*, VI, 14; VIII, 258. Also VIII, 164.

46. By Maitland in D.N.B. article. The story is in Roger of Hoveden, II, 286; "Benedict," I, 314–315.

47. *Giraldi Cambrensis Opera*, v, 299–300.

48. "Benedict," I, 66–67; Roger of Hoveden, II, 62.

49. "Chronique de Jordan Fantosme," *Chronicles of the Reigns of Stephen, Henry II and Richard I*, III, 334–396. The lines referred to are 1366, 1980. The story of the messenger is also in William of Newburgh, I, 189.

50. For references see Maitland in D.N.B. mostly derived from "Benedict."

51. Haskins, "Henry II as a Patron of Literature," p. 72.

52. Possibly he was the Randulfus, *praepositus* of Norfolk, who appears in 1160–63: *Pipe Rolls 7–9 Henry II* (Pipe Roll Society), IV, 6; V, 64; VI, 30. "In the reign of Stephen he was receiver of the forfeited Earldom of Conan, and the collector of the Crown rents in the counties of Yorkshire and Westmorland," Glanville-Richards, p. 27. No source is given; the information would be valuable if verified.

53. *A Medieval Miscellany for Doris Mary Stenton* (Pipe Roll Society no. 76, 1962), 16. "The Anstey Case," by Patricia M. Barnes, pp. 1–24.

54. *Ibid.*, p. 21.

55. J. R. Strayer, "The Two Levels of Feudalism," in R. S. Hoyt ed., *Life and Thought in the Early Middle Ages* (Minneapolis, 1967), pp. 51–65, esp. pp. 54–57, 61–65.

56. J. C. Russell, "The Triumph of Dignity over Order," pp. 137–50.

57. David, *De Expugnatione Lyxbonensi*, pp. 45–46.

CHAPTER 10

Hereford and Arabic Science in England about 1175 – 1200

For a country located so far from the Mediterranean the share of England in the spread of Arabic science was rather astonishing. Professor Haskins has shown the significance of that country in this movement by identifying the translations of a series of Englishmen who took part in it.[1] About most of these men little else was known. With such a small amount of personal information available it has been difficult to detect the institutional connections, if any, of these men or to place their work in the background of cathedral school or university development of the century. In the course of research primarily for biographical information about thirteenth century men of letters in England a number of items turned up about ROGER OF HEREFORD, DANIEL OF MERLAI, ALEXANDER NECKAM, and probably ALFREDUS ANGLICUS. They tend to show—I believe—that Hereford, possibly through a cathedral school, was a center of this learning in the second half of the twelfth century.[2]

"ROGER OF HEREFORD," says Professor Haskins, "was a teacher and writer on astronomical and astrological subjects who was still a young man in 1176, and who, two years later, adapted astronomical tables of Arabic origin to the use of

Hereford.[3]" Professor Haskins also notes a number of items in contemporary records which might refer to him: a Master ROGER OF HEREFORD attesting a York charter of 1154–1163, a ROGER OF HEREFORD witnessing a document of GILBERT FOLIOT of 1173–74, a ROGER vice-dean of Hereford, owner of certain manuscripts, and a ROGER clerk of Hereford and itinerant justice. To these may be added a Master ROGER OF HEREFORD who attested a charter of Archbishop RICHARD OF CANTERBURY (1174–1184).[4] The frequency with which the title master is given makes one hesitate to accept any identification of the astronomer with a name not so prefixed. The chief difficulty seems to come from the popularity of the name ROGER at Hereford.

The *Compotus* of 1176 has in the Digby MS. the title, "Prefatio magistri Rogeri Infantis in compotum." The gloss on a work of ALFREDUS ANGLICUS called him *Rogerus Puer*.[5] Since the preface itself states that the author was still young it was possible to conjecture that *Infans* or *Puer* was an inference from the preface. This puzzle is settled by the appearance in a Hereford charter of 1195 of a Master ROGER Infans as a witness.[6] The astronomer's name was probably the Anglo-Norman *Lenfant* or the English *Child*. This lead does not seem to carry one far. A WILLIAM CHILD, it is true, connected with Hereford, appears in the Pipe Roll for 21 HENRY II.[7] His son would be, of course, *filius Willelmi de Hereford*. In a Rawlinson cartulary there is a series of Hereford documents which mention a ROGER *filius Willelmi de Hereford* and several relatives including an uncle ROGER *filius Mauricii de Hereford*.[8] The latter is probably that canon of Hereford described by THOMAS DE MARLEBERGH as a great man whom the abbey of Evesham ejected from the position of Dean of Christianity for the churches of the Vale of Evesham about 1202.[9] The temptation to identify the astronomer as a member of this family is discouraged by the fact that the charters do not call any member of the family *Infans* nor master either.

The attestation of Master ROGER INFANS in 1195 prolongs his career nearly a score of years beyond the date of his treatise of 1178. If we may identify him with the Master ROGER who appears frequently in Hereford charters of the period, once as early as 1172, he may be assumed to have spent much of his time there.[10] The preface of his *Compotus* mentions that he had taught several years but does not give the place of his school. If his astronomical tables were written for school use the fact that they were prepared for the meridian of Hereford may be significant. Was there a school at Hereford? If so did it conform to the pattern of studies which ROGER OF HEREFORD inserts in the preface of the *Compotus?*

Before taking up these questions let us examine a treatise which seems to disclose the concluding chapter of the life of ROGER OF HEREFORD. This book has an acrostic of the table of chapters which the preface says gives the name of compiler and corrector, ROGERUS COMPOTISTA ET REGINALDUS DE WALSINGHAM MONACHI SANCTI EDMUNDI REGIS.[11] In just such an acrostic was revealed the authorship of the *Compotus* of ROGER OF HEREFORD. The work is entitled *Expositiones Vocabulorum que sunt in Biblia* and has been assigned to a ROGER COMPOTISTA of the fourteenth century. Examination shows that it was probably earlier: the manuscripts themselves may be of the thirteenth century. The work is prefixed by a very remarkable index of the words commented upon. Arranged in approximately alphabetical order with reference to book and section number this index gives the impression that its author had a precise and orderly mind. But this might be expected of any computist. The heading of the Laudian manuscript to the introduction is "Prologus Promathei." This brings to mind at once the *Corrogationes Promethei* of ALEXANDER NECKAM whose interests were in many ways similar to those of ROGER OF HEREFORD. The *Corrogationes Promethei* have been explained by Paul Meyer as the collections of one who was idle as Prometheus bound.[12] It would be as appropriate for ROGER OF HEREFORD in a monastery after a busy life as it was for NECKAM in very similar circumstances.

The date of the work may be determined to a certain extent from the citations. The library at Bury was a large one: one might expect that up to date books would be there. The authorities are several. ALEXANDER NECKAM is cited very frequently. JOHN OF SALISBURY, among modern writers, is cited several times.[13] Others were PETRUS HELIAS,[14] WYDO DE

CREMA,[15] HILDEBERT,[16] PETRUS COMESTOR,[17] and the Architrenius of JOHN OF HANVILLE[18]. Two editions were apparently made. The Laud MS represents the first, and does not contain items which appear in the later, fuller edition. The latter, for instance, contains references to the *Physics* and *Nicomachean Ethics* which do not appear in the other.[19] NECKAM's *De Naturis Rerum* was written before the revision of ROGER's work.[20] It is difficult to determine whether the first edition was also written before this work. Of more importance is whether it was written before NECKAM's *Corrogationes Promethei*. In this respect however the evidence is clear. NECKAM's work preceded even ROGER's first version.[21]

Interesting as the information is that ROGER had before him the *Corrogationes* of NECKAM, a more important question is the extent of his borrowing. As samples let us take the books of Joshua and of Maccabees: both works are arranged according to the books of the Bible. In the former NECKAM comments upon about 15 words or phrases and ROGER upon 36.[22] Of these only 3 are identical. In Maccabees NECKAM comments upon 22 items and ROGER 87: they have 23 in common, a much higher percentage. How much ROGER took from other writers must await further investigation, but there seems reason to believe that some is original. In one important respect ROGER differed from NECKAM: the latter used the old arrangement of the Bible while ROGER already had the new, usually attributed to STEPHEN LANGTON.

In all of this there is no book which could not have been secured in the early years of the thirteenth century. There is nothing to prevent identification of this ROGER COMPOTISTA with ROGER OF HEREFORD. If the astronomer became a monk of St. Edmund's he probably died before 1214: his name does not appear in the very long list of monks who took part in the election of that year.[23] His coauthor, REGINALD OF WALSINGHAM does not appear either. Among the miracles attributed to St. Edmund recorded by the contemporary abbot was one to ROGER DE HASELEYA, canon of Hereford, and his chaplain, ROGER DE AVESTANE.[24]

Another character of greater importance in the transmission of Arabic knowledge from Spain to northern Europe was

ALFREDUS ANGLICUS or ALFRED OF 'SARECHEL'.[25] "We know from ROGER BACON and from internal evidence that he visited Spain."[26] He dedicated works to ROGER OF HEREFORD and to ALEXANDER NECKAM. Certain facts about the latter make it possible to give a conjectural date for the dedication.[27] The title of ALFRED's work reads, "Liber magistri Alvredi de Sareshel ad magistrum magnum Alexandrum Nequam de motu cordis."[28] This assumes that NECKAM was probably still a teacher and that he was not yet canon of Cirencester. In the latter capacity he appears as early as the spring of 1203. It assumes also that his interests were largely in science, although this is not so certain. NECKAM taught theology at Oxford for several years. Since theology usually was a man's ultimate interest the date of his interest in science should probably be pushed back. On the other hand NECKAM was seeking a school as late as 1183 and would hardly have been called a magnum magistrum earlier. These indications point to the decade 1185–1195 as the most probable period for the dedication.

In the course of an examination of chartulary and printed documents for evidence of thirteenth century literary men I found that the name ALFRED was very uncommon. The following are the instances. A Master *Aldredus* appears at Hereford as a witness ca. 1153–55 and ca. 1175 according to the editor.[29] A Master *Aldredus* was a chaplain of Dean GEOFFREY OF HEREFORD.[30]. Three Hereford books once belonged to Master ALVEREDUS: the cathedral library, *MS 02 IV*: Jesus College, Oxford, *MS 26*, and All Souls College, *MS 82*. His *obit* was on IX kal. January.[31] A Master ALFRED was canon of St. Peter of Exeter about 1205.[32] SENATUS BRAVONIUS of Worcester who died about 1207 dedicated a book to a Master ALFRED. These items may belong to the same career—that of the translator, ALFREDUS ANGLICUS. The dedication to ROGER OF HEREFORD whose connections as well as his name were—of Hereford— makes this highly probable.

Two such distinguished Arabists at Hereford would make this a scholarly center of some importance. Was there a school there? In a poem addressed to GERALD OF WALES inviting him to come to Hereford SIMON DE FRESNE makes a rather clear statement that such existed[33]:

> Flos et honor cleri, nostram te transfer ad urbem,
>   Sunt ubi philosophi, summus habendus ibi,
> Urbs Herefordensis multum tibi competit, in qua
>   Proprius est trivii quadriviique locus,
> Floruit et floret, in hac specialiter urbe
>   Artis septenae praedominatur honos.
> Hunc, ubi tot radiant artes, de jure teneris,
>   Cum sis artis honos, artis amare locum.

The poem mentions the failure of GERALD OF WALES to receive high preferment. This may have occurred any time after 1176 but would be especially appropriate about 1200.

SIMON DU FRESNE, designated in the manuscripts of the poems, as canon of Hereford, was also the author of two Anglo-Norman poems, *Le Roman de Philosophie* and *La Vie de Saint Georges.* In both poems the author gives his name in an acrostic: it seems to have been a Hereford custom. He witnessed, ca. 1200 according to the editor, a convention between WILLIAM the treasurer and the chapter of Hereford.[34] He attested a charter of Bishop WILLIAM DE VERE (1189-1199)[35] and one of H, abbot of Salop.[36] By the time of THOMAS, abbot of Gloucester (1224-1228) he had died.[37] His obit was on 15 July.[38] SIMON's information about Hereford refers then to the time or slightly later than the time of ROGER and ALFRED.

Another Master SIMON at Hereford might be confused with SIMON DU FRESNE did not the two appear together in the same charter.[39] Unfortunately in a number of instances the mere citation Master SIMON does not indicate which one is meant.[40] This other Master SIMON is called Master SIMON MELUD or Melun or the Theologian.[41] Since the man's surname is known it seems probable that his other name *theologus* was given for achievement or occupation. He probably taught theology at Hereford.

Let us turn to the preface of ROGER's *compotus.* It reads as follows[42]:

> Cum non sit humane benevolentie rem pluribus sed quod magis est, singulis necessariam infra terminos facilitatis includere, de compoto, quamvis difficillimum sit tante rei a viris summis sepe et diligenter tractate aliquid novi addere, sed et presumptuosum videatur

juvenem tot senum scripta retractare, multorum tamen
petitionibus quos ad hoc hujus scientie invitavit excellen-
tia scribere compellor. Hoc namque, ut asserit Timeus
Platonis, in beneficio oculorum seminarium totius extitit
philosophie, que primo considerata mirabili motuum ac
temporum variatione se erexit ad liberrimas humane nature excellentias, sermonem videlicet ac rationem exor-
nandasi sermonem quidem recte loquendi vel scribendi
ad intelligentiam (gloss, gramatica), argute vero dis-
serendi ad fidem (gl. dialectica), ornate decorandi ad per-
suasionem (gl. retorica); sed et rationem ipsam, ut sicut
cuncta numero (gl. arismetica), pondere (gl. musica), et
mensura (gl. geometria) consistunt, ita horum trium sci-
entiis ad rerum naturam investigandum et superiorum
(gl. astronomia) et inferiorum (gl. phisica) pervexit. Nec-
non et ipsa theologia que est de creatoris cognitione, hanc
sibi tanquam de eximia artium astronomia suam elegit
portionem non solum sibi sed omni vite tam communi
quam studiose maxime necessitatem. Hanc tamen tante
excellentie scientiam astrologi, nature superiorum secreta
motuumque tam celi quam stellarum certitudinem inves-
tigantes, compotumque ab illa certitudine multum dis-
crepare reperientes, falsam ab omni philosophica disciplina abjiciendam arbitrantur.

The preface continues with a statement of the battles of
the computists together with the author's statement that he
has been kept busy for many years in the schools and by
personal affairs.

The preface gives a rather interesting outline of study: the
seven liberal arts, theology and the sciences, especially astronomy, astrology and physics. Of the seven liberal arts,
grammar, logic, and rhetoric are regarded as only means to an
end, the study of the subject matter itself, arithmetic, music,
geometry, and astronomy. Even theology had much to learn
from astrology and astronomy. How does this fit into what we
know of Hereford? SIMON DU FRESNE told us that the seven
liberal arts flourished there. SIMON the theologian was there.
ROGER OF HEREFORD and ALFREDUS ANGLICUS, if we have
identified him correctly, were eminent scientists. There is a
striking similarity of interests. There is, moreover, in both the

preface and in our knowledge of Hereford a notable absence of references to medicine and law and that in a century in which both were popular in the schools. Since ROGER probably used the schools in which he taught as an illustration it seems very likely that we have here a picture of the interests of the school at Hereford—probably a cathedral school.

In the movement for the spread of Arabic science in England DANIEL OF MERLAI is a character of considerable interest. He gives some autobiographical information in his *Philosophia*. [43] He tried the University of Paris but was bored by the instruction and proceeded to Spain where he listened to the great translator GERARD OF CREMONA who died in 1187. His book was dedicated to JOHN, Bishop of Norwich (1175–1200). While these dates indicate the time of his activity others define it even more clearly.

In the Pipe Rolls of 1184–1187 there are references to a debt which he contracted along with three other men with a few, DEULEBENEIE. [44] How much earlier than 1184 was the date of the transaction is uncertain. He next appears in a Curia Regis Roll of 1198. [45] In the following year in the same suit he appears as parson of Flitcham, in which capacity he seems to have acted the year before. [46] For the Trinity term of 2 John (1200–1201) he appears in a Curia Regis Roll in regard to a question of land tenure at Cambridge. [47] The *Rotulus Cancellarii* shows him owing three marks *de Gernemue* also of Cambridge. [48] On 2 September, 1205 the bishop of Norwich confirmed to the church of Flitcham a small piece of land over which G. de Norfolk and the parson, Master *D. de Merleia* had had a suit. [49] As parson of Flitcham DANIEL OF MERLAI seems to have been succeeded by a JOHN OF MERLAI. It has been suggested that this JOHN was a son of DANIEL but of that there seems no evidence in the Holkham deeds. [50] Other items may belong to this man or to a later man of the same name: the donor of a gift to the priory of Castleacre, [51] and a debtor of 200 marks for disseisin in 1230. [52] In any case the student interested in Arabic science lived near the end of the twelfth century.

Now let us turn to a paragraph in the treatise of DANIEL OF MERLAI's *Philosophia* which has been the subject of much controversy:

Vocatus vero tandem ab amicis, et invitatus ut ab
Hispania redirem, cum pretiosa multitudine librorum, in
Angliam veni. Cumque nuntiatum esset mihi quod in
partibus illis discipline liberales silentium habet, et pro
Tito et Seio penitus Aristoteles et Plato oblivioni daren-
tur, vehementer indolui. Et ne ego solus inter Romanos
Grecus remanerem, ubi huiusmodi studium florere di-
diceram iter arripui. Et in ipso itinere obviam habui
dominum meum et patrem spiritualem, Johannem Nor-
vicensem episcopum, qui me honorifice ut eum decebat,
recipiens, valde meo gratulabatur adventui.

We may suspect that the friends of DANIEL were fellow
students of his pre-Spanish days. Where? This would depend
upon the subjects which DANIEL had studied. Obviously not
theology or he would not have been so bored with Paris. Since
he went on to Spain it seems probable that he was already
interested in Arabic science. Was this study at Hereford? It is
the one place where our present evidence points to a probable
school. The reference to Roman law probably indicates Oxford. "In illis partibus" is broad enough to include Hereford if
one is in Norfolk. Indeed, the use of the plural requires explanation if only Oxford was meant by DANIEL. One may conjecture that DANIEL had studied at Hereford before his departure
for Spain sometime previous to 1187 and on his return before
1198 he found a great decline in interest in ARISTOTLE and
others coming in by way of translations from the Arabic.

What were the antecedents of the interest in Arabic learning at Hereford? Professor Haskins has pointed out a group of
Lorrainers eminent in science who came to England in the
second half of the eleventh century and the first half of the
twelfth. Among the greatest were ROBERT DE LOSINGA, bishop
of Hereford[53], and WALCHER, prior of Malvern, not so far from
Hereford. It is perhaps significant that the two other great
names of the scientific movement, ADELARD OF BATH and
ROBERT OF CHESTER, indicate the rather sparsely settled western part of England. For the period even farther back Professor
Thompson has written of "The introduction of Arabic science
into Lorraine in the tenth century."[54]

As to the successor or successors of the school of Hereford
we may well look to the Franciscan school at Oxford, whose

interests have been so well described by Dr. Little.[55] After
mentioning the great stress upon study of the Bible and the
languages, he quotes ROGER BACON for its interest in mathematics and physical science as follows:

> "There have been found some famous men, such as
> Robert Bishop of Lincoln, and friar Adam Marsh and
> some others, who have known how by the power of
> mathematics to unfold the causes of all things and to give
> a sufficient explanation of human and divine phenom-
> ena; and the assurance of this fact is to be found in the
> writings of these great men, as, for instance, in their
> works on the impression (of the elements), on the rain-
> bow and the comets, on the sphere, and on other ques-
> tions appertaining both to theology and to natural philos-
> ophy."

All very much like the remark of Master ROGER INFANS.
This Bishop ROBERT was a chaplain or one of the clerks of
Bishop WILLIAM DE VERE of Hereford (1189–1199). His name
occurs several times in the Balliol cartulary previously mentioned.[56] This confirms the statement of GERALD OF WALES to
the effect that ROBERT GROSSETESTE was a member of the
household of Bishop WILLIAM. GROSSETESTE was the first master of the Franciscan school at Oxford and set the stamp of his
personality upon it.

If the school declined or interest in Arabic science lessened
it was not because the pioneers in this science were subjected
to ecclesiastical censure or restriction. NECKAM died abbot of
Cirencester. DANIEL OF MERLAI became a parson. ROGER OF
HEREFORD probably ended his days as a monk of Bury St.
Edmund. ALFREDUS ANGLICUS may have become canon of
Exeter. All died in the good graces of the church. After all, it
was Aristotelian metaphysics and its Arabic commentators
rather than the other work of the Greeks which brought down
the ecclesiastical prohibitions of 1210 and 1215. These pioneers
do not seem much interested in theological discussion based
on the new material.

Along several lines some advance in knowledge is made.
The lives of ROGER OF HEREFORD and DANIEL OF MERLAI have
been more precisely defined. ALFREDUS ANGLICUS has been

identified with some probability as the Master ALFRED whose activity is evident about Hereford in the second half of the twelfth century. The presence of these men together with other evidence points to a cathedral school at Hereford at which the liberal arts, theology, and Arabic science were taught. Some surmises as to the antecedents and subsequent influence of the group are easy but conjectural. On the side of research the study suggests the possibility of supplementing by examination of unprinted records the careful study of translations and other treatises by such scholars as Professor Haskins.

Notes

1. *Studies in the History of Mediaeval Science* (Cambridge 1927), ch. II "Adelard of Bath," ch. VI "The Introduction of Arabic Science into England;" and to some extent chs. XV and XVIII.
2. My interest in these men began in the fall of 1923 in a seminar in which Professor HASKINS took up certain questions raised in the above mentioned work. My research was as a fellow of the Guggenheim Foundation in 1930−31. I am glad to acknowledge the advice and suggestions of my colleague Professor L. C. MacKINNEY.
3. *Op. cit.*, p. 126.
4. *Archeologia Cantiana*, V, 201−202.
5. HASKINS, *op. cit.*, 125.
6. Oxford, Balliol College, *MS 271*, fol. 6*or*.
7. P. 70.
8. Bodleian Library, *MS Rawlinson B 329*, fols. 123*r*−126*v*.
9. W. D. MACRAY, ed. *Chronicon de Evesham* (London, 1863, Rolls Series), 196, 264.
10. Balliol College, *MS 271*, fol. 16*r*, other instances on fols. 6*r*, 16*r*, 36*r*, 39*r*, 44*r*, 67*v* and 71*r*. He always appears after the canons of Hereford.
11. Oxford, Bodleian Library, *MS Laud Misc.* 176, all 160 fols: *MS Bodley* 238, fols. 200*v*−262*r*; Magdalen College, *MS* 112.
12. *Notices et extraits des MSS*, XXXV, 2, 649, 651−654.
13. *MS Bodley* 238, fols, 216*v*, 229*v*, 233*v*, 248*r*, 250*r*, 251*r*.
14. *Ibid.*, fol. 213*v*.
15. *Ibid.*, fol. 228*v*.
16. *Ibid.*, fols. 232*v*, 236*r*.
17. *Ibid.*, fol. 240*r*, 225*v*, 234*v*.
18. *Ibid.*, fol. 214*r*.
19. *Ibid.*, fols. 234*v* and 250*r*.
20. *Ibid.*, fol. 248*r*. Magister Alexander Nequam dicit in libro suo de natura rerum.

21. *Ibid.*, fols. 121r, 121v, 133v, 243v: MS *Laud Misc.* 176, fols. 61r, 67v, 126v, 142v.
22. For NECKAM's work I have used MS *Bodley* 550.
23. T. ARNOLD, ed. *Memorials of St. Edmund's Abbey* (London, 1896, Rolls Series, no. 90), II, 75–76.
24. *Ibid.*, I, 207–208.
25. HASKINS, *op. cit.*, 128.
26. *Ibid.*, p. 129.
27. For these facts see my "Alexander Neckam in England," *English Historical Review.* XLVII (1932), 260–268.
28. C. BAEUMKER, *Des Alfred von Sareshel Schrift de motu cordis* (Münster i.W 1923), I.
29. W. W. CAPES, ed. *Charters and Records of Hereford Cathedral* (Hereford, 1908), 17 and 27.
30. Balliol College, MS 271, fol. 37v.
31. GOUGH, *The History and Antiquities of the City and Cathedral Church of Hereford*, etc. (London, 1717) (31).
32. J. H. ROUND, ed. *Calendar of Documents preserved in France* etc., 918–1206. (London, 1899), 279: Brit. Mus. MS *Cotton, Vitell. D.* IX, fol. 33v.
33. J. E. MATZKE, ed. *Les Œuvres de Simund de Freine* (Paris, 1909), VII.
34. CAPES, *op. cit.*, 38.
35. Brit. Mus, MS *Arundel* 19, fol. 31r.
36. Balliol College, MS 271, fol. 54r–v.
37. *Ibid.*, fol. 70v.
38. GOUGH, *op. cit.* (17).
39. CAPES, *op. cit.*, 38.
40. *Ibid.*, 19, 23, 24, 25, 37.
41. GOUGH, *op. cit.* (6). Oxford, Balliol College, MS 271, fols. 52r, 61r.
42. Bodleian Library, MS *Digby* 40, fol. 21r. Printed by T. WRIGHT, *Biographia Britannica Literaria* (London, 1846), II, 90–91.
43. For bibliography see HASKINS, *op. cit.*, p. 126–127.
44. Pipe Rolls, 31–33 Henry II, see index: the same item is repeated for these years.
45. P. 35.
46. WALTER RYE, ed. *A Short Calendar of the Feet of Fines for Norfolk* (Norwich, 1885), p. 64.
47. P. 177. Cf. also WALTER RYE, *Pedes Finium* etc. *of Cambridge* (Cambridge, 1891, Cambridge Antiquarian Society), 4.
48. P. 31.
49. *Catalogue of Miscellaneous Deeds belonging to the Rt. Hon. the Earl of Leicester*, no. 703, at Holkham Hall, Norfolk. Used by courtesy of the Earl and with the assistance of the librarian, Mr. JAMES. The Flitcham deeds seem to have been misplaced.
50. Hist. MSS Commission, *Report on Various Collections*, IV, 317. JOHN's name appears in the Holkham catalogue in nos. 704, 705, 706, 708, 713, 714, 715, 716, 717, 718, 719, 720, 722, 724, 728, 730, 731, 732, 737. JOHN's

brother RICHARD occurs in most of those from no. 718.
51.   Brit. Mus. *MS Harley* 2110, fol. 38*v* : FRANCIS BLOMEFIELD, *An Essay towards a Topographical History of the County of Norfolk,* VIII, 390, 465.
52.   P. 340.
53.   HASKINS, *op. cit.* 333–335.
54.   *Isis* XII, 184–193 (1929).
55.   *Archivum Franciscanum Historicum* XIX, 810 (1926).
56.   *MS* 271, fols. 6*v*, 56*v*, 79*v*, 88*v*.

CHAPTER 11

Alexander Neckam in England

Although Alexander Neckam occupies a prominent place in the intellectual history of England at the end of the twelfth century, much remains to be done before his position is thoroughly understood. The only recent catalogue of his writings must be regarded, as its compiler warned us, as a tentative list.[1] To it should probably be added, as Professor Haskins has shown, an unusual and valuable outline of university study.[2] The catalogue shows that from the thirteenth century England possessed the greater part of the manuscripts of Neckam's writings. This requires explanation since Neckam's academic life is usually associated with Paris. It suggests that research is needed upon the English side of his career. Professor Powicke has shown that there was a second and contemporary Master Alexander of St. Albans with whom Neckam might be confused.[3] Further evidence, however, exists, which clears up some obscurity about his writings, and shows that Neckam spent many of his mature years in England as a teacher at Oxford and as canon of Cirencester.

According to one chronicler Neckam was born on the same night as Richard I, 13 September 1157, and had this prince as a foster brother.[4] From the short autobiographical account at the end of his *Laus Sapientie Divine* it is clear that he spent his boyhood and received his early training at St. Albans. He then spent several years studying at Paris. Unfortunately, the account breaks off here, leaving it uncertain whether he carried on advanced study elsewhere.[5] For a time he taught at Dunstable, and while there was summoned to teach at St. Albans. Here he was followed by Warin, the nephew of both the abbot and prior. This Warin is stated to have been like a brother to his two uncles and to have excercised power with them as a triumvirate at St. Albans. The indications are that Warin must have been master of the schools at St. Albans for a considerable portion of his uncle's term as abbot, thus pushing Neckam's incumbency back to the early years of the abbot.[6]

References which Tanner culled directly or indirectly from a sermon preached at the Council at Basel and from William of Worcester indicate that Neckam was associated with Oxford,[7] and this connexion is confirmed by an autobiographical note buried in one of the least interesting of Neckam's works, his 'Commentary on the Song of Songs'.[8] His story reads:

> Ego ipse, qui hec scribo, dum publice legerem in theologia, vehemens eram assertor quad dies conceptionis beate Marie celebrandus solempnitur non esset. Unde et quotannis illo die legere publice decreveram sicut in profectis diebus consueveram. Sed testor solem iustitie quod repentino morbo vexatus sum Oxonie singulis annis in illo die ut nullo modo susceptum magisterii officium exequi valerem, sive id casus ageret sive divina voluntas. Sed et viri prudentes, qui me tunc temporis in scholis audierunt, diligenter hoc consideraverunt, me secreto corripientes eo quod impugnare velle videbar celebrantes diem festum conceptionis beate virginis. Ecce ego doceo, assero, credo non indiscrete agere illos, sed potius in hoc commendandos qui pie et devote diem sepe dictum celebrare agunt in honorem perpetue virginis Marie.

It is curious that this story, which was apparently known to Wood, has escaped the notice of later historians of the university. After all, facts about Oxford in the twelfth century which throw such light upon its life are quite scarce.[9]

The story, in a different form, of Neckam's conversion to belief in the Immaculate Conception of the Virgin Mary appears in at least two collections of *exempla*.[10] It is as follows:

Referunt quidam fidedigni quod[11] Alexander Nequam frequenter asserere consuevit quod conceptio virginis[12] Marie celebrari non debet, et ad firmationem opinionis sue omnes quas potuit rationes induxit. Cum autem quadam die[13] ora matutina dictus magister[14] in lecto suo quiesceret, apparuit ei beata virgo; cui sic improperanda[15] est locuta, 'Cur me persequeris?[16] Cur solemnitatem conceptionis mee impedire niteris? Ad hoc enim ingenium tuum et studium tuum[17] usque direxisti. Quod si ab temeraria[18] presumptione cessare nolueris, scito quod graviter punieris'. Quo audito cepit assertationes suas revocare. Unde[19] postmodum in quadem religione abbas constitutus fecit[20] eandem conceptionem solempniter celebrari.[21]

Neckam's connexion with Oxford may also be deduced from the colophon of one of his sermons. The sermon, which in a Merton manuscript has the heading, *Alexandri in primo adventu scolaribus Oxonie*, appears also in a great Bodleian collection of his homilies.[22] It begins:

Tu exurgens misereberis Sion:
    Quia tempus miserendi eius, quia venit tempus. Psa. ci. 14.
In patre unitas, in filio equalitas, in spiritu sancto unitatis equalitatisque connexio. In patre unitas auctoritatis, in filio equalitas prima, in spiritu sancto, qui est spiritus fidei, amborum est concordia. Prima, igitur, arismetica equalitas in unitate reperitur.. Si vero dicatur duo et apponatur denominatio talis bis duo, maior numerus resultat. Et ita se habet res et aliis numeris. Si vero dicatur unum et fiat denominatio talis semel unum, non procreatur maior numerus. Similiter dicatur semel, major vero excrescit numerus. Si dicatur bis duo...Sed in unitate equalitas reperitur sive adiciatur sive substrahatur. Est igitur pater qui unum, filius qui semel unum, spiritus sanctus qui semel unum semel. Ecce unus, duo, tres.

One has only to examine the introductory textbook on theology usually ascribed to Alan de l'Isle to realize how close to the theological classroom is this sermon.[23]

For the chronology of Neckam's life a composition before papal delegates in 1205, published by Madox in his *Formulare*

Anglicanum, is important.[24] The delegates are Robert, abbot of
Malmesbury, Walter, prior of Llanthony, and Master Alexander of St. Albans, canon of Cirencester. Furthermore, the
composition recites the papal letter of delegation of 8 May
1203, which names the same delegates. From this it is clear that
Neckam was quite well known as Alexander of St. Albans, a
fact which is suggested by several manuscripts.[25] It shows also
that he was an Austin canon of Cirencester by the spring of
1203. Elastic though it was, the Austin Rule would hardly have
allowed Neckam the extended absences from Cirencester
which teaching at Oxford must have demanded.

Neckam's entrance into religious life as a regular was
probably the occasion for a letter of Peter of Blois. Addressing
him as Master Alexander of St. Albans, Peter speaks of *lit-
teratura vestra* and says, 'Honorem magisterii, laudemque
hominum, et inanem hujus seculi letitiam exspuisti'. These
phrases point to Neckam rather than to the little known Alexander the Mason of St. Albans, who was still a royal clerk
after the death of Peter of Blois.[26] Mr. Cohn has shown that
this letter was probably not in the first recension of Peter's
collection compiled probably by 1189, but was included in the
second.[27] Peter was probably still archdeacon of Bath.[28] Since,
however, he apparently held his office as late as 1202 and
possibly till 1205, the title is not very helpful in determining the
date of the letter.[29] Rather light verses on wine by both of these
men appear in a manuscript together.[30]

As canon of Cirencester, Neckam seems to have served
the king as well as the pope. Twice in 1212 there were royal
payments to messengers going to Master *Alexander Nequam* at
Cirencester, one to Neckam's clerk, Walter, and another to
Henry of Germany.[31] On 30 August 1213 the king ordered him
to accompany John of Hastings, the constable of Kenilworth,
and a clerk of the archbishop of Canterbury to inquire into the
royal rights in the priory of Kenilworth.[32] This service, in the
time of the interdict we should remember, helps explain the
election of Neckam as abbot of Cirencester in this same year.[33]
The temporalities were restored by a writ of 19 May 1214.[34]

In the summer of 1215 Neckam was at court preparing to
attend the Fourth Lateran Council. At Marlborough on 8 July

the king ordered the seven hundreds of Cirencester to be restored to the abbey of Cirencester.[35] The following day the abbot attested a charter and secured other privileges for his abbey.[36] On 15 July the king ordered letters patent to be issued to Neckam and to other ecclesiastics who were leaving for the council, and on 19 August he ordered a boat for the abbot.[37] On 13 September Neckam attested a charter at Dover, presumably just as he was leaving for the council.[38] Since the bishop of Worcester attests the same charter, the tradition seems correct which makes him accompany Neckam.[39]

Neckam seems to have been on very good terms with the successor to this bishop, since he died at Kempsey, a manor of the bishops of Worcester, and was buried in Worcester Cathedral.[40] William of Worcester has a curious note to the effect that the bishop of Worcester did not wish Neckam to be buried at Cirencester and excommunicated him on his return from Rome.[41] Neckam died early in 1217, for by 27 April the king had announced his approval of the election of Walter the Cellarer as abbot of Cirencester.[42] Neckam was buried in the same cathedral as King John, where his mutilated tomb is still thought to remain.[43]

The career of the other Master Alexander of St. Albans[44] deserves study, if for no other reason than that it may be separated from that of Neckam. Wendover called this man *Magister Alexander dictus Cementarius*.[45] He is apparently the Master Alexander of St. Albans who was involved in some litigation of 1212.[46] The incident of 1215 has been told already by Professor Powicke[47] and need not be retold here.

The career of this Master Alexander may be pushed back some years. Professor Stenton has used his attestation of a charter of John de Grey, bishop of Norwich, as an instance of a royal clerk who had previously served in a bishop's curia.[48] Several other instances occur, enough to justify Tanner's statement, 'Quidam Alex. de S. Albano frequenter occurrit testis cartarum Johannis de Oxon. episcopi Norivc.'[49] Five dated charters fall within the sixth year of the pontificate of Bishop John between 13 November 1205 and 3 March 1206.[50] Since Neckam was a canon of Cirencester by this time, the existence of two Alexanders at this date is indicated.

An interesting possibility is that this Master Alexander of St. Albans may be the *Magister Alexander Cementarius* who appears as the *Cementarius* of the cathedral church of Worcester in a series of documents.[51] The editor speaks of him as of the time of King John, but that is a little doubtful. Two documents are of the time of Bishop Walter Cantelupe (1236–66), but since Alexander's son appears with him, his career doubtless goes back many years.[52] However, two witnesses of other documents seem to appear in charters of 1249–50.[53] While chronology may tend to prevent the identification, a master mason was obviously a man of importance about a cathedral and might well have been a royal clerk.[54] In the field of the fine arts should be noticed a John of St. Albans of 1257–8 and Walter of Coleworth, sacristan of St. Albans of 1220: St. Albans was a place from which an architect might be expected.[55]

The thirteenth-century compilation from the writings of Neckam in MS. Gg. vi. 42 of the Cambridge University Library enables us to proceed a little farther with the definition of his works. This is arranged as a devotional treatise. Geoffrey, its poetically inclined author,[56] dedicated his work to *Sol Meldunensis et cinthia lux monachorum*. If Neckam's fellow delegate, Robert of Melun, abbot of Malmesbury, had not died so many years before Neckam, one might suspect him of being the patron, since both elements of his name might be *Meldunensis*. A letter of Prior S. of Malmesbury to a canon of Cirencester, Walter Melidie, praising Neckam's writings, exists in at least two manuscripts.[57] Geoffrey wrote the names of treatises and sermons in the margin, so that it is relatively easy to locate references. Not all of Neckam's works were used. The evidence derived from this compilation is given in the appendix.

In Leland's *Itinerary* there is what purports to be an exchange of hostile epigrams between Philip of Repton, abbot of Leicester, and Neckam.[58]

> *Versus Nechami Cirencestris ad Philippum Repingdunum Leircestr. Abbatem.*
>
> Phi nota fetoris, lippus malus omnibus horis;
> Phi fetor, lippus, totus malus ergo Philippus.
>
> Philippi responsio.

Es niger et nequam dictus cognomine Necham.
Nigrior esse potes, nequior esse nequis.

That Neckam was one of the participants is clear from the second couplet, but Philip of Repton lived too late to have been the other.[59]

Appendix

A. Comments upon writings in Esposito's catalogue.

The numbers are those of his list. References to folios of Geoffrey's compilation (C.U.L. MS. Gg. vi. 42) are given when citations are not numerous.

4. Ex libro de naturis rerum. Geoffrey cites separately as ex tractatu super ecclesiasticen the last three books of this work.

5. Ex libro qui intitulatur laus sapientie divine. Fos. 69^r, 71^r.

6. Ex libro qui intitulatur corrogationes Promothei.

7. Ex tractatu super Cantica Canticorum. *Laus Beatissime Virginis* (Esposito, p. 470) is probably not a subtitle of this. See supplementary list no. 2 below.

9. Ex glosa super psalmum v (fo. 66^r): xxiii (fos. 98^r, 162^v), xxiv (fo. 162^v), xxxvi (fo. 12^r), xxxvii (fo. 9^v), xlviii (fo. 75^v).

11. Ex tractatu super Parabolas.

12. Ex tractatu qui intitulatur speculum speculationum. Fos. 70^r, 143^v.

13. Ex tractatu super conversionem admirabilem beatissime Magdalene. Fos. 98^v, 99^v.

14. Ex questione scolastica. Fos. 12^r, 74^v, 75^v. Not checked against the Lambeth manuscript, however.

30. Ex tractatu super mulierem fortem.

B. Supplementary list.

1. Ex tractatu super Ecclesiasticen. Usually called books III—V of the *De Naturis Rerum*.

2. Ex libro edito in laudem gloriose Virginis. Fos. 7^v, 16^v, 18^r, 19^r, 22^v, 24^r, 32^r, 40^v, 46^v, 48^v, 50^v, 57^v, 150^r, 202^r. This was probably a commentary on Genesis, as Neckam's statement suggests. 'Si quis autem diligentiorem explanationem principii Geneseos inspicere desiderat, legat opus nostrum quod in

laudem beatissime Virginis scripsimus, et opus morale quod intitulavi solatium fidelis animé (*De Naturis Rerum* (Rolls Series), p. 16).

3. Ex libro qui intitulatur solatium fidelis anime. Fos. 66ᵛ, 80ʳ, 88ᵛ, 89ʳ – 90ᵛ, 91ʳ, 93ʳ, 112ʳ, 113ʳ, 119ᵛ, 120ʳ, 125ʳ, 127ᵛ, 141ᵛ, 142ʳ, 143ᵛ, 150ʳ, 165ᵛ, 169ʳ, 201ʳ. From Neckam's statement, quoted above, it seems that this treatise is also a commentary on Genesis and probably exists in a Canterbury MS. (B. vi): 'Biblia Latina Thomae de Banchester cui prefigitur Tractatus Moralium super Genesim qui dicitur Solatium fidelis anime' (*Catalogue of Books, etc. of Christ Church, Canterbury* (1802), p. 115).

4. Ex libro qui intitulatur corrogationes novi Promothei. Fos. 70aʳ, 72ᵛ, 147ᵛ. Esposito, pp. 457–60.

5. Ex glosa super epistolam secundam ad Thessalonicenses. Fo. 75ʳ.

6. Ex glosa super Matheum. Fos. 9ᵛ, 14ʳ, 193ᵛ.

7. Ex glosa super Quicunque vult. Fo. 8ʳ.

C. Sermons from C.U.L. Gg. vi. 42.

The sermons from which extracts are made are indicated in this fashion, 'Ex sermone qui sic incipit'.

Abraham mortuus est, 197ᵛ.
Absterget Deus, 8ʳ, 9ᵛ, 65ʳ.
Ad locum unde exeunt flumina, 81ᵛ, 98ᵛ, 99ʳ.
Ad te, Domine, levavi animam meam, 161ʳ.
Agar ancilla Saray, 88ʳ, 88ᵛ, 169ʳ, 169ᵛ.
Apertis thesauris suis, 117ʳ.
Ascendit Deus in jubilo, 159ʳ.
Beati pauperes spiritu, 13ʳᵛ, 14ʳ, 73ʳ–82ʳ, *passim.*
Cantate Domino, 95ʳ, 100ʳ, 117ʳ, 149ᵛ.
Cum appropinquasset Jhesus, 163ᵛ.
Cum esses minor, 12ᵛ, 163ʳ.
Cum exaltatus fuero a terra, 42ᵛ, 105ᵛ.
Cum (ergo) natus esset, 149ᵛ, 150ʳ.
Cum (ubi?) venit plenitudo temporis, 161ᵛ.
Dabo uobis cor carneum, 23ᵛ.
Debilitata est fortitudo portantis, 163ᵛ, 165ʳ.
Dixit Christus Patri, 79ᵛ.

Dixit Jhesus Petro, 155ʳ, 172ʳ, 201ʳ, 211ʳ, 212ʳ.
Dixit Deus fiat lux, 30ʳ, 34ʳ, 38ᵛ, 39ᵛ.
Ductus est Ihesus in desertum, 87ᵛ, 129ʳ, 148ʳ, 183ᵛ, 184ᵛ.
Domine si inveni gratiam, 80ᵛ.
Dulce (est) lumen, 4ᵛ, 160ʳ.
Ecce ego mitto angelum meum, 24ʳ.
Ecce ego omnia facio nova, 131ʳ.
Egressus Petrus de carcere, 60ʳ, 62ᵛ, 65ʳ.
Erunt signa in sole et luna, 73ʳᵛ, 74ʳ.
Et tu turris gregis, 41ʳ, 42ʳ, 43ʳ, 80ᵛ.
Exeamus extra castra, 78ᵛ – 113ᵛ *passim.*
Filii hominum, 135ʳ, 154ᵛ, 212ᵛ.
Filioli manete nunc in Christo, 146ʳ, 149ᵛ.
Fuit homo, 3ʳ.
Funes ceciderunt, 154ʳ.
Grata erat serenitas, 107ᵛ.
Hic est dies, 8ʳ.
Hi sunt viri misericordie, 11ᵛ, 12ʳ, 66ʳ, 82ᵛ, 83ʳ, 93ʳ.
Hodierna die noster dominus, 74ᵛ.
Inclinavit celos, 30ᵛ, 79ʳ, 113ᵛ, 155ᵛ.
Ingredere Petram, 19ʳ.
Impulsus eversus sum, 201ʳ.
Letare Jerusalem, 38ᵛ.
Mane nobiscum, Domine, 126ᵛ.
Memento homo, 193ᵛ.
Misit Herodes, 61ᵛ, 197ᵛ.
Nox precessit, 8ᵛ, 40ʳᵛ, 74ᵛ, 211ᵛ.
Numquid ad preceptum tuum, 93ʳ.
Nuptie sancte sunt, 77ʳ, 80ᵛ, 150ᵛ.
Obsecro vos tamquam advenas, 144ʳ, 146ᵛ.
Omnia tempus habent, 4ᵛ, 88ʳ, 143ʳ, 198ᵛ.
Operamini opus vestri, 94ᵛ, 100ʳ, 109ᵛ, 130ᵛ, 165ʳ.
Pascha nostrum, 156ʳ.
Ponam tabernaculum meum, 24ʳ, 33ʳᵛ.
Ponite corda vestra, 119ʳ, 180ᵛ, 194ʳ.
Probasti cor meum, 151ʳ, 152ʳ.
Quare appenditis argentum, 157ᵛ, 159ʳ.
Que est ista que ascendit de deserto, 24ʳ.
Quem queritis, 211ʳ.

Scio quod redemptor meus vivit, 4ᵛ, 6ʳ, 123ᵛ.
Si obliti sumus, 154ᵛ.
Si quis vult venire post me, 105ᵛ, 106ᵛ.
Spiritus intelligentie, 14ᵛ, 43ʳ, 57ᵛ.
Spiritus Domini, 201ᵛ.
Tamquam aurum in fornace, 8ᵛ.
Transeamus usque Betheleem, 32ᵛ, 43ᵛ, 194ʳ.
Tu autem cum ieiunas, 13ʳ, 112ʳ.
Tu es pastor, 150ᵛ.
Tu es qui venturus es, 37ʳ, 38ᵛ, 41ʳ, 43ʳ, 78ᵛ, 80ʳ.
Tu exurgens misereberis Sion, 34ᵛ.
Ubi est qui natus est, 126ᵛ.
Venit mater Salomonis, 54ʳ.
Videte, vigilate, et orate, 156ᵛ.

Notes

1. M. Esposito, *ante*, xxx. 461–71.
2. *Studies in the History of Mediaeval Science* (2nd ed., Cambridge, Mass., 1927), pp. 356–76.
3. 'Alexander of St. Albans, a Literary Muddle,' *Essays in History Presented to Reginald Lane Poole*, ed. H. W. C. Davis (Oxford, 1927), pp. 246–60.
4. T. Tanner, *Bibliotheca Britannico-Hibernica* (London, 1848), p. 539. The existence of a similar story about Abbot Alexander of St. Augustine's and John throws this story open to a certain amount of suspicion. See Powicke, *op. cit.*, p. 247.
5. *De Naturis Rerum*, ed. T. Wright (Rolls Series), p. 503.
6. *Gesta Abbatum Monasterii Sancti Albani*, ed. H. T. Riley (London, 1867), i. 195–6.
7. *Op. cit.*, pp. 538–9.
8. British Museum, MS. Royal 4 D. xi, fo. 5ᵛ: Oxford, MS. Balliol 39, fo. 7ᵛ. This item is not noticed by Edmund Bishop, *Liturgica Historica* (Oxford, 1918), chap. x.
9. Anthony à Wood, *The History and Antiquities of the University of Oxford*, (Oxford, 1792), p. 190.
10. British Museum, MS. Royal 5 A. viii, fo. 148ʳ (xiii cent.): MS. Harley 206, fo. 103ʳ (xv cent.). The text is that of the Royal MS. with divergent Harley MS. readings in the notes. For reference to another version see *Hist. Litt. de la France*, xxv. 83.
11. 'Ut narratur quidam magister nomine'.
12. 'beate virginis'.
13. 'in quadam die'.
14. 'dictus magister' omitted.

15. 'imparando'.
16. 'inquid persequeris'.
17. 'huic'.
18. 'huiusmodi' before 'temeraria'.
19. 'in' before 'post'.
20. 'iussit'.
21. 'festinari'.
22. MS. Merton 180, fo. 161^{rv} and Bodleian, MS. Wood empt. 13, fo. 3^v.
23. Migne 200, cols. 617–84. Compare the section with the opening sentence (col. 625): 'In patre unitas, in filio equalitas, in spiritu sancto unitatis equalitatisque connexio'. In MS. Gg. i. 5 of the Cambridge University Library this treatise is attributed by a late hand to Neckam, as Esposito notices, p. 465.
24. (London, 1702), p. 25: 'Mense Augusti proximo post obitum H. Cantuariensis episcopi'. The composition is between the rector of the church of Henbiry and the monks of Bordesley touching tithes of the grange of Holewey.
25. *De Naturis Rerum*, MS. Reg. 12, F. xiv, flyleaf; MS. Harley 3737, fo. 2^r; MS. Reg. 12 G. xi, fo. 4^r. *Symbolum Athanasii*, MS. Harley 3133, fo. 100^r. *Questiones*, MS. Lambeth 421, fo. 124^r.
26. Migne 207, cols. 404–8, no 137.
27. E.S. Cohn, *The Manuscript Evidence of the Letters of Peter of Blois, ante* xli. 51.
28. Mr. Cohn believes that the title given in the letters is usually trustworthy. He tentatively identified the addressee of the letter with Neckam.
29. J. Armitage Robinson, *Somerset Historical Essays* (London, 1921, The British Academy), pp. 132–3.
30. C. U. L., MS. Gg. vi. 42, fos. 223^{rv}, 225^v, and 228^r for Neckam, and 223^{rv} for Peter of Blois.
31. Henry Cole, ed. *Documents Illustrative of English History, &c.* (London, 1844), pp. 242, 266.
32. *Rotuli Litterarum Patentium,* ed. T. D. Hardy (London, 1835), p. 103 b.
33. *Annales Monastici* (Rolls Series), i. 63; ii. 289; iii. 40; iv. 409.
34. *Rotuli Litterarum Clausarum,* ed. T. D. Hardy (London, 1833), p. 204 b.
35. *Rot. Litt. Pat.,* p. 149.
36. *Rotuli Chartarum,* ed. T. D. Hardy (London, 1837), p. 212 b; *Rot. Litt. Claus.,* p. 220.
37. *Rot. Litt. Pat.,* p. 149; *Rot. Litt. Claus.,* p. 227.
38. *Rot. Chart.,* p. 218 b.
39. *Dict. Nat. Biog.,* sub Alexander Neckam.
40. *Ann. Monast.* iv. 409 (Worcester): notices of his death are in the Annals of Waverley, *ibid.,* ii. 289, and Tewkesbury, *ibid.,* i. 63, as well as in Robert of Gloucester (Rolls Series), lines 10502–3.
41. *Itineraria Symonis Simeonis et Willelmi de Worcestre,* ed. J. Nasmith (Cambridge, 1778), p. 279.
42. *Rot. Litt. Claus.,* p. 307 b.

43. J. F. Floyer, 'On a mutilated effigy in the cloisters of Worcester Cathedral said to represent Alexander Neckam', *Assoc. Archit. Soc. Reports*, xxiv (1898), pp. 188–96; *Register of Worcester Priory* (Camden Society), p. 107 b: 'De Anniversario Alexandri Abbatis de Cyrenstr.' Next title, 'De Anniversario Regis Johannis.'

44. I confused the two in my 'The English Court as an Intellectual Centre (1199–1227),' *Colorado College Publication* (December, 1927), pp. 62–6.

45. Rolls Series, ii. 53.

46. *Rot. Litt. Claus.*, p. 121.

47. *Op. cit.*

48. F. M. Stenton, 'Acta Episcoporum,' *The Cambridge Historical Journal*, iii. 8 (1929). He notices MS. Cotton, Faustina B. i, of 13 January 1206.

49. C. U. L. MS. Ee. v. 31, fo. 90^v, 91^r; *Rot. Cott.* ii. 21 (7), (10). Also see next note, Tanner, *op. cit.*, p. 539.

50. MS. Cotton, Tib. E v, fo. 217^r; id. November; MS. Harley 3697, fo. 40^v, vi kal. December: MS. Harley 2110, fo. 127^v, 3 January; MS. Cotton, Faust, B r, fo. 44^{v,} 13 January; MS. Cotton, Claud D, xiii, fo. 43^v (Dugdale, iii. 348), v non. Mart.

51. *Original Charters relating to the City of Worcester in possession of the Dean and Chapter* (Oxford, 1909: Worcestershire Historical Society), pp. 3, 5, 7(2), 119; also Charter B 598 of the Worcester Cathedral Muniments, *Register of Worcester Priory* (Camden Society), p. 109 b.

52. *Original Charters*, &c., p. 7.

53. Adam *filius Petri* and Alexander Edwyne, p. 36.

54. Cf. Victor Mortet, *Recueil des Textes relatifs à l'Histoire de l'Architecture* (Paris, 1911), in glossary, *Cementarius*; W. R. Lethaby, *Westminster Abbey and the King's Craftsmen* (London, 1906), pp. 151, 362–3. Dr. Rose Graham was kind enough to advise me in regard to the master mason.

55. Lethaby, *op. cit.*, 245; Matthew Paris, *Hist. Anglorum* (Rolls Series), ii. 242.

56. His lines occur on fo. 3^r, 71^v, and 212^v.

57. Brit. Mus., MS. Reg. 5 C. v, fo. 57^{rv}; Bibliothèque Nationale, MS. latin 11867, fo. 240 ff., much of which is published by Meyer, *Notices et Extraits*, xxxv, 2, 657. An S., prior of Malmesbury occurs in a document of 20 April 1246 (*Sarum Charters and Documents*, ed. W. Rich Jones and W. D. Macray (London, 1891), p. 301).

58. 3rd ed. Oxford, 1769, vi. 51.

59. Dugdale, *Monasticon Anglicanum*, vi. 462, 1393–1404.

CHAPTER 12

The Early Schools of Oxford and Cambridge

The formative period of the medieval English universities was largely over by 1265, although, of course, these institutions underwent great and extensive changes later.[1] A hundred years earlier England had had many schools, but no universities. Such places as Northampton, Lincoln, and Winchester, as well as Oxford, attracted students, and few differences were apparent among them in the documents of the period.[2] They had a few masters and relatively few students, but they were already institutions with fairly fixed customs and a definite function in English society. The university of 1265 was quite a different institution. Indeed, so different was it that historians have neglected the study of the schools for the light which might thereby be thrown upon the ideas and influences surrounding early university development. It is our purpose to consider certain of these ideas and influences and the factors which produced only two permanent institutions of higher education out of the many promising centres.

Such a study has been rendered easier by the appearance of a number of writings. On the university side are Emden's revision of Rashdall's *Medieval Universities* and his *Oxford Hall in Medieval Times*.[3] The problem of the relationship of the papacy to schools and universities has been studied by Post.[4] Two studies upon the schools have appeared, prepared by scholars with somewhat different approaches to the subject.[5] The quasi-university of Northampton and early legal study at Oxford have been discussed by Richardson,[6] while Hunt has written upon status of English learning in part of the period.[7] Other phases of the subject remain to be studied: the influence of changes in number of ecclesiastical and clerical positions, clerical and secular attitudes toward teaching, evidence for university growth, and influence of the selection of Oxford and Cambridge, among others. For several of these the evidence is not too clear but at least it can be the basis for further discussion.

Perhaps the greatest single problem of early English university history is why the cathedral schools did not develop into universities. Even in the early part of the twelfth century York, London, Salisbury, and Lincoln were known as great clerical centres.[8] Before the end of the century, other schools had arisen at Canterbury,[9] Exeter,[10] and Hereford.[11] Most of them had become important quite as soon as had Oxford and all of them long before Cambridge became a center of education. In their bishops and chancellors these centres had definite leaders in education, supported by benefices. Yet none became a university. Of course a certain element of chance existed since London was so similar to Paris, as to royal and episcopal status, that it might have become a university site. The result may have been accidental but the statistical chances are heavily against it.

I

The discussion of the rise of universities has been restricted by the sources which are rather few and largely limited to the more advanced subjects of study. Some additional information may be secured if questions which vitally concern any academic institution are asked and answers sought in unusual sources. Students usually attend school to secure an education for definite careers and plan to study the subjects which prepare them for those careers. During the period of study they have the problem of their support, a problem of great weight if the preparation requires many years. These factors influence universities today and should have been important in the Middle Ages.

Medieval education led into the clergy and the related clerical subjects of law, medicine, and business. The opportunities in those fields increased greatly from 1066 to 1265, first in the purely ecclesiastical field and then in the clerical. At the time in which English population was growing from about 1,100,000 to 2,750,000, the monastic population jumped from less than a thousand to probably over 7,000, even if the mendicants are not included.[12] The number of parishes increased from about four thousand to over eight thousand, but the pattern of expansion is not clear chronologically. Moreover, the number of vicarages and lesser positions increased also. On the clerical side, initiative and example came from the central government, producing an enthusiasm for documents and records which required an ever growing number of writers who had some knowledge of legal processes.

The use of written financial accounts became of importance even for private estates in the thirteenth century as England became more conscious of the value of financial records. The monks, rectors, vicars, and better paid clerks were quite affluent, but the literate group included many poorly rewarded clerks, particularly parish clerks whose status was often little better than peasant freemen.[13]

The sheer weight of numbers seeking education probably would have created permanent institutions of a different character from the earlier schools. Contemporary economic life, in which a parallel expansion occurred, developed first the gild merchant and later the craft gild. To the latter the university was similar in many respects. The study of the forces which created the gilds is still not well advanced and has little light to throw upon university origins yet.

The curricula of the schools followed closely the needs of the students. The priests and monks were expected to be literate: for this a general arts course was sufficient although a knowledge of some theology was advantageous. Many aspired to higher study, especially those whose social background needed strengthening by academic prestige.[14] Not much attention was devoted to the study of medicine.[15]

As monasteries acquired property, they needed better ad-
ministrators, particularly men versed in law. The newer class
of administrative and clerical students also took to law and its
close relative, the *ars dictandi,* the art of writing letters and
documents.[16] Here was a shift away from the classics toward
the more practical subjects.

Means of support was no less important. Monasteries
usually educated their younger members either within the
walls or at external schools. The early students were apt to
come from families which could supply them with liberal al-
lowances or benefices. If they went to cathedral schools, they
learned from masters supported by prebends who might receive gifts but who were not expected to demand fees. As
greater numbers of opportunities opened for the literate, more
and more poor boys were attracted into education, so that even
serfs were freed by small payments that they might become
clerks. For the poor the prospect of advance was brighter in the
church than elsewhere.[17]

The trend throughout the twelfth and early thirteenth
centuries is clear. Earlier, promotion was rapid for students,
most of whom were well cared for while at school and took
liberal arts to meet the needs of literacy in their career. Later,
more and more students struggled for poorer paying places
after difficult times at school, studying, in many cases, the
newer and more practical subjects. Thus we have a sort of
dualism of development with a kind of law of diminishing
returns in early education. Furthermore, the newer students
and newer subjects were less specifically religious in character.
A village priest or vicar with "cure of souls" or a prospective
monk obviously was in the heart of the ecclesiastical system. A
village clerk, devoting his time largely to writing charters,
wills, and to farming was useful in the church service but
hardly essential, while clerks writing up baronial or manorial
accounts had little to do with the church. Yet they had the
same elementary education.

This duality had interesting implications. Insofar as education led into the clergy it should have been, according to
church theory, free to all. To charge students for such study
was like charging for holy orders and was regarded also as

simony. For education in other subjects, the Church was not responsible and had no more interest in them than it did in the work of the gilds of the time. The possibility of conflict of interests is clear and will be taken up next.

II

Certain definitions are necessary before proceeding to consideration of the problem of early teaching. The master's degree in the schools simply allowed the successful candidate to teach in that school. It was like the mastership in a gild and in this period was not a general certificate to teach. The license to teach granted by the chancellor of a cathedral conferred upon the candidate the right to set up his school in the area, usually only the city and its suburbs, over which the chancellor had the ecclesiastical patronage. These had different meanings later but they do not affect the early teaching problem. The problem which the chancellor faced was, who should be permitted to teach in the schools.

On the one hand the Pope had very definite ideas in regard to the obligations of the chancellors.[18] He felt that all properly qualified persons should be permitted to teach without paying any fee to the chancellor. Furthermore, he urged that as far as possible all teaching should be available to students gratis. The Pope obviously regarded learning as a religious exercise primarily. He was aware, however, that this wish for free opportunity to teach was usually prevented by a certain "bad and illegal custom."[19]

This custom prescribed that teaching, like other economic opportunities in the Middle Ages, was subject to monopoly control.[20] The teacher must secure someone's permission to teach, no matter how excellent his credentials. Usually the right to appoint a teacher in a parish belonged to the church's patron.[21] Probably the priest would perform this service himself unless he was willing to allow someone else to do it.[22] School patronage and clerical patronage were not always coextensive. The chancellor of a cathedral city usually had the patronage of the whole area, as we have mentioned, and often religious houses possessed it over the whole of a large place.[23]

Apparently, the right to appoint the schoolmaster belonged to the oldest parish and did not belong to later parishes carved out of the original parish.[24]

How did the patrons exercise their rights of appointment? A clerk, John Jekyll, who had tried to teach at Winchester, lost his appeal about 1159 against the master, Jordan Fantosme, the poet, who was acting in place of a chancellor since Winchester had a monastic chapter.[25] No other clear cases seem to occur in this period, but the fact that universities did not develop in the cathedral cities is evidence enough that the chancellors did not encourage the free licensing of teachers. The problem then becomes one of trying to fathom the reasons for this attitude on the part of the educational patrons.

The attitude of the Papacy was probably one factor. The bishops and chancellors may well have felt that their duty toward the education of the clergy was satisfied by the provision of one or two masters in elementary education, theology, and music, supported by benefices. Additional masters, if licensed, must have been supported in large part by either gifts or tuition. The problem of simony would be a delicate matter. Perhaps it might have been faced if there had not been the further complication of additional students.

The problem of discipline in the twelfth century might well be feared by the cathedral chancellors. The students were often quite young. They lived, for the most part, where they pleased. Some were clerks, and therefore at least theoretically exempt from lay jurisdiction. Others pretended that they were clerks and used their immunity for unlawful purposes.[26] Under these circumstances a chancellor might well have hesitated about licensing many masters and bringing in large numbers of students, even if constant reports of disorder at the continental institutions had not come to his ears.

Another danger, more evident to the medieval chancellor than to the modern scholar, was the possibility of the loss of legal jurisdiction. Medieval law generated spontaneously in any group with special interests and identity of its own. Medieval gilds, for instance, had their own laws. Thus a group of masters and students might easily form a university and shut out the chancellor, if they became strong enough. The king might claim that, since students came from all parts of England, he was their overlord and could grant them liberties and immunities from the control of the chancellor. Had not the University of Paris secured a charter from Philip Augustus in 1200? Or even the Pope might allege that, since clerks came from all over Christendom, he could legislate for them.[27] Had not Fantosme appealed to the papacy in the Winchester case? Any of these developments would be at the expense of the chancellor's authority.

Unfortunately, no chancellor unburdened his mind with reference to the refusal to license more teachers so that these surmises may never be more. The attitude of ecclesiastical patrons distinctly limited the number of places where institutions might arise and thus influenced greatly their later history. Universities developing at Norwich, or Bristol, or London might have been quite different from those developed at Oxford and Cambridge.

III

Curiously enough the question of the educational patronage of the early schools of Oxford and Cambridge has never been raised, largely because its significance was not understood. We may notice at once that, although the connection of early education in both places has been suggested with local religious bodies, none has been proved with any plausibility.[28] None ever claimed any jurisdiction over either institution. Had there been any claim it would almost certainly have appeared.

Now Rashdall noticed that the university at Oxford grew up in the neighborhood of the parish church of St. Mary and that the university sermons were preached in it.[29] This church was in the patronage of the king, and all other evidence seems to show that the king was the educational patron of the university.[30] This fact seems to be a point of very great importance. At Cambridge the schools also seem to have been in the patronage of the king, in the parish of St. Mary where university sermons were preached at an early date.[31]

This royal patronage does not explain why the king should have taken a different attitude toward education than

did the chancellors, however. One should have expected him
to appoint masters or at least to interfere in the choice of
masters of the schools. The problems of jurisdiction and of
discipline do not seem to have disturbed the English kings. In
fact even in a time of disturbance Henry III had written:[32]

> You are aware that a multitude of scholars from di-
> vers parts, as well from this side the sea as from overseas,
> meets at our town of Cambridge for study, which we hold
> a very gratifying and desirable thing, since no small ben-
> efit and glory accrues therefrom to our whole realm; and
> you, among whom these students personally live, ought
> especially to be pleased and delighted at it.

In this case distance lent enchantment. Furthermore, the kings
seem to have avoided Oxford in this period even though it was
so near their favorite seat at Woodstock.[33] Perhaps a clue to the
mystery is that the king regarded the university as another gild
in its early days and left it alone as he would other gilds,
recognizing its monopoly of education. These are problems
which require further examination.

The most likely site for a university after Oxford and
Cambridge was Northampton. During the decade before 1192,
the schools of Northampton "had more to offer . . . than the
schools of any cathedral town."[34] It was an outstanding centre
of arts, legal studies, and even theology.[35] Like the other two
places, Northampton was in the middle of England and was a
relatively large place. The exact location of the schools within
the city is uncertain, but there was one important parish whose
patronage was contested by the king.[36] Probably damaged
seriously about 1192 by a disturbance from which Oxford
profited,[37] it still attracted large migrations from Oxford in
1238 and 1261.[38] The cause for its twelfth century failure is not
clear. Possibly it was because it was not protected by the king.

The year 1265 saw the end of official countenancing of
Northampton. The royal document which closed that institution states:[39]

> that our borough of Oxford, which is of ancient
> foundation, and was confirmed by our ancestors kings of
> England, and is commonly commended for its advantage

to students, would suffer no little damage from such University.

The idea of educational monopoly is apparent again. Oxford and Cambridge were in possession of the sites of higher education in England, and no other such developments were to be permitted to which the original universities objected.

IV

Another interesting question is the rate of growth of the universities, a matter of considerable speculation. Early Cambridge history seems fairly clear. From probably a small school,[40] it jumped to a university status through a migration from Oxford in 1209. Afterward in our period it remained a small institution. Oxford history bristles with thorny controversies, perhaps the most vigorous in regard to the alleged migration from Paris in 1167.[41] The evaluation of the early evidence for its implications about university attendance is difficult.

At the universities were both grammar students and students of the advanced faculties. The latter left more early evidence than the grammar students and their teachers. Even the very remarkable schools of London in the twelfth century would be little more than names if it had not been for the description by Fitz-Stephen.[42] The problem then arises. If evidence of theological or legal faculties appears, must we assume also grammar schools coeval or even earlier? We know occasional instances where students supported themselves by tutoring.[43] Did grammar masters also study the higher subjects while teaching? If they did we may perhaps assume that grammar schools were necessary to help students through the advanced courses, but the questions arising here are many.[44]

The attraction of places for advanced students may be tested by another method based on the theory that migration to centers of learning will be affected by distance, by placing on a map of England the towns used as surnames of masters at a given time. In this case we use the names appearing in the close, patent, and charter rolls of the time of John.[45] In general

we can assume that a clerk by the name of Master Alexander of
St. Albans, to use one illustration, was born in or came from St.
Albans. Any notable concentration of names should indicate
that a center of learning was within it. For earlier periods, the
method would be more difficult since no great lists of documents from all over the country remain. It should be obvious
that, if the documents are from one diocese or one part of the
country, the names of masters will be in large part from that
area also.[46]

The map for the early thirteenth century shows an unmis-
takable concentration in the territory near Oxford, showing
that it was drawing heavily from the Thames Valley. A smaller
group is near Cambridge, but its significance is harder to
estimate. The eastern part of England, particularly East Anglia, was the most heavily populated area in the country, an
area which should have sent students in some numbers even
to Oxford. The small number of names in the north of England
is to be accounted for partly by the sparseness of population
there and partly by the drag of distance on migration, in this
case to the king's court. Probably this method of approach can
be refined by use and experience.[47]

V

The location of universities at Cambridge and Oxford
fixed the environment of higher education in England for
centuries, imposing upon it the limitations which the size and
position of the cities presented. These limitations have not
been studied carefully and have, indeed, been regarded rather
as advantages in their college town picturesqueness. Rashdall
has pointed out that the freedom of Oxford from royal and
episcopal control was due in large part to its location.[48] The
same held true for Cambridge in less degree. Probably the
limitations only gradually appeared or operated as hindering
influences in university growth in this period.

Cambridge and Oxford, then, were growing county
boroughs of about three to six thousand population, not
noticeably different from other boroughs in England. Grammar and theology, of course, might be taught anywhere. Ac-

tions in the county courts might be used as illustrations of pleading in lectures on manorial management.[49] Common law and medicine did not do well then. The study of the former centered about the law courts in London. These subjects are usually encouraged by adequate clinical facilities which were not available in the university boroughs. The failure of these facilities to develop may have been one result of the location and size of the towns. This was a serious loss since these faculties are usually more closely in touch with current advances than some other faculties.

The size of the cities may have aided in developing in the hall system a better day and night control over students housed in them.[50] This was the system in effect during the period before 1265. It is possible that this system in turn produced an environment which was satisfactory to the great families of England. The presence of their children is attested by their participation in the siege of Northampton in 1265.[51]

> The clerks of Oxford University, which by the barons' orders had been transferred there, inflicted greater losses on the attacking force which came in through the breach than the rest of the barons, by their slings and bows and balistas. They had their own flag, which they held up on high against the king, which so enraged him that he swore that when he got in he would hang them all. On hearing this many of them shaved their heads and fled as quickly as possible.
>
> When the town was quiet, the king ordered the execution of his oath. But they said to him, "Far be this from you, king, for the sons of your great men and others of your realm came here with your University, and if you hang or behead them, those who are now on your side will rise against you, as they will not allow the blood of their sons and relations to be shed if they can help it." So the king was pacified and his anger against the clerks cooled.

From allowing the clerks to attend was but a step to allowing their brothers to attend: the activity of the latter could hardly have been more belligerent than the former. Already the universities were becoming the training ground for the ruling class of England, clerical and feudal.

In this study several questions have been examined for
which answers are needed. Possibly the raising of the questions is more valuable than the tentative answers presented.
The gradual change in numbers, needs, and subjects studied
in the twelfth century produced a problem for the early
schools. Apparently the ecclesiastical patrons did not wish to
undertake the enlargement of the schools and prevented their
growth by refusing to appoint additional teachers. This
canalized the academic growth through the institutions over
which the king was patron: Oxford and Cambridge. Their
growth may possibly be defined by a study of master's names.
Finally, the chance that the site and size of the university
towns may have helped shape the higher educational development is considered, probably stunting rather than encouraging it. Given the medieval and geographical factors
present in the situation, the English medieval university development seems very natural.

Notes

1. This study is revised from a paper read before the Erasmus Club of Duke
   University and benefits from the subsequent discussion, notably by
   Professors Nelson and Quynn of Duke and A. C. Krey of Minnesota.
2. The early documents concerning education in England have been edited
   in large part by A. F. Leach, *Educational Charters and Documents 598 to 1909*
   (Cambridge, 1911).
3. Hastings Rashdall, *The Universities of Europe in the Middle Ages,* edited by
   F. M. Powicke and A. B. Emden. 3 vols. (Oxford, 1936). The third volume
   relating to England and certain general phases of university life is edited
   by Emden. A.B.Emden, *An Oxford Hall in Medieval Times* (Oxford, 1927).
4. Gaines Post, "Alexander III, the Licentia Docendi, and the rise of Universities," *Haskins Anniversary Essays* (Boston, 1929), pp. 255–277.
5. A. W. Parry, *Education in England in the Middle Ages* (London, 1920); A. F.
   Leach, *The Schools of Medieval England* (London, 1915). Leach's work is
   without footnotes, but the references can usually be traced without
   difficulty in his *Educational Charters.*
6. H. G. Richardson, "The Schools of Northampton in the Twelfth Century," *English Historical Review,* LVI (1941), pp. 596–606; "The Oxford
   Law School under John," *Law Quarterly Review,* LVII (1941), pp. 319–338.
7. R. W. Hunt, "English Learning in the late twelfth century," *Transactions
   of the Royal Historical Society,* 4th series, XIX (1936), pp. 19–42.
8. Leach, *Educational Charters,* pp. 105–107.

9. W. Stubbs, *Seventeen Lectures* (Oxford, 1887), pp. 156 ff.
10. R. L. Poole, "The Early Lives of Robert Pullen and Nicholas Breakspear," *Essays in Medieval History presented to T. F. Tout* (Manchester, 1925), pp. 62–63.
11. J. C. Russell, "Hereford and Arabic Science in England about 1175–1200," *Isis*, XVIII (1932), pp. 14-25; Hunt, *op. cit.*, p. 23.
12. These figures for the lay and clerical population come from my unpublished study on *Medieval British Population*.
13. Unfortunately no study of the "clerk" in medieval England has been made. It would be a very valuable addition to our understanding of the educational needs and organization of the period. On one phase, see L. C. Gabel, *Benefit of Clergy in the Later Middle Ages* (Northampton, Mass., 1929).
14. On the attraction of scholars to monasteries, see Hunt, *op. cit.*, pp. 27–28; on the literacy of monks, Gerald of Wales, *Opera Omnia* (Rolls Series), II, p. 347.
15. In his dissertation, E. A. Hammond has a chapter upon medical schools and libraries but could find little evidence of medical training in England in this period. *The Medical Profession in England in the Late Middle Ages* (Chapel Hill, 1941, unpublished doctoral thesis).
16. For recent study upon the *ars dictandi*, see C. H. Haskins, *Renaissance of the Twelfth Century* (Cambridge, 1927), particularly ch. IV and its bibliography.
17. No study of the support of medieval students seems to have been undertaken. It should be well worth the effort.
18. This is the subject of Post's article (*cf.* note 4). *Cf.* Leach, *Charters*, p. 123.
19. Leach, *Charters*, p. 119.
20. Parry, *op. cit.*, p. 92; Leach, *Schools*, pp. 112 ff.
21. Parry, *op. cit.*, pp. 94, 100; Leach, *Educational Charters*, pp. 75, 89.
22. This is apparently the meaning of an item formulated by the Council of Winchester in 1200. Leach, *Educational Charters*, p. 139.
23. Leach, *Educational Charters*, pp. 95-97, 109, 117, 129, 133.
24. Parry, *op. cit.*, p. 95. Parry does not discuss the question of a second parish starting a school if the first parish had failed to do so. In theory, presumably, the second parish could, since no monopoly had as yet been established.
25. Leach, *Educational Charters*, pp. 113–155.
26. *Cf.* Cambridge in 1231. Leach, *Educational Charters*, p. 149.
27. G. Post, "Parisian Masters as a Corporation, 1200–1246," *Speculum*, IX (1934), pp. 426, 437. The popes did legislate more and more for the universities.
28. This was one of Rashdall's very strong points. *Op. cit.*, pp. 10, 227.
29. Rashdall, *op. cit.*, p. 10.
30. For royal patronage of the church, see *Rot. Chart.*, p. 126; *Calendar of Patent Rolls, 1225–1232*, p. 402. On the relations of king and university, see J. F. Willard, *Royal Authority and the Early English Universities*

(Philadelphia, 1902).

31. Rashdall, *op. cit.*, p. 279, note 3; *English Historical Review, L* (1935), p. 687.
The royal patronage is shown in *Calendar of Patent Rolls, 1232 –1247*, pp.
36, 531, 581. The university at Cambridge also had some connections with
the church of St. Benet, whose patronage I did not discover.
32. Leach, *Educational Charters*, pp. 151, 153.
33. *Annales Monastici* (Rolls Series), IV, pp. 142, 143, 264, 449.
34. Richardson, "The Schools of Northampton," pp. 602–603.
35. Hunt, *op. cit.*, p. 20.
36. St. Peter's. R. M. Sarjeantson, *A History of the Church of St. Peter, Northampton* (Northampton, 1904), pp. 11–17. *Cf.* also *Calendar of Patent Rolls,
1216 –1225*, p. 342; *Ibid., 1241 –1258*, pp. 143, 146.
37. Richardson, *op. cit.*, pp. 603–604. Richardson suggests that possibly the
authority over the schools was disputed.
38. Leach, *Educational Charters*, pp. 155, 159–163.
39. Leach, *Educational Charters*, p. 163.
40. Rashdall, *op. cit.*, pp. 276–279. Richardson ("The Schools of Northampton," p. 602) suggests that Daniel of Morley may have been at
Cambridge in the last few years of the twelfth century. Richard of
Bardney (Russell, *Dictionary of Writers of Thirteenth Century England*, p.
136) said that Robert Grosseteste studied at Cambridge at about this time.
41. Rashdall, *op. cit.*, pp. 12–16 and literature there cited.
42. Printed many times. See Leach, *Educational Charters*, pp. 82–85.
43. See Russell, *Dictionary of Writers of Thirteenth Century England*, under John
Peckham.
44. Teaching of undergraduates by graduate students is, of course, a feature
of American universities today.
45. Respectively the *Rotuli Litterarum Clausarum* (London, 1837), *Rotuli Litterarum Patentium* (London, 1837), and the *Rotuli Chartarum* (London,
1837).
46. One assumption is that 'Master' indicates an academic master rather than
a gild master, an assumption that is apparently wrong occasionally. If the
'master' indicates some other than academic mastership, the trade is
usually stated.
47. A test for the last quarter of the twelfth century based upon a few sets of
documents did not seem sufficiently exhaustive to deserve publishing.
No such concentration near Oxford appeared, however, and more centered about Northampton. Many of the places seemed to be monastic
sites, as if the monastery was the source of inspiration rather than the
university.
48. Rashdall, *op. cit.*, p. 46.
49. Compare, for instance, the case of John of Morbiry. Russell, *Dictionary of
Writers of Thirteenth Century England*, p. 69.
50. On the halls see Emden, *An Oxford Hall in Medieval Times*, particularly the
first two chapters.
51. Leach, *Education Charters*, pp. 161, 163.

CHAPTER 13

The Patrons of "The Owl and the Nightingale"

Literature is determined largely by its traditions, its patrons and its authors. The tradition in which *The Owl and the Nightingale* falls has been discussed extensively and well by E. G. Stanley in his recent edition.[1] The poem covers a wide range of debatable ideas current at the end of the twelfth century. It gives some indications about the authors, but the guesses based on them have not been very helpful. For unexplained reasons little attention has been given to the patronage of the poem. Obviously, if its purpose was directly or even indirectly to provide livings for Master Nicholas of Guildford, the author should have had some patrons in mind. Two assumptions are made in this study: that the poem was written for definite patrons and that the author, as a quite sophisticated person, alludes only indirectly or obliquely to events and ideas without making it necessary to regard the owl and the nightingale identical in all respects to persons concerned in the references.

There is some evidence for dating the poem. It refers to Henry II as dead (line 1091),[2] mentions an astronomical conjunction of 1186 (1145-1330), and plays upon the name, Foliot (868), presumably that of Gilbert Foliot, Bishop of London who died in 1187. The ideas about the birds resemble those in the *De natura rerum* of Alexander Neckam and in the fables of Marie de France. The poem was thus presumably written in 1189 or

181

later, perhaps not much later since the datable items fall in the years 1186-89. The problem then is to find someone in that period who might be appealed to by the ideas set forth in the poem. We shall try to show that the principal patron was probably Geoffrey, son of Henry II and Archbishop of York, 1189-1212, that Master Nicholas of Guildford was Master Nicholas of Aquila, a canon lawyer and professor, and that the poem might have been written for an Oxford audience which included Geoffrey in December 1189.

In a recent article, M. Angela Carson, O.S.U., has shown that the author of the poem has followed the Classical rules of rhetoric and apparently knew its authorities well.[3] Yet he has not given the names of those authorities, as, indeed, he did not mention either Alexander Neckam or Marie de France. One possible reason is that the occasion or the patron did not call for a display of academic erudition. The use of English also might have been dictated by similar considerations.

The patron ought to have been someone who could reward Master Nicholas of Guildford generously. Since the author suggests that Nicholas' decisions might be appealed to Rome (1016), they should have concerned canon law: other lines also suggest canon law (541-55, 1087-1101 among others). In this field bishops were the most promising patrons. Since poets had for some time mastered the art of appealing for largess or livings by flattering patrons or by playing upon their interests, the poem should provide clues for detecting the patron or patrons. What strikes one as unusual at once is the large number of times references to the proverbs attributed to King Alfred appear.[4] They are the only specific references to an authority in the poem. The pious line about Henry II and apparent reference to his faithful follower, Gilbert Foliot, indicate that association with English royalty flattered the patron. In that period such an appeal would be most appropriate to Geoffrey, natural son of Henry II who became Archbishop of York not long after his father's death.[5] The question then is whether other remarks in the poem might have been received favorably by Geoffrey.

As Bishop-elect of Lincoln in the years 1171-82, Geoffrey

had filled the chapter with scholars. Thus criticism (1773-6) of bishops making unworthy appointments would not apply to him. He was following the tradition of literary patronage set up by his father in the course of his long reign.[6] As to his education there are opposing opinions: Gerald of Wales in his biography of Geoffrey wrote "that from childhood Geoffrey was given to studies and liberal disciplines," while Gervase of Canterbury called him "illiterate, stammering and stuttering."[7] Clearly Geoffrey aroused strong feelings, not surprising in view of his many controversies. Walter Map wrote an amusing story of Geoffrey's attempt to resign his bishopric of Lincoln before Archbishop Richard of York at Marlborough. The latter did not understand Geoffrey's French, but before he could repeat it, Walter, according to his own account, broke in brightly and quipped, "He is talking French of Marlborough,"[8] an allusion to the belief that drinking water there confused one's speech. It might suggest that Geoffrey spoke only English well,[9] but it may refer only to his stuttering.

Further examination of the ideas in the poem, especially about references to the owl, shows more which seem appropriate to Geoffrey. The owl did not take a serious view of adultery (1568-70), considerate in view of Geoffrey's birth. The purity of Geoffrey was well known.[10] The owl was not a churchman (1211): Geoffrey, in spite of being a bishop-elect for many years, became a priest only on September 23, 1189 at Southwell, where he was consecrated by his suffragan, the Bishop of Galloway (Whithorn, *Candida Casa*). In the poem (910) Galloway is mentioned along with Ireland, Scotland and Norway, a baffling combination.[11] A long series of lines suggest the north of England or going north. One of the owl's good points was that he stayed in the north in the winter (999-1014). Master Nicholas's work (1757) improved even Scotland. In the fall of 1189 Geoffrey, as representative of the king, went to the Tweed in Scotland and escorted the Scottish king, William the Lion, to a meeting with King Richard. Even the line (176) "well fights who flies well" would be appropriate in view of Geoffrey's flight, along with Henry II, from Le Mans in 1189.

Even more impressive is the coincidence of three stages of the owl's fortunes in the poem with Geoffrey's luck in the summer and fall of 1189. At the beginning of the poem the owl suffered an initial setback from an early offensive by the nightingale, then he put on a successful rebuttal, but at the end his enemies converged upon him, leaving the decision uncertain. Now Geoffrey shared Henry II's defeat at the hands of Richard and John (assisted by Philip Augustus of France), being driven (as mentioned above) from Le Mans to Chinon, where Henry died on July 6. As the one loyal son, Geoffrey brought a measure of dignity to his father's last hours by encouraging him to fulfill his religious duties. Geoffrey's fortunes then changed. Richard I nominated him as archbishop of York on July 20, the York chapter elected him on August 10, and Richard accepted the election on September 16. The king then sent Geoffrey to bring William the Lion to a conference with Richard at Canterbury on December 5. At about this time Geoffrey's enemies converged on him, trying to prevent his consecration as archbishop. However, just before leaving England on December 14 with the king, the papal legate, Cardinal John of Anagni, confirmed the election. The reference (1016) to the good man from Rome would bring this act to mind, although the line referred to a visit of a papal representative to the northern countries probably several years earlier.

Since the owl's fortunes seem to have parallels to the successes and failures of Geoffrey's career, those of the nightingale might be suspected of paralleling Richard's activities. The nightingale spoke first: this conforms to medieval ideas of social status, the king before even an archbishop. The Latin title has the same order: *altercatio inter philomenam et bubonem.* Both Richard and Geoffrey were excellent army leaders: the poet points out, however, that "verbal deeds and not deeds of martial prowess will win the day" (1067-74, 1707-16). The nightingale's forces are termed the *here* (1702, 1790), that is, a group fighting out of the country, as Richard's crusaders would do, while those of the owl (1684) were called the *ferde* (fyrd), more like a militia. The nightingale was celebrated as a sweet singer, while Richard was a writer and singer of songs: both also were associated with the warm south rather than with the cold north (412-62). If the hypothesis about parallels mentioned above is accurate, then many other references to contemporary conditions may be discovered.

The assumption that the author had the king and archbishop in mind (although not identifying them too closely with the birds) would also assume a judge of rank to match their high status and thus that Master Nicholas of Guildford was a person of importance, at least in the eyes of the patrons. Among the important canon lawyers of the time, discussed in that very fine study of the Anglo-Norman group by Stephan Kuttner and Eleanor Rathbone, only one was named Nicholas, which was not a common name then.[12] He was Master Nicholas of Aquila. Since Aquila means 'eagle', the relevance to a debate between birds arises. In one rather outstanding collection of canon law tracts, Nicholas, according to Kuttner and Rathbone, seems to have supplied the core,[13] indicating his importance among several well-known professors, presumably at Oxford. His opinion might well have influenced England as far as Scotland (908, 1758), if that is what those lines mean. Nicholas became dean of Chichester in 1197 and was elected bishop of Chichester in 1209 but was never consecrated.

The only gap in the evidence lies in the inability to show that the Oxford professor was called "of Aquila." In a parallel case of the well-known Richard de Mores, his other name "of Lincoln" appeared only in a poem, written by himself, among the many references to him. The chief seat of the rather prominent Aquila family was at Witley in Surrey, only seven miles from Guildford! A contemporary Master Gilbert de Aquila was a very prominent doctor, physician to both Archbishop Hubert Walter and later to King John.[14] The chance that Nicholas of Guildford was Nicholas of Aquila is thus very good. If true, Nicholas was probably prominent socially as well as intellectually, even if his only holding was at Portesham.

Was the poem merely sent to Nicholas to read in private? If so why was it written in English, when Nicholas, as a learned man, would have been more flattered to have it written in Latin or French? Far more likely the poem was designed to be read aloud. "It is true—that medieval poems, other than those written for private devotions or for evangelical instruction, were 'occasional' poems, composed for an audience assembled for some specific occasion."[15] If so, what audience?

Now one would expect that the readers or patrons would be persons who knew Nicholas. If he were only a country celebrity living in Dorset near Portesham, it would be odd to refer a debate of any kind to him. The reference to Dorset (1753) as if one did not know just where it was, would indicate that the site of the reading was not near there. The reading should have occurred wherever Nicholas was known: if he was a professor at Oxford presumably there. Did the matter of the poem have an interest for an Oxford audience as well as for the archbishop, assuming him the main patron? Is there material in the poem which was current as well as appropriate for an Oxford audience in 1189-90?

The very well known story by Gerald of Wales tells how he, a few years earlier than this time (1186), read his *Topographia Hibernica*, on three days: the first part before "all the poor scholars of the whole town," the second before "all the doctors of the different faculties and such of their students as were of greater fame and note," and the third before "the rest of the scholars, together with many knights, townsfolk and Burghers". He was proud that "neither the present nor past age recall anything like it in England."[16] Such gatherings were unusual only for the lavishness of the arrangements.

Such a gathering with Geoffrey present was possible. As formerly bishop-elect of Lincoln which had the archdeaconry of Oxford within its widespread boundaries, Geoffrey should have endeared himself to the schools by his favors to literary men. He was already in serious difficulties in his archbishopric in 1189-90 and needed the assistance of canonists: he employed an outstanding one, Honorius, by 1195.[17] His retinue of clerks and laymen should also have appreciated a reading in English. Geoffrey does seem to have been popular. On the occasion of his quarrel with his chapter at York in January 1190 he was said to have enjoyed popularity, and two years later he again proved popular when he was released after being arrested and placed in Dover prison.[18] Geoffrey was virtuous, loyal and cantankerous: a combination often liked in

England. He may also have represented something like a nascent nationalism: pure English returning to influence after a century of subordination to Norman, Flemish, Italian and Jewish aliens after the Conquest. This nascent feeling of patriotism nearly always invokes persecution of elements which do not integrate: the Jews felt it in 1190.

Such gatherings as Gerald describes, included persons of many interests to whom appeal could be made. If we may believe Gerald, Oxford had even in 1186 many masters of several faculties. Eleven masters, presumably in canon law, witness a document of 1192, while the works of several of them have been examined and described by Kuttner and Rathbone.[19] The poem has something to interest them. The connection of the virtues (707-836) concerned the theologians.[20] The new sciences were important at Oxford: presumably the section on astrology would interest them. The poet's following of the rules of rhetoric has been mentioned: enough of logic appears to appeal to the logicians. He may have been one of the brilliant young teachers who were making Oxford a great intellectual center at the time. As Atkins observed, "The poet has spoken to his generation of things of the mind."[21]

The poet also presents ideas which would probably have appealed to the non-academic side of both the students and townspeople. The unfavorable remarks about the backwardness of the north, Scotland and Norway sound much like the usual student insults to regional "nations." Fifty years later Oxford students were apparently organized into southern and northern groups; perhaps the division existed earlier, at least informally. And where in England would one know how an Irish priest would chatter (322), except in a metropolis or Oxford? And the poem certainly has a rural background. The log section on forms of love was probably much like the usual student discussions of love and sex life, while the eulogy of married love and of the devoted wife would please a lay audience and even suggests the presence of women. Less admirable activities such as cock fighting (1619) and gambling (1666) presumably also might interest members of a town-gown assembly: the "merchant, knight, bondmen" (1340-49) as well as the guild of professors and students.

A conjecture may be made as to date. The silence about the crusade, unless the casual reference to the smallness of the nightingale's forces is a sidelong glance at the smallness of the crusading group, suggests that Richard had left, and thus dating the poem after December 14, 1189. The poet does not give the impression of victory for the owl, which, assuming a parallel, would have been justified by the cardinal's approval of his election. Geoffrey may have accompanied William the Lion back to London and thus have left Canterbury soon after December 5, and he was at York on January 5, 1190. Six days to Oxford would get him there by the 11th and allowing ten days to get from Oxford to York, he should have left there immediately after Christmas. Christmas is, I believe, the only day mentioned specifically in the poem (481). The lodge at Woodstock near Oxford was a favorite stopping and hunting residence with English royalty. The poet must have known of the coming visit weeks before if the hypothesis is accurate. One wonders if Geoffrey gave a feast for the schools and the town.

If the hypothesis presented above is correct, *The Owl and the Nightingale* acquires greater significance than just that of a good English poem of the end of twelfth century. Like Gerald's story of his reading at Oxford, it throws much light on the culture of that city and its schools. The construction rests heavily on parallels in the poems to current events, particularly in the life of Geoffrey and less so of Richard I. The nearness of Guildford to the Aquila manor makes the identification of the two Nicholases more attractive. The material of the poem would appeal to such an audience as was alleged to have listened to Gerald's readings, only a few years before. If the poem was not written for a special occasion, a visit by Geoffrey to Oxford in December 1189, the poet wrote a poem most appropriate for precisely such an occasion.

Notes

1   Eric Gerald Stanley (ed.), *The Owl and the Nightingale* (London, 1960). The possibility that Alexander Neckam was the author should be considered, but this is essentially a literary problem.

2. Besides the arguments already given, a line near the end (1731) which says that the king is neither dead nor feeble might be interpreted to mean that Richard was neither dead like Henry II nor feeble like Stephen.
3. "Rhetorical Structure in the Owl and the Nightingale," *Speculum*, XLII (1967), 92−103.
4. Lines 235, 294, 299, 349, 569, 685, 697, 761, 942, 1074, 1223, and 1269.
5. The account of Geoffrey's career in the *Dictionary of National Biography* is a convenient biography.
6. C. H. Haskins, "Henry II as a Patron of Literature," *Essays in Medieval History presented to Thomas F. Tout*, ed. A. G. Little and F. M. Powicke (Manchester, 1925), pp. 71−77.
7. *Giraldi Cambrensis Opera* (Rolls Series) IV, 363: Gervase of Canterbury (Rolls Series) I, 520.
8. *De nugis curialium*, ed. Kuno Meyer (Oxford, 1905), pp. 246−47.
9. As suggested by *DNB*.
10. *The Historians of the Church of York* (Rolls Series), II, 400−01.
11. The bishop was apparently consecrated as bishop only four days earlier. If the reference to Nicholas and Scotland means more than just influence of writings, perhaps he had gone there earlier in the employ of a bishop or abbot, such as Simon de Tonei, monk of Melrose, who became in succession abbot of Coggeshall and then bishop of Moray 1172−87.
12. "Anglo-Norman Canonists of the Twelfth Century," *Traditio*, VII (1949-51), 279−358. Nicholas is discussed on p. 320.
13. Kuttner-Rathbone, p. 331.
14. For Richard, Kuttner-Rathbone, p. 317 n 7. For Gilbert the Physician, C. G. Talbot and E. A. Hammond, *The Medical Practitioners in Medieval England* (Wellcome Historical Medical Library, new ser., vol. VIII, 1965), pp. 58−60.
15. D. W. Robertson, "The Historical Setting of Chaucer's Book of the Duchess," *Mediaeval Studies in Honor of Urban Tignor Holmes, Jr.* (1965), p. 172.
16. *Giraldi Cambrensis*, I, 72−3. Conveniently translated by H. Wieruszewski, *The Medieval University* (1966), p. 156. The date is that given by Kuttner-Rathbone, p. 324.
17. Kuttner-Rathbone, p. 305.
18. *Chronicon Magistri Rogeri de Hoveden* (Rolls Series) III, 31; for 1191−92, Roger of Wendover (Rolls Series) I, 194; *Giraldi Cambrensis*, IV, 395.
19. Kuttner-Rathbone, p. 326.
20. Stanley, *Owl and the Nightingale*, p. 120.
21. J. W. H. Atkins, *The Owl and the Nightingale* (1922), p. lxxxv.

CHAPTER 14

The Triumph of Dignity over Order in England

A critical period of early English constitutional history seems to lie between 1166 and 1322. Upon the earlier period "self-government at the king's command" regularizing a feudal setup has been generally accepted. At the other end the Statute of York has been subjected to intensive research recently.[1] Among other problems falls the question of what influence of the lesser people of England had upon constitutional development. Recently Professor Powicke has discussed the general principles upon which the controversy has been based, showing that different parties have not agreed upon the types of evidence which should be admitted. He finds the lesser people an important factor as "an active and intelligent element in the social, economic, and administrative life of the country" and emphasizes the position that "we have not to seek here and there for isolated signs of political assertiveness; we have rather to watch the gradual adjustment of this middle class to a political life which could not exist without it."[2] This study would suggest that the influence of the lesser people is to be sought in the field of ideas rather than of "political assertiveness" and attempts to point out some evidence of such influence. However, one instance, the triumph of dignity over order, is of such importance as a key principle of the constitution that it has seemed best to give the study that title.

One of our great difficulties is to place in proper historical perspective the different groups of the society of medieval England while considering their influence upon the constitution. We remember that the king had the executive power in the government and that the nobles had considerable influence as outstanding leaders of the country in the great council and outside. What we easily forget is that this left the lesser people with relatively little direct influence, partly by the poor positions which precedence allowed them if they attended meetings and partly by the meagerness of their prestige in an age which paid large attention to social status.[3] Generally the lesser people accepted their position as natural, were not "politically assertive," and waited upon the words of their social superiors. If we focus our attention upon them in Parliament we shall miss the whole point of their influence; there in the presence of the great they appeared at their worst.[4] Even separated from the rest of the Parliament, the knights probably seated and the burgesses and freemen standing,[5] they were hardly the self-assured, competent men who ran the shires so smoothly.

Yet we do know that in some respects the influence of the lesser people was powerful. Their language, English, became the language of the whole people although for two centuries after the Conquest French had the prestige of the nobility and Latin that of the Church. Even though French became the language of the law courts and Latin the language of administration English won out largely by the end of the fourteenth century. The lesser people might be expected to have had less influence in political institutions in which the ruling classes had solid vested interests. However, ideas diffuse easily. We might expect to discover the influence of the lesser people in the history of ideas more easily than in the activity of institutions. Using the axiom that legislation is largely in response to political pressure from the benefitted groups we shall point out first evidence of the influence of the lesser people in the early statutes of the kingdom. We shall take up then the evidence which comes from the arrangement of witness lists in the charters of the royal court and of two significant areas in England at the end of the twelfth century. These tend to show the passage of a very important conception of society, previously mentioned, from the lesser people to the greater in England.

If we examine the statutes of the reign of Henry III we have a reasonable picture of the pattern of reformation of the realm which existed then, even though they include only the Statute of Merton of 1235, the Provisions of 1259, the Dictum de Kenilworth of 1266 and the Statute of Marlborough of 1268. We assume that the items included in the statutes were the result of pressure on the part of those benefitted by the provisions. The feudal lords obviously benefitted greatly.[6] Nevertheless a quite considerable number of items were for the advantage of the lesser people. Occasionally a provision which would seem designed to protect the great, such as a prohibition of disparagement in the marriage of heiresses, turns out to protect the freeholder as well, since the denial of marriage to villains could only refer to heiresses in the freeholder class.[7]

The right of a freeholder to be represented by attorney in the local courts was important, since attendance upon the frequent sessions of local courts might be very inconvenient at times.[8] Similarly judges were forbidden to fine townships if all of their males over 12 years of age failed to appear for inquests.[9] Likewise essoins (excuses), usually for failure to attend ordinary courts, need no longer to be warranted.[10] In all of these the ordinary freeholder was relieved from technicalities which could be penalized by fines.

Even when a provision seems directed against the lesser people an effort seems to be made to see that justice is rendered and guaranteed to the lesser persons. So while we see that social status is definitely recognized and assumed as part of the setup of contemporary society, there is a very large emphasis upon the responsibility as well as the privileges of the great. Furthermore we see indications of another movement. The privileges granted to the lesser people with respect to court attendance and freedom from irksome technicalities had been enjoyed by the greater people for some time. It is a part of the process which led the king to extend the summons to the lesser people to attend the great council through their representatives as a part of the regular development of the constitution. The lesser people are thus being invited to share the common political and legal life of the kingdom upon terms comparable to those already granted to the great people of England.

When we turn from the statutes to the charter witness lists we find a quite different type of evidence. Charters were written records of transactions in the presence of witnesses who would be willing to testify to the authenticity of the transactions in court if necessary.[11] The scribes of the charters wrote in the lists of the witnesses at the end of the documents, usually in a very definite order. Since the clerks read the charters aloud in meetings at which the witnesses and others were present, we assume that the arrangement of names in the lists met public satisfaction and represents current ideas of social status.

The medieval chroniclers when speaking of groups occasionally state that the persons were arranged "secundum ordinem et dignitatem."[12] That is, the clergy as one order sat to the right of the presiding personage and the laity to the left. The most important persons, those with the most dignity, sat closest to the presiding officer and those of lesser dignity sat farther away; each man usually knew his place. Now when a clerk wrote down the list of witnesses he could give the names in two possible arrangements. He could list all of the clerks first and then all of the laity, as in the following list:[13]

> Testibus: Wintoniensi episcopo, magistro Waltero de Constantiis, Godefrido de Luce, W. de Sancte Marie Ecclesia, comite Baldoino de Rivers, et fratre eius, et pluribus aliis.

He might have listed the witnesses by their dignity, the highest clergy first followed by the highest laymen, and the lesser clergy and laity farther on, as in the following list:[14]

> Testibus: Ph.Dunolm. episcopo, R. abbate Ebor., Robert de Turnham, Willi. de Stutewill., A., archd. Carleol. et Dunolm., H. de Welles, J. de Brancaster, etc.

Turnham and Stuteville were barons of considerable importance and outranked the archdeacons of Carlisle and Durham as well as the clerks, Hugh of Welles and John of Brancaster.

The clerk then could arrange the witnesses by order or by dignity. The choice would, of course, probably be determined by current social feeling rather than the preference of the clerk in what was to him merely a routine operation. The lists are good data from which to determine which was regarded more highly as a basis for social stratification, order or dignity.

The charter witness lists have great advantages as sources, since their great number and widespread origin, covering both great geographical areas and a long period of time, provide evidence for the diffusion of ideas in time and space in England. As yet, however, the study is hindered by the lack of published collections of charters and by the failure to assign accurate dates or even any at all to the published charters. Fortunately a good beginning can be made by the use of the collections of royal charters and two significant collections made by very able scholars: H. E. Salter's *Cartulary of Oseney Abbey* and F. M. Stenton's *Documents Illustrative of the Danelaw*.

The evidence of the royal charters is rather conclusive in regard to the practice of the chancery. In the reigns of the Williams the preference was apparently for arrangement by dignity but the problem was complicated by the use of 'signa' instead of witnesses in many documents and by chaos of precedence in others.[15] However, in the reigns of Henry I, Stephen, and Henry II the usual arrangement was by order although sufficient exceptions remain to show that the other arrangement was always a possibility.[16] The reign of Richard I finds a remarkable increase in the preference for dignity, so that nearly half of the charters are arranged in this fashion.[17] In the reign of John but very few charters have lists of witnesses proceeding according to order rather than to dignity—and this continued to be the standard arrangement. The change might be accounted for by the fact that the clerks of Henry II were mostly French in origin while those of John were largely English, but this discounts too heavily the fact that most chanceries develop diplomatic traditions, which obviously in England were moving from arrangement by order to arrangement by dignity. Let us see what was being done by the clerks of the lesser people at this time as illustrated by the Danelaw and Oxford charters.

The Danelaw charters provide information which can be compared with the diplomatic of the royal court. Before 1180 the number of charters is relatively less than after, but the number arranged by order is usually larger than that by dignity. The later twelfth century charters we divide into two groups, assuming them to represent roughly the decades 1180-90 and 1190-1200. Among the former we include those charters which are designated by Professor Stenton as "late Henry II" and among the latter the charters dated as "late twelfth century." The second group probably represent even with all possible qualifications a group later as a whole than the former and thus supply us with a suitable sample of diplomatic trend in the territory of the charters. We notice that for the earlier decade the number of lists arranged by order is about the same as the number arranged by dignity.[18] For the last decade of the century there is almost a five to three advantage for the lists arranged by dignity.[19] In short it appears clearly here that dignity was winning out.

Some of the most satisfactory evidence comes from the collections of charters of Oseney Abbey in Oxford. Here we find that there is little information about the arrangement of lists from before 1180, but that little would seem to show about an equal number arranged in each fashion. In the period 1180-90, lists arranged by dignity outnumber the other by a considerable margin,[20] and continue to do so until in the thirteenth century lists arranged by order seldom appear.[21] Oxford at this time was a great center of legal education and of the training of clerks. It may well have been the center for the diffusion of ideas about diplomatic and for the political ideas which they illustrate. The Oxford evidence is thus of peculiar importance.

While we may suspect that a good many of the charters included in the groups above emanated from the county and hundred courts, the real centers of local political life, none is absolutely certain. One charter from the Hertfordshire county court in 1191 shows the persons arranged as follows: knights, clerks, sergeants of the hundreds, others.[22] The arrangement is clearly by dignity, since the knights and sergeants were laymen.

Two facts emerge from the evidence of the charter collections examined. The first is that the triumph of dignity over order at the royal court took place in the reign of Richard I and was completely finished in the reign of John. The second is, as far as evidence from such significant places as Oxford and the Danelaw shows, the change came among the lesser people first and then diffused to the royal court. The evidence is doubly valuable since it comes from official records and is thus acceptable to nearly all students of English constitutional and general history. Let us take up the meaning of this evidence in English development.

In theory the difference between a society based upon dignity and one based upon order might not seem very great; in practice it affected such things as the seating arrangements none at all at first. Yet order did stand for large privileges to distinct groups which was a decisive influence in the culture of those states which were divided by estates. Dignity, however, emphasized the importance of the individual as a member of society. The supremacy of dignity associated members of the clergy whose duties and responsibilities were almost always important with their peers among the laity and stimulated them by example. In its operation it tended to correlate wealth, political responsibility, and social status so that the possession of one or two of these presumed an acquisition of the rest.

Several instances show the progress of this concept. As early as 1189 the nearest heir of the Mandeville title did not secure it because he did not have sufficient means to secure the succession and therefore presumably to support the title properly.[23] Instead it went to Geoffrey Fitzpeter, who had a secondary claim only but who was justiciar of England.[24] Within the same era both William Marshall and Hubert de Burgh arose from relatively obscure positions through executive ability to the top rank of English nobles.

The feeling that dignity implied responsibility included within its scope even the dignity of kingship. Irresponsibility was the unforgivable crime that caused the deposition of Edward II and Richard II. One of the complaints against Henry III was that he gave in-laws and half-brothers and their friends the rewards which should have gone to the great men of the kingdom.[25]

> The King ought to honour with escheats and wards
> his own people, who can help him in various ways, who,
> by as much as they are more powerful by their own
> strength, are so much the more secure in all cases.

Feudalism provided many methods of rewarding retainers of reasonably high dignity: heiresses as well as escheats and wardships.

Very early the tradition was firmly established which encouraged ability among royal officials by ample rewards, replenished the nobility and gentry by giving able husbands to heiresses, and caused the upper classes to regard active participation in county and national government as part of their dignity. By 1363 the sumptuary statute which prescribed the proper apparel for Englishmen arranges persons by income groups as well as by social status,[26] practically assuming a correlation between them in law. And up to the present it has usually been not too difficult for the wealthy to join the gentry and nobility by appropriate procedure. Thus dignity superseded order in England and then rebuffed the rise of interest in "order" in the fourteenth century, when England faced the diffusion of the estate idea from the continent.[27]

Closely allied with the idea of dignity was the concept of the "commune of England," that of an integrated society in which all parts had their proper function.[28] In government the king, the clergy, the nobility, and the lesser people had a definite series of political responsibilities. Although by 1215 the nobles had learned of the advantages of this pattern of culture the possibility of reversion to feudal chaos always remained. The king was even more likely to swerve from his proper place in the scheme since he, as an individual, had both the power and opportunity to act by himself. The lesser people had no hope of securing power for themselves. As a result when all groups were in agreement it was upon the idea of the "commune;" when they differed it was for the benefit of king or nobles. The lesser people thus acted as a kind of balance wheel between forces pulling toward feudalism and absolutism. Their function was the smooth operation of local government and its connections with the central government under ordinary circumstances and protest against aberrations from the ideal in unusual times.

The second point of importance is that the idea of the superiority of dignity over that of order appeared first at the courts of the lesser people before it was accepted by the clerks of the royal court. It seems clear evidence that ideas could and did pass from the lesser people to the greater in England. It also suggests that other ideas possessed first by the lesser people may have gone across in the same way. About 1200 the shire and other local courts were characterized by regularity of meeting, wide competence, and something approaching a definite membership. At the same time the great council met as called by the king at increasingly regular times,[29] advised him in such matters as he saw fit to inquire about, and, while usually including the greater men, hardly had anything which could be called membership.[30] Two centuries later we see that Parliament had moved much nearer to the ideas which the local courts had exhibited by 1200. Since this was not typical of the continental parliaments it cannot be attributed to diffusion of ideas from abroad. It is much easier to see the influence of the lesser people of England here as in the case of the statutes mentioned earlier or of the triumph of dignity over order.

The fact of influence by the lesser people is interesting, but the means and course of the passage of that influence invite speculation and research. The circulation of ideas in the medieval period was discussed once by Professor Haskins,[31] but it is a relatively little worked vein in early English constitutional history. The following are but a few prefatory remarks. There were many places where the greater and lesser people could and did meet. While barons had largely ceased from regular attendance of the local courts by the thirteenth century, they still probably attended some of them or had in early life. Some were judges and thus came in contact with these courts. Many of the suitors of these courts were bailiffs of the

great men and thus naturally in touch with them. The operation of administration and of common law drew together a
large body of able, well-trained men who enjoyed political life.
The opportunities for the intercourse of ideas were obviously
present.

Let us note the relative numbers of persons in the courts
and the amount of their experience. The greater people meeting in Parliament perhaps three times a year numbered probably not more than two hundred annually. On the other hand
the county courts usually met several times a year, the
hundred courts every few weeks, and the borough courts at
frequent intervals. For every person who got his experience in
the central assembly many received a more extensive experience in the lesser courts. Granted the circulation of ideas
among the classes of England the sheer weight of numbers and
experience lay with the lesser people.

That there was a circulation of ideas—of wrong ideas,
according to the authorities—is clear from an early statute
leveled against the telling of tales harmful to the administration.[32] There is some evidence that unofficial reports went
from London to interested persons in the province.[33] The
whole subject needs more careful study.

———

Approaching the problem of the influence of the lesser
people upon the constitutional history of England from the
standpoint of the history of ideas we see possibilities for further understanding. In the case of the statutes of the reign of
Henry III provisions to extend to the lesser people certain of
the privileges already enjoyed by the greater were made. The
triumph of dignity over order as a basis for English culture is
seen to have occurred first among the lesser people and then at
the royal court, both by the beginning of the reign of King
John. Other constitutional ideas appear first at local courts and
may well have proceeded thence to the Parliament. These
require further study particularly from the angle of the circulation of ideas among the social classes of England.

Notes

1. The author is professor of history at the University of New Mexico. On the first topic see A. B. White, *Self-Government at the King's Command* (Minneapolis, 1933) and F. M. Stenton. *The First Century of English Feudalism* (Oxford, 1932). On the Statute of York see Gaillard Lapsley, "The Interpretation of the Statute of York." *English Historical Review*, LVI (1941), 22–51, 411–46. J. R. Strayer, "The Statute of York," *American Historical Review*, XLVII (1941), 1–22, and B. Wilkinson, "The Coronation Oath of Edward II and the Statute of York," *Speculum*, XIX (1944), 455–69, and other literature cited in these.

2. F. M. Powicke, "Recent work on the origin of the English parliament," *L'organisation corporative du Moyen Age à la Fin de l'Ancien Régime* (Louvain, 1939), pp. 138 and 139 respectively.

3. See my "Early Parliamentary Organization," *American Historical Review*, XLIII (1937), 1–21.

4. See the description of the Commons in Parliament at the end of the fourteenth century in H. Cam, "The relation of English members of Parliament to their constituencies in the fourteenth century," *L'organisation corporative....*, pp. 143–53.

5. *Ibid.*, p. 151. That Mr. Richardson's interpretation of the expression is correct would appear from a second reference to the situation early in the reign of Edward II. T. Wright, *Political Songs of England* (London, 1839), p. 183.

6. A good illustration is the protection of loss by the lord in infeudation. *Statutes of the Realm*, i, 2.

7. *Ibid.*, i, 3.

8. *Ibid.*, i, 4. Fines for beaupleader were also eliminated. *Ibid.*, i, 9, 22.

9. *Ibid.*, i, 11, 25.

10. *Ibid.*, i, 10, 23, 24.

11. On the questions involved in charter witnessing see my "Attestation of charters in the reign of John," *Speculum*, XV (1940), 480–98, and the literature there cited.

12. For a discussion of these terms see *American Historical Review*, XLIII (1937), 4–10.

13. L. Delisle, *Recueil des Acts de Henri II* (Paris, 1909), no 580.

14. *Rotuli Chartarum* (London, 1837), p. 39b.

15. H. W. C. Davis, *Regesta Regum Anglo-Normannorum, 1066–1154* (Oxford, 1913), I. Lists by order appear in nos. 10, 74, 77, 146a; by dignity in nos. 4, 8, 22, 28, 29, 39, 46, 76, 103, 107, 118; by signa or mixed arrangement in nos. 121, 125, 126, 131, 147, 158, 168, 172, 173.

16. For the documents of Henry I see W. Farrer, "An Outline Itinerary of Henry I," *English Historical Review*, XXXIV (1919), 303–82, 505–79. For the reign of Stephen see a few in J. H. Round, *Calendar of Documents preserved in France* (London, 1899), 377, 504, and in *Ancient Charters* (Pipe

Roll Soc.), pp. 48–9. For the documents of Henry II see L. Delisle, *Recueil des Acts de Henri II*, I (Paris, 1916). Those apparently arranged by dignity are nos. 43, 70, 83, 93, 440, 532, 618, and 674, although there is some doubt about a few of these. Arranged by order are nos. 79, 87, 113, 124, 153, 154, 165, 168, 195, 199, 204, 206, 247, 256, 257, 269, 271, 274, 275, 289, 293, 295, 308, 309, 311, 312, 313, 317, 353, 354, 394, 395, 411, 413, 414, 416, 423, 433, 443, 444, 447, 459, 481, 485, 494, 539, 549, 554, 564, 570, 573, 574, 576, 581, 583, 591, 592, 593, 594, 598, 600, 604, 609, 613, 615, 616, 621, 622, 628, 630, 631, 632, 633, 675, 682, 683, 684, 721, 744, 748, 755, 762, 763, supp. 34, 35.

17. Lionel Landon, *The Itinerary of King Richard I* (London, 1935, Pipe Roll Soc). By dignity nos. 8, 32, 54, 57, 147, 268, 276, 299, 313, 324, 390, 395, 402, 405, 416, 420, 423, 424, 445, 452, 453, 476, 478, 483, 486, 492, 501, 505, 510, 515, 517, 519, 533, 562. By order nos. 233, 286, 308, 314, 388, 392, 394, 397, 398, 399, 408, 425, 426, 427, 432, 439, 454, 457, 460, 463, 468, 474, 477, 478, 482, 488, 490, 491, 493, 499, 500, 531, 543, 477 (p. 139), 544, 546, 340 (p. 140), 548, 37 (p. 141), 479 (p. 141), 553, 554, 555, 132 (p. 142), 560.

18. Stenton, *op. cit.*, by order, nos, 7, 10, 21, 33, 40, 43, 102, 153, 166, 220, 224, 225, 259, 291, 292, 293, 294, 315, 319, 330, 397, 426: by dignity, nos. 20, 22, 48, 51, 76, 84, 112, 136, 179, 180, 216, 231, 268 (?), 320, 347, 356, 395, 396, 408, 517, 553.

19. *Ibid.*, by order, nos. 17, 18, 29, 42, 45, 46, 55, 65, 66, 68, 69, 74, 75, 79, 81, 104, 129, 130, 135, 137, 154, 169, 170, 191, 213, 254, 288, 295, 346, 360, 424, 459, 524; by dignity, nos. 16, 34, 35, 36, 49, 50, 53, 54, 78, 83, 86, 99, 115, 138, 193, 196, 197, 217, 226, 227, 228, 234, 252, 267, 269, 278, 321, 322, 323, 349, 361, 362, 365, 366, 374, 384, 388, 389, 410, 418, 442, 487, 493, 510, 511, 526, 543, 546, 550, 554.

20. *Op. cit.* for order: I, 83, 172; II, 29, 81, 479; IV, 416, 445, 466. For dignity, I, 71, 266; II, 5, 55, 82, 433, 463, 481; IV, 19, 34, 153, 155, 258, 259, 368, 374, 389, 413, 463.

21. *Op. cit.* for order in 1191-1200: II, 252, 281, 338, 396; IV, 408, 498. For dignity: I, 84, 127, 305; II, 23, 49, 195, 196, 197, 434, 446; IV, 58, 66, 89, 90, 171, 241, 326, 337, 338, 466, 505, 517.

22. *Historical Manuscripts Commission*, IX Report, app. i, pp. 32b–33a.

23. The succession was rather complicated. See *Dictionary of National Biography* under Fitzpeter, Geoffrey.

24. In social status Fitzpeter ranked at the top of the lay nobility. *Cf. Speculum*, XII (1937), 324.

25. From the Song of Lewes. Wright, *Political Songs of England*, pp. 86–7.

26. *Statutes of the Realm*, i, 380–2.

27. S. B. Chrimes, *English Constitutional Ideas of the Fifteenth Century* (Cambridge, 1936), pp. 105–26, particularly p. 105.

28. For recent interpretations of the "commune" see D. Rayner, "The Forms and Machinery of the 'Commune Petition'," *English Historical Review*, LVI (1941), 204 and J. R. Strayer in *American Historical Review*, LVI (1941), 11.

29. Recently made clearer by J. E. A. Jolliffe, "Some factors in the beginnings of Parliament," *Transactions of the Royal Historical Society,* 4th series, XXII (1940), 101–39.
30. In this study we have not touched upon the problem of representation.
31. C. H. Haskins, "The spread of ideas in the Middle Ages," *Speculum,* I. (1926), 19–30.
32. *Statutes of the Realm,* i, 35.
33. H. Cam. *L'organisation corporative,* p. 146.

CHAPTER 15

Social Status at the Court of King John

Social status is an important factor in society at all times, not merely as the legal condition of social groups, which has received much scholarly attention, but also as the pattern of social relationship of men and groups.[1] A man's status has meaning to him as a position in human society relative to other people. He is intensely interested in that position whether it is in the *Notitia Dignitatum* of the later Roman Empire or at a Washington dinner. The sum of these individual opinions about social status is a collective social custom which operates to unite and divide society into a wide variety of groups. This study is an effort to analyze the types of social grouping which existed at the court of King John of England (1199–1216) and is based largely upon the evidence afforded by the witness lists of the royal charters of that reign.[2]

The reign of King John was selected for study because the witness lists of his charters are published.[3] The royal charters were transcribed on rolls which have been preserved in the archives of England. Since they were copied at the time of the issuance of the original charters, they are probably accurate transcripts. The charters were among the more formal royal documents and thus the names of witnesses were written in them. These documents were probably written by royal clerks under the direction of the officials whose names are given.[4]

The variety of names from day to day is an indication that these are genuine lists of witnesses who were actually present. Indeed, we may assume that the recipient of such a charter would insist upon the inclusion of the names of the persons who had actually witnessed the charters; it was a very serious matter for him since he might need them to testify in court that the charter was not a forgery.

I

If we subject these witness lists to even elementary tests for precedence, we find that the names of persons appear in a well-defined order.[5] The variation from this order amounts to about 6.5 per cent, which may be explained as follows. If two people, A and B, stand in a row, there is one possibility for misplacement, that is, BA instead of AB. If three people are present, arranged ABC, there are three chances for misplacements: that is, BA, CA, BC, instead of AB, AC, and BC. The problem is one of combinations rather than permutations, to use the language of our early arithmetic; 6.5 per cent is equivalent to the misplacing of two people standing together in a line of six. This is a low rate of misplacements, since the rate of variation if the names of witnesses were written without order would be about 50 per cent. We have then to assume that there is a definite order and that there must be reasons for it.

The amount of variation, although small, rules out an official list because the use of such a list would have precluded any but copyists' mistakes which would have probably been less than 6.5 per cent. Moreover, no *Notitia Dignitatum* has come down to us from this period, and no reference appears to such a schedule even in the lively debates over precedence at the coronation of Henry III.[6]

A second hypothesis is that the clerk simply recorded the names of persons in the order in which they were seated or standing or in which they would usually be seated or standing. This has in its favor two strong assumptions: first, that the clerks who had to record witnesses would naturally adopt an orderly method preferably based upon visual evidence, and second, that they would hardly have had such definite ideas about arrangement if their contemporaries had not had them also. In short, the obvious explanation of the orderliness of the witness lists is that the clerks merely recorded the names of the persons as they sat arranged according to the customary group of the time.

This hypothesis can be tested with respect to the bishops of England, since statements of their precedence remain. The most detailed explanation is the following:

> In the same assembly Lanfranc inquired of the senior bishops what was the order of sitting in council established by ancient usage. After careful consideration the reply was made, that when the archbishop of Canterbury presided, the archbishop of York was on his right hand, with the bishop of Winchester next him, and the bishop of London on his left. If for any reason the archbishop of York presided, he had the bishop of London on his right and the bishop of Winchester on his left. The other bishops sat according to priority of consecration.[7]

This order holds true for the bishops of the time of King John and is especially accurate for long lists drawn up upon solemn occasions.[8]

The charter witness lists are thus also seating lists. From a study of them there should come an understanding of the pattern and the principles of arrangement of groups and individuals. It must be remembered that this study is merely a beginning in a field of some complexity. Its results will be very tentative,[9] and will require confirmation from further research.

II

The names of charter witnesses usually follows the order which so frequently appears in the chronicles: archbishops, bishops, and abbots, earls and barons. Since these persons were the most important men of the realm, their names would have been welcomed as witnesses. Many times, however, few or no ecclesiastical or lay nobles were present. Then it was necessary to write in the names of archdeacons, lesser barons, and even clerks.

We notice that there is no confusion in regard to the relative positions of groups of archbishops, bishops, abbots, priors, archdeacons, and clerks. Similarly there is none among the earls, barons, and knights. When members of both were present and of about the same rank questions did arise, however. Sometimes earls appeared before abbots, and at least once after them.[10] The names of archdeacons occasionally interrupt a series of names of barons, perhaps dividing it into groups of greater and lesser barons.[11] Even the clerks appear occasionally before men who were probably lesser barons.[12] It is obvious that the writers of the charters were uncertain as to the relative status of these groups. The easiest explanation of this confusion is that the clerical and lay groups sat apart. Thus while it was a fairly simple matter to determine the relative status of groups within the clergy or within the laity, the status of a lay group with respect to a clerical group was more difficult. In two instances, at least, the clerks wrote all the clerical names before proceeding to the lay names.[13]

The arrangement of the groups would appear to be as in the diagram below.

Clergy		Laity	
	King		
Archbishops			
Bishops	Earls		
Abbots			
Priors	Barons, greater	Mayor of London	
Archdeacons			
Clerks	Barons, lesser	Aldermen (?)	

The division of groups is by function and of importance of duties. The functionaries of the church are separated from those of the state. At this time also very heavy administrative responsibilities rested upon the shoulders of the earls and barons in their own lands. The Norman and Angevin rulers had established a tradition which required themselves and their lords to participate in English government with excellent results; the peace of England was hard to parallel elsewhere. The scope of function as the basis of social status included even London; the committee of twenty-five nobles (which was formed in 1215 to watch King John) included the mayor of London.[14] We shall find other instances of individuals of status which might have been considered questionable, who rose to high rank through administrative achievement.

This evidence seems to show that by 1200 English society was taking a different course from that of France. There society was divided into three distinct orders: clergy, knighthood, and workers. A theory in regard to it had been developed by the twelfth century which has been summarized by Luchaire as follows:[15]

> Society is divided by Divine will into three classes or castes, each of which has its proper function and which is necessary to the existence and life of the social bodies; the priests, who are charged with prayer and conducting mankind to salvation; the nobles, on whom devolves the mission of defending the nation by arms against its enemies and causing justice and order to reign; the people, and peasants and burghers, who by their labor nourish the two upper classes and satisfy all their desires for luxuries as well as necessities.

This division of society into orders was vaguely apparent in England, but remained subordinate to the concept of division by importance of responsibilities. It is perhaps not an accident that the two charters in which the clerical and lay witnesses are separated were written in France.

Besides the variability in the order of the groups in the royal charters there are cases of persons who appear in more than one group. The most conspicuous instance is that of William Longsword, earl of Salisbury and half-brother of the king. These two items about him seem to explain the variation. As half-brother of the king he might join the royal entourage and thus have his name placed in the list ahead of the earls. As earl of Salisbury he had a place about halfway down the list of earls; this was the less common position. A second instance is that of the Templar, Alan Martel, who appeared in a much lower position when he was the only Templar present than when he was with the master of his order in England.[16] Instances of the presence of fathers and sons or brothers at the same time do not seem to appear in these records; among the

210 of 290

charters of lesser places the name of son or brother usually
follows that of the father or elder brother. In our charters the
sons occupy lesser places than do their fathers.[17]

The explanation of this problem is probably to be found in
the custom of having retainers or relatives near one. Professor
Stenton has shown that this was a very important custom in
twelfth-century England.[18] The greatness of the feudal lord
was more easily appreciated by the strength of his armed
following than by his inherent importance. Seeing the men
together the clerks recorded the names of important relatives
or retainers as witnesses along with those of their lords rather
than farther along in the list where their names would have
been, had they been there without their lords. This is another
and rather important indication that the clerks recorded what
they saw. The number of retainers was part of what was
termed a man's dignity.

III

Dignity was indicated in part by a man's position even
within his own group. The low rate of variability among the
witnesses shows that these positions within ranks were quite
well fixed. The large amount of evidence in regard to the
precedence of archbishops, bishops, earls, and barons enables
us to determine their positions with some accuracy and even to
state reasons for precedence for some with certainty and to
give a tentative explanation for others. The order of precedence of the archbishops and bishops has already been given
and seems certain. The reasons for the orderliness of earls and
barons is not so easy to understand.

Even though the order of precedence among the archbishops and bishops seems clear enough there are misplacements among their names in the charter witness lists. The
names of Eustace, bishop of Ely, and John, bishop of Norwich,
frequently appear at the head of the list of bishops, before the
names of the bishops of London and Winchester and of
bishops who were consecrated before them. Since these two
men seem to have had no office in addition to their bishopric
which might have raised their dignity, some other explanation

must be sought. They were very close friends of the king during most of his reign and were frequently at court. Probably they were regarded as royal chaplains and thus part of his entourage.

An interesting tradition had grown up in the English church whereby the bishops of London and Winchester were considered the dean and subdean of the province of Canterbury. In the struggle between the archbishop, Stephen Langton, and King John, a partizan of the archbishop refers to the bishop of London, William de Sainte-Mere-Eglise as Stephen's John the Baptist in the following verse:

> Joannes nostri temporis
>   surgit decanus Anglie,
> canus mente, ui roboris
>   stratam uadit iustitie,
> canit laudum preconia
> qui iure de ecclesia
> Marie nomen accipit,
> dum conflictum hunc suscipit
>   sacre deuotus Virgini.[19]

By 1221 the bishop of Salisbury was claiming that he was regarded as the precentor of the province and therefore entitled to a permanent place after the bishop of Winchester. The bishop of Rochester also asserted he had special prerogatives as the chaplain of the archbishop of Canterbury.[20] This conception of the prelates of the province of Canterbury as a cathedral chapter is an instance of English unity.

Below the abbots who probably sat by priority of consecration[21] was the Master of the Templars, Aimeric de St. Maur. Except for the evidence of two charters in which the names of earls precede his own, Aimeric might have been placed first on the side of the laity.[22] Unfortunately his name does not appear in the same charters with the names of archdeacons so that it cannot be stated whether he outranked them or not. The archdeacons may have had rules for their own precedence, but the available evidence is apparently too slight for its determination.[23]

The evidence in regard to the precedence of the earls and barons presents the following schedule of dignities:

Earls

1	Essex, Geoffrey Fitzpeter	8	Surrey, William of Warenne
2	Chester, Randulph de Blundeville	9	Sussex, Arundel, William Aubigny
3	Pembroke, William Marshall	10	Huntingdon, David
4	Leicester, Robert Beaumont	11	Derby, William Ferrars
5	Norfolk, Roger Bigod	12	Oxford, Alberic de Vere
6	Salisbury, William Longsword	13	Hereford, Humphrey de Bohun
7	Hertford, Richard of Clare		

Barons

1	William de Braose	14	Warin Fitzgerald
2	William de Stuteville	15	Robert de Vipont
3	Hugh Bardulf	16	Thomas Basset
4	Robert Fitzroger	17	Thomas of Sandford
5	Roger de Lacy, constable of Chester	18	Peter of Stoke
6	William Brewer	19	William de Cantelupe
7	Peter de Préaux	20	Simon de Pateshull
8	Roger de Tony	21	Hubert de Burgh
9	Walter de Lacy	22	James de Poterne
10	William de Aubigny	23	John Marshall
11	Robert de Turnham	24	Geoffrey de Lucy
12	Hugh de Neville	25	Peter de Mauley
13	Eustace de Vescy	26	Geoffrey Luttrell
		27	Brian de Lisle

The title of an earl probably conferred a definite place in the order of precedence. An earl's son seems to have taken the position which his father held before him.[24] This precedence apparently bore some relationship to the knight service which the earl owed the king. The arrangement was probably traditional rather than one which was constantly being revised. As J. H. Round has shown in a notable article, William the Norman after his conquest of England, assigned to his followers definite quotas of knights in units of five or ten.[25] These remained the basis for the feudal army until well into the reign of Henry II, when certain alterations were made. Examination of the records of the holdings of these men shows some shifting of lands even in England, while their possessions in Normandy and Ireland were often either precarious or actually lost by this time. Round has pointed out that in some instances men did not know how many knights were in their quota.[26] Had the actual number of knights determined status this number would have been very important for the lords. Furthermore, the precedence of the earls seems to have corresponded roughly to the number of their knights' fees, which ranged from about 175 to about 50.[27] Probably the original status of the earl after the conquest determined his quota and remained as a traditional status for the earldom.

For the barons the evidence is less satisfactory: the term baron was not as yet a title. A few of them seem to have held more fees than some of the earls.[28] This probably explains why the earls and greater barons were considered together so frequently: they were the group of lords with the larger holdings. The correlation of the holdings of other barons with their precedence does not seem to be very close. Probably knight service was merely one factor in their position. Other factors such as family prestige or administrative office may be tentatively suggested. The names of the sons of the earls of Norfolk and Hertford (Clare) appear in the lists among those of the lesser barons.[29] Many of these barons held offices under the king which may have conferred more prestige than the knight service which they owed.

By the use of this schedule of lay dignities, it is possible to make certain estimates about the individual importance of the leaders who opposed King John. It has been asserted that Robert Fitzwalter, leader of the anti-royalists, was a baron of secondary rank who was lower in the social scale than the heads of the houses of Aubigny, Vipont, de Lacy, Basset, Cantelupe, Neville and Brewer.[30] Fitzwalter's position, like his holdings, ranked high among those of the great barons and was about the position of William Brewer but above those of the other houses mentioned above.[31] The terrible treatment of the wife and son of William Braose was one of the worst instances of John's cruelty. That Braose was one of the greatest of the barons of England made the act startling evidence of the danger of royal despotism.

Usually there were enough men of prominence present to enable the charter clerks to satisfy the record. Sometimes, however, the shortage of great names caused the adding of quite unimportant people. Their appearance is in the nature of an accident and gives very little satisfactory information about their precedence.

In this study of groups and individual dignity it should be possible to come to some opinion in regard to the meaning of the word, peer (*par*), which occurs several times in Magna Carta and was to have an important place in English political language. One of the outstanding grievances of the anti-royal forces was that they had not been allowed their right to legal judgment by their peers.[32] At first sight it might seem that there was no such thing as an equal, since every man had his place with respect to all others. It should be noticed that the percentage of variation increases in proportion to proximity within each group so that a distance of two or three seats among friends would seem to have made little difference. Two opinions in regard to the meaning of peer seem plausible. One is that a man's peer was a member of his own group. For instance, an earl was the peer of earls and perhaps even of the greater barons. The other is that a man's peer was a person who ranked above him in social status. Either would probably have been satisfactory in law, although the first meaning is probably much preferable.

IV

Another cause for misplacement among the names of charter witnesses is that of change in status or, as it usually is called, social mobility. In general, corrections have been made for such changes in the calculations given above. That is, in such a short period as fifteen years, a man was apt to have held one position for a good part of the time. Wherever possible, the items which definitely saw him in other positions were discarded. Nevertheless, there are probably many misplacements included in the calculations that are the result of changes in status which were apparent to the clerk but not to us. These changes are of two types: vertical, that is, from a lower to a higher status, and lateral, from one social group to another.

Because there was practically no inheritance of clerical

positions by the time of King John, the higher clergy had to come from other classes and was recruited from several groups. Langton, the archbishop of Canterbury, had been a professor at Paris and had come from a relatively unimportant Yorkshire family. The archbishop of York to 1212 was the half-brother of the king, Geoffrey. Other bishops came from such feudal families as those of Braose or De Lucy, or from lesser families. Most of the bishops had been either professors or royal administrative officers,[33] usually rising to their episcopal eminence by way of the office of canon or archdeacon.

The abbots, no less than the bishops, were frequently drawn from the schools. The ranking abbot, John de Cella, of St Albans, was a physician and poet. Abbot John of Ford was apparently a friend of the king and received notable gifts from him; he was likewise a scholar. Another royal friend and scholar was that Alexander Neckam who became abbot of Cirencester toward the end of the reign of John: his mother had been the nurse of King Richard and was probably of minor social status. With legal entanglements so frequently a problem of the monastery the advantage of having an authority on law as administrator was obvious. Richard Mores, prior of Dunstable, had been a famous writer and teacher at Bologna before entering the monastery and while there wrote a chronicle which is almost a legal history of his house. Of course, the exploits of Thomas of Marlborough as monk and legal defender of Evesham are well known.[34] The inner history of Bury St Edmunds is probably better known than that of any other house through the pen of Joscelin of Brakelond and the anonymous account of the election of 1214.[35] The relative equality of the brethren and their heavy collective responsibilities enabled the more capable and energetic to rise upon their ability.

Among the earls and barons, men arose most frequently by succeeding to the positions of their fathers. However, some men advanced by royal appointment to high office. There is the case of Hubert de Burgh, whose career can be followed more easily than that of most others. In the early charters of the reign, he appears in the position given him in our list. In the introduction of Magna Carta he is called seneschal of Poitou

214 TWELFTH CENTURY STUDIES

and has risen to a place between Warin Fitzgerald and Thomas Basset.[36] Within a month he was justiciar of England and was now ranked ahead of the barons.[37] Another method of advancement was by way of marriage to great heiresses, sometimes as a reward for royal friendship or help. In our period we have the rise of Saer de Quincy who first had a rank equivalent to that of William de Cantelupe, but rose to the level of William Brewer, and finally became earl of Winchester.[38] The great feudal hero, William Marshall, commenced his career as a knight without wealth and finally succeeded King John as master of England.[39]

In the cities and especially in London opportunities for rising were more frequent. The mayor of London, an elective officer, was numbered among the lords who were to watch the king in 1215, as we have seen. The mobility achieved by acknowledging that an elected officer of a borough was worthy of the dignity of a baron was very important. Mobility from burgess ranks was lateral also. Reginald of Cornhill was numbered among the barons, although he came from a London family. Hugh Neville, a greater baron, married a city heiress. Indeed, in one way London was a kind of miniature England. In or near it were the palaces, not merely of the king and bishop of London, but those also of the archbishop of Canterbury, and of other nobles. Robert Fitzwalter was lord of Castle Baynard and Richard Munfichet, of Munfichet Castle, while sokes in the city were held by the bishops of Ely and Worcester, the earls of Huntingdon, and Gloucester, Hugh Neville and Warin Fitzgerald.[40] As an organism it was typical of the unity of England.

This lateral mobility was also possible from the burgess ranks into the church. The great saint of mediaeval England, Thomas Becket, came of a London family.

Geographical limitations were not very effective restraints upon social mobility. The Angevin Empire still included parts of France even though John had lost most of them. From them came men like Peter des Roches who was bishop of Winchester and Saer de Quincy who became earl of the same place. From Germany had come the family of Arnald Fitzthedmar, a chronicler and an important official of London. The papal legate Pandulf who eventually was chosen bishop of Norwich was from Italy.

Thus far we have discussed the factors which favored the advancement of men. There were elements which discouraged or retarded such mobility. The existence of such a strong feeling for social status must in itself have been a retarding factor, even though it was less in England than in France. A second element was formed by family prestige and by rights of inheritance, even beyond the natural advantages which wealth and its associations bring. On the other hand there is something to be said for the idea that these feelings for family and social status may have been powerful aids in the building up of strong personalities. They gave to men confidence that they 'belonged' and were a part of a solid social structure.

This sense of belonging was increased even more by the social security which the people of England enjoyed at the time. The archbishops, bishops, abbots, and priors held office for good behavior which usually meant life. The same was true for the feudal lords. Once they had succeeded to their inheritance, they could be forced from their lands only with the greatest difficulty.

Even this sense of security might have been an anti-social factor if the lords had been a lazy, pleasure-loving, predatory group. In England the kings had usually set good examples of attention to administrative duties: the bishops and lay lords followed naturally or were forced to follow in the same path. The precedence of the clergy implied acknowledgment of a superior standard of ethics and education than that of the feudality, capable and intelligent as it was then.

As we have said, such conclusions as may seem advisable are still very tentative. This study does, however, give some clues to the social structure of the court of England, in the time of John. That, in itself, is important: for as Professor Powicke has written, 'The reign of King John, is to a degree found in no period of previous history, a commentary upon the development of the *Curia Regis.*'[41] This court possessed a very definite social pattern which was reflected in the charter witness lists and in the seating and arrangements of persons. Society was divided faintly into the clergy and laity, and these groups more sharply into smaller divisions: archbishops, bishops, abbots, and priors, military orders, archdeacons, clerks; and earls, greater barons, lesser barons, knights, freemen, serfs. Even though members of the groups called each other peers, precedence existed among them. The boundaries of these groups were not too difficult to cross, either laterally or vertically. To the ambitious and capable, advancement was possible and was largely based upon administrative ability. Among the men of high rank there were relatively few sinecures and little of the luxuriousness and indolence of the early modern courts. This advancement was protected by a large degree of social security. The picture is that of energetic and intelligent leadership. It is not surprising that such a group should have set out upon the road which led to democratic control of geographical areas wider than those of the city-state.

Notes

1. Little seems to have been done toward analyzing social status in terms of social distance and relationship in the middle ages. Even such an outstanding book as Luchaire's *Social France at the time of Philip Augustus* (trans. E. B. Krehbiel, New York, 1929) touches upon it only incidentally, as on pp. 382 and 391.
2. For the methods and some results of the examination of charter witness lists, see my 'Significance of Charter Witness Lists in Thirteenth Century England,' *New Mexico Normal University Bulletin* (August, 1930, supplement).
3. T. Hardy, ed. *Rotuli Chartarum* (London, 1837). In the calendars of charter rolls of later reigns the charter witnesses are not included.
4. The charters usually have the statement, 'Datum per manum' (of some official), but it is hardly likely that the clerical labor would have been done by such important men. By this time these officials had clerks, according to the *Dialogus de Scaccario*, Stubbs, *Select Charters* (Oxford, 1921), pp. 206–208.
5. A somewhat more detailed description of the method is given in my 'Significance of Charter Witness Lists in Thirteenth Century England,' *loc. cit. supra.*
6. Hubert Hall, ed. *Red Book of the Exchequer* (London, 1896, Rolls Series), pp. 755–760.
7. *Willelmi Malmesbiriensis monachi de gestis regum Anglorum* (London, 1889, Rolls Series), II, 353. The translation is that of A. W. Goodman, *Chartulary of Winchester Cathedral* (Winchester, 1927), p. 184.
8. Stubbs, *Select Charters*, pp. 283, 292, 350.

9. What seems to me now the very obvious hypothesis that charter witness lists are seating lists entirely escaped me when I wrote the 'Significance of Charter Witness Lists in Thirteenth Century England,' cited above.
10. *Rotuli Chartarum*, pp. 186a, 202b, 203b.
11. *Ibid.*, 115b, 155b, 156b, 189b, 191a.
12. *Ibid.*, pp. 105b, 199.
13. *Ibid.*, pp. 57, 177b. In one instance the clerk included the archdeacons' names before he began with those of the earls. *Ibid.*, p. 107a.
14. Stubbs, *Select Charters*, p. 303. By the fifteenth century the mayor and aldermen of London were claiming that they possessed the dignity of earl and baron respectively. H. T. Riley, ed., *Liber Albus* (London, 1861), pp. 13, 29.
15. Luchaire, *Social France in the Time of Philip Augustus*, p. 382.
16. *Rotuli Chartarum*, 198b, 202b, 212b, 221.
17. *Ibid.*, pp. 113a, 174a(2), and 186a.
18. F. M. Stenton, *The First Century of English Feudalism* (Oxford, 1932), pp. 30, 58, 128, 175 ff.
19. T. Wright, *The Political Songs of England* (London, 1839), p. 12. Wright missed the point of the verse, since he did not know of the tradition. The usual picture of this bishop is not so flattering.
20. J. C. Russell and J. P. Heironimus, *The Shorter Latin Poems of Master Henry of Avranches relating to England* (Cambridge: Mediaeval Academy of America, 1935), p. 82. H. G. Hewlett, ed., *Flowers of History of Roger of Wendover* (London, 1886, Rolls Series), I, 319.
21. W. Stubbs, ed., *Historical Works of Gervase of Canterbury* (London, 1880, Rolls Series), I, 251. H. R. Luard, ed. *Matthaei Parisiensis Chronica Majora* (London, 1877, Rolls Series), III, 337. Matthew Paris says that the abbot of St Albans had the first place.
22. *Rotuli Chartarum*, pp. 217b, 218b. He appears as witness also on pp. 128b, 214a, 221a.
23. The precedence of one group was apparently: Wells, Carlisle-Durham, Gloucester, Worcester, and Salisbury, and of another: Stafford, Hunts, and Salop. See *Rot. Chart.* under the names of the archdeaconries. These men were often royal officials and might have been present as episcopal retainers. The problem of their precedence was complicated by several factors.
24. *Feudal England*, p. 225 ff.
25. *Ibid.*, pp. 244, 257.
26. *Ibid.*, pp. 244, 257.
27. H. Hall, *Red Book of the Exchequer*, under names of the earls.
28. For the possessions of William de Braose, see *ibid.*, pp. 112, 114, 123, and 152; for Roger, constable of Chester pp. 165, 490; for Walter de Lacey, pp. 114, 158 and 496; for Warin Fitzgerald, pp. 53, 169, and 544; for Robert Fitzwalter, pp. 98, 175, 476 and 498. The term, greater barons, is used in Magna Carta, ch. 14.
29. *Rot. Chart.*, pp. 113[a], 174[a] (2), 186a.

218 TWELFTH CENTURY STUDIES

30. Kate Norgate, *John Lackland*, p. 219.
31. *Rot. Chart.*, see index under *Filius Walteri, Robertus*. His names appears with hardly enough frequency to warrant giving him a position in the schedule.
32. Magna Carta, chs. 21, 39, 52, 56, 59. Stubbs, *Select Charters*, pp. 296–299.
33. On the background of the episcopate at this time, see M. Gibbs and J. Lang, *Bishops and Reform, 1215–1272; with special reference to the Lateran Council of 1215* (London: Oxford Historical Series, 1934).
34. For these men see my *Dictionary of Writers of Thirteenth Century England* (London, 1936).
35. The latter is published by T. Arnold, *Memorials of St Edmunds* (London, 1892, Rolls Series), II, 29–130.
36. Stubbs, *Select Charters*, p. 292; *Rot. Chart.* pp. 200–201.
37. *Ibid.*, pp. 210–221 *passim*.
38. *Ibid.*, see index under *Quency, Saer. de.*
39. His biography has been written by Sidney Painter, *William Marshall, Knight Errant, Baron, and Regent of England* (Baltimore, 1933).
40. William Page, *London, Its Origin and Development* (London, 1923); p. 131 ff.
41. *Cambridge Medieval History*, VI, 218.

CHAPTER 16

Attestation of Charters in the Reign of John

More than two centuries ago Thomas Madox published his *Formulare Anglicanum* in which he assumed that a charter witness had seen and heard the document upon which his name appeared.[1] This remained the usual attitude toward attestation until a generation ago when Warner and Ellis published facsimiles of many early charters and some other documents. Among them were a charter and a letter about the charter which, according to their interpretation, proved that the witnesses of the charter had never seen it before it had been delivered,[2] and they pointed out two similar instances. From this arose the hypothesis among paleographers and historians of the 'constructive presence'[3] of witnesses about the end of the twelfth century,[4] at least as regards private charters. Recently the hypothesis has been extended to the royal charters of the period with little additional evidence.[5] The argument thus far has been raised upon only a narrow base of evidence although there exists enough information upon the subject to lift it from its present conjectural level.

The usual scholarly use of charter witness lists is biographical, but recently its social implications have been presented. These studies indicated that there was a definite order of witnesses in thirteenth century lists, that this order represented customary seating lists based upon social precedence, and that these arrangements could be used to illustrate and explain the organization of the English central assembly.[6] These studies have been attacked upon the grounds that the mathematical method of computation was incorrect and that witnesses were not usually present at transactions.[7] Unlike many historical problems the question of a method determining variation from a given order by frequency distribution is capable of proof beyond any doubt. *The method is correct.*[8] It proves beyond the solemn assertions that the 'method is not accepted' of even the most weighty of historical authorities that there is a high degree of orderliness in the charter witness lists.

The high degree of order in the witness lists cannot be dissociated from the question of the witnesses as a group together. It is true that even chroniclers tended to follow a definite pattern in naming social classes and in listing individuals. But when lists of persons were written by people who did not see the groups together the percentage of variation often runs very high.[9] In other words the existence of a consistently high degree of order creates a presumption that the groups were probably seen together.

With this as a background the question of attestation may be discussed according to the social status of the witnesses— the divine and saintly witnesses, the persons of high social status of the royal charters, and the witnesses of local charters, mostly lesser folk. The first is important only in theory. The second involves research into the actual presence of witnesses at the times and places given in the charters since the witnesses were of sufficient importance for their movements to be followed at times in other evidence. Unfortunately this cannot be done for the lesser folk, but there is a considerable body of evidence which can be used to explain their diplomatic practices.

I

In his *Formulare Anglicanum* Madox gave several instances of charters in which the names of divinity and of saints were used as witnesses, saying of the practice[10] 'and sometimes the

Attestation has been expressed in Unusual (I think I may say Fantastical) terms.' In view of this the recent presentation of a charter having some saints' names in the witness list hardly ranks as a discovery of any sort.[11] Its presentation as an illustration of attestation by *absent persons* is even more amazing. Supernatural beings hardly are of the category of persons in a legal sense.[12] If we must consider the matter with regard to theory then we must accept the medieval point of view and regard saints as present at the transactions for which their witness was invoked.[13] Far from proving that 'constructive presence' was common the invoking of saints tends to show the opposite. If it were easy to write in the names of persons without their knowledge or consent the scribe would merely have included the names of the nearest important men instead of invoking saints or divinity.

II

The problem of the attestation of charters at the royal court was somewhat different from that of the private charters, but since local clerks tended to imitate those of the great center, we might expect that their practice might follow that of the royal clerks. The king's court possessed a sufficient complement of men of great 'dignity' for the attestation of any other than the most exceptional charter and in its clerks the means of regular and effective administration of such documents. Thus there was no need to add the names of men who were not present. On the other hand the very authority of the charter with the royal seal might make the names unimportant since the witnesses would probably never be summoned to answer questions about it. This situation or some other cause did operate to make the charter witness lists of the fourteenth century somewhat unreliable.[14] But the thirteenth century was a different century and its practices were its own. We use the charters of King John because they are printed and thus easier to control than the witness lists of later kings which, in spite of Maitland's appeal decades ago, still remain unprinted.[15]

Fortunately for the attestation of the royal charters it is possible to do what is virtually impossible with respect to the private charters, actually 'control' the presence of witnesses by the use of other documents since they were such important men. Some were bishops who can be followed at times in episcopal documents, although, it must be admitted the lack of *Acta Episcoporum* is a handicap. Many of the witnesses of royal charters can be traced occasionally in the chronicles which usually show us when they were not at court. Many of these persons also appear frequently in royal documents of other types such as the close and patent rolls which tend to corroborate evidence of presence rather than to show persons absent. We must grant that the evidence does not provide a day by day account and that care must be taken to avoid arguments from silence. Yet if 'in general the evidence is against' the 'assumption that witnesses were present at the time of the transaction'[16] it should be easy to catch the clerks in mistakes especially in regard to the great men. Mr Haskins, let us note, does not produce a single instance of 'constructive presence' of a witness in an English royal charter.

Furthermore Mr Haskins' argument from analogy with the royal charters of France is superficial. He knows that the names of the great officers of state appear on French charters and authenticate them. Such authentication is conducive to 'constructive presence,' normally by deputy. As we shall see this was apparently happening in England to the justiciar's authentication of fines at this time. But Mr Haskins is at pains to point out that in England the use of official titles in charters was diminishing:[17] attestation was thus personal rather than official. There is not the slightest indication that any official's name was necessary and one of the most convincing bits of evidence is the great variety of names in the royal lists. If lists were 'cooked' they reveal an amazing ingenuity on the part of the clerks. Maitland's remarks upon the reliability of the witness lists of the royal charters of Henry III can be paralleled with instances in the charters of the reign of John:

> A doubt may well occur to us as to whether there may not be fictions lurking in the charter rolls, when we read that on a given day the king delivered a charter with certain men as witnesses, we are entitled to infer that on that day those men were really and truly, and not by way

of fiction in the king's presence. But having looked at a good many rolls of the thirteenth century (I must not speak of much later times) this doubt seems to me to be unwarranted. We see the witnesses changing day by day and can in some measure account for the changes. At one time the king is enjoying himself at one of his rural manors or hunting lodges; the witnesses will be for the most part officers of the household, though it may happen that some bishop or earl will be paying him a casual visit, and if so will be named in the charter. Then the king comes to Westminster for the dispatch of business; the number of charters he has to execute increases, and the quality of the witnesses changes; the great officers of state are mentioned, and, it may be, some of the judges. The king holds a parliament; the quality of the witnesses changes once more; four or five bishops, four or five earls or great barons will attest his deeds. Further, it often happens that several charters are dated on the same day and that the lists of the witnesses coincide but partially. If the scribe of the charter had before him some rota of 'gentlemen in waiting,' and took his list of supposed witnesses, we should surely expect that our list would do duty for a whole day.[18]

Let us turn to an actual check of the movements of men whose names appear frequently in the lists, first to the negative type of evidence which shows persons absent from the witness lists when they are known from other sources to have been away from court. Thus William Longsword, earl of Salisbury, who fought in and was captured at the battle of Bouvines, was out of the lists for a considerable period both before and after that battle.[19] The civil war provides a series of such instances. The chief conspirators, Robert Fitzwalter, Eustace de Vescy, the earl of Clare, William Mowbray, Fulk Fitzwarin, William Mallet, Simon de Kyme, John Fitzrobert, Maurice de Gaunt, Richard de Munfichet, William de Lanvalet, Geoffrey de Mandeville, William de Huntingfeld, Robert de Greslei, John, constable of Chester and Thomas Multon all disappear from the witness lists at about the proper time.[20] The rather faithful earls of Warenne, Arundel and Salisbury remain in the lists until just before they went over to

Prince Louis in the spring of 1216.[21] At about the same time
King John assigned the defense of certain distant castles to
Philip Ulcotes, Robert Vipont, Brian de Lisle, Geoffrey de Lucy
and the earl of Albemarle, who are thenceforth as absent from
the witness lists as the conspirators.[22] Even earlier the custody
of the castle of Rochester kept William d'Aubigne away.[23]

As has been mentioned, the attempt to collate episcopal
movements with charter records is disappointing. The most
detailed record is that of Hugh of Wells, bishop of Lincoln,
who apparently brought to Lincoln an ethusiasm for administrative documents which he had acquired as a clerk of the royal
court,[24] and began the long series of records which Lincoln
cathedral possesses. In the *Liber Antiquus* are many dated
charters of this period, but they begin only in 1214. Previous to
this the charter rolls show the bishop at Winchester and Corf
on the 21 and 24 of July 1213 and at St Paul's on 3 October.[25] For
1214 there are but few references in either series of documents.[26] In 1215 he appears in London on 9 and 15 January[27]
and at Banbury and Lincoln on 7 February and 21 March.[28]
Royal charters have him at Runnymede on 20 June and at
Oxford on 18, 19, 20, and 23 July.[29] Then there follows a series
of items which show him moving toward the Lateran Council:
Banbury (28, 29 July), Kyldeby (7, 8 August), Oxford (18, 21
August), London (28, 29 August), Maidstone (30, 31 August)
and Canterbury (1 September).[30] That he went to Rome for the
Council is known from a Lincoln document.[31]

The Lateran Council late in 1215 attracted a group of
eminent persons from England, several of whose names appear as witnesses at Dover early in September; the proctors,
Geoffrey de Craucomb on the first and the abbot of Beaulieu on
the fourth,[32] the bishop of Worcester and his friend, Alexander
Neckam, a famous writer, on the eighth.[33] In the same charter
with the bishop and Neckam appears William of Cheriton, a
local Kentish magnate and father of another writer, Odo of
Cheriton.[34] Two years earlier a band of prelates returning from
their exile during the Interdict, landed at Dover on 16 July and
proceeded to Winchester on St Margaret's Day.[35] The bishops'
names appear in charters dated at Winchester on 21 July and
Corf on 24 July.[36] Later in the year we read of a three day

session of prominent men at London followed by the resigna-
tion of the English crown into the hands of the papal legate at
St Paul's. The document reciting this act is in the rolls with its
list of important witnesses.[37] Arrangements were made for a
council at Reading, first in November and then postponed to
December, at which time the presence of many important men
is again seen in the witness lists.[38] Two days later the usual list
of witnesses appears at Reading.[39]

As samples of the evidence provided about officials let us
take the cases of Simon de Pateshull and Geoffrey Fitzpeter.
Simon was a judge of the curia regis throughout the portions of
John's reign covered by the charter rolls. We can thus compare
the evidence of the fines with those of the charters, and we see
that Westminster sessions from which he was absent usually
occur at times in which the charter witness lists indicate his
presence with the itinerant king.[40] However, he did not rank
among the greater barons, and thus the clerks of both the
charters and the charter rolls often stopped enrolling names
before they came to him. In 1 John he was apparently with the
king just before the Easter term but only two attestations
occur.[41] In the second year both fines and charters show him at
Dorchester on 19 April[42] and in the fifth year they find him at
Westminster about 26–27 January,[43] and at York on 19–26
February.[44] The sixth year sees coincidences of date and place
on 26 August at Aslacton, 9 December at Melkesham, 6–8
March at York,[45] while letters close and charters agree in
having him at Kenilworth on 10 March, at Feckenham on
19–20 March, and at Woodstock on 25–26 of the same
month.[46] Such coincidences for the seventh year show him at
York on 9–12 February and at Winchester-Clarendon on 18
April.[47] The ninth year a fine and a charter place him at
Hereford on 20 April,[48] while the fourteenth year sees him at
Westminster on 12 November and 1–2 December in fines and
charters.[49] Against this rather impressive record of agreement,
there is not a single discrepancy.

For purposes of controlling the presence of witnesses of
royal charters Geoffrey Fitzpeter's career is probably most
important. As justiciar and earl of Essex his name normally
appears at the head of the lists of lay witnesses. Furthermore,

his hand appears in all types of documents; patents, charters, fines, all bear his name. The evidence of the fines is especially important although the method of dating many of them makes it possible to fix the time of composition only within a week apparently. It was already the custom to date them so many weeks after Trinity, or Michaelmas, or Hilary, or Easter and apparently this means in the week following the first date. Thus a fine was dated at Hereford in the quindena of Easter, 1208 (April 20).[50] The charter rolls show the court at Tewksbury on 20 April, at Gloucester on 22 April and at Hereford on 24 April.[51]

For at least 60 days the places specified on charter rolls attested by Fitzpeter can be checked by data from fines, patents and letters close. Over three-fourths of these show the same place and for the others but few miles separate the places, except for a few instances. Of them only eight are of fines coinciding with the charters.[52] Usually when he was acting as judge, normally at London, he was absent from the witness lists of the royal charters if it was elsewhere but, as we shall see, there were important exceptions.[53] There are indications that at York (where the fines are dated accurately) that when present at fines he usually does not appear as witness in charters. Table 1 gives the numbers of charters, fines, and patents in which his name appears during a session at York in February and March 1204.[54] Thus two-thirds of the fines were executed on days when no other activity is recorded for Fitz-

TABLE 1. Number of Documents Signed by Geoffrey Fitzpeter, 19 February to 2 March, 1208

Document	February										March	
	19	20	21	22	23	24	25	26	27	28	1	2
Charters			2	1		1	2	2	1	1	5	
Fines	8				11	3		2		3		
Patents						1						1

peter. The unfortunate custom of dating fines by weeks precludes any definite results from the London evidence, but the York data together with the paucity of instances in which his name appears for fines and charters on the same day would tend to show that such work usually occupied his time on the days assigned to it.

However, a comparison between the dates and places of fines and charters shows that at times something is wrong. The first instance is of a charter at Porchester and a fine at Westminster on 26 April, 1200 but a defect in the fine complicates the problem.[55] In the spring of 1204 another series of Westminster fines and southern English charters bearing Fitzpeter's name seem incompatible.[56] Similar difficulties appear for the autumn and possibly for other times.[57] The most serious case of contradiction is in the late autumn of 1200. There the charters tell a coherent story of Fitzpeter's presence with the king at some distance from London from 19 October to 29 November.[58] Yet in the same period occur many cases of fines at Westminster in which his name appears.[59] Hoveden tells us that Fitzpeter was among the great men who witnessed the homage of the king of Scotland on 21 November and were present at the funeral of Bishop Hugh two days later.[60] Finally Fitzpeter's name appears in two fines of St. Katherine's Day, one at Lincoln and the other at Westminster.[61] Since no 'constructive presence' is suspected of the other judges of the two fines it would seem that the legal fiction had developed only in the case of the justiciar at Westminster when he was possibly served by deputy.[62]

This examination might be pursued at greater length by comparing the data for other men of the reign, but this is probably an adequate sample of the whole situation. We have seen thus far no case in which 'constructive presence' is suspected except in the case of Geoffrey Fitzpeter which is evident in the fines but not in the charters. It is obvious that legal fiction of the presence of officials had developed, possibly by deputy, but in view of the very personal character of attestation 'constructive presence' can hardly be extended by analogy to the charter witness lists.

III

Thus far we have the testimony of the witnesses, but what can the actual charter rolls themselves tell? When compared with the originals the standard of accuracy in detail is not high.[63] The scribes occasionally omit the names of witnesses, usually those at the end of the lists. Not all of the charters were enrolled: the most notable exception was Magna Charta. The copying was evidently done by ear, at least in some instances, since a considerable difference of spelling exists between original and roll which can be more easily explained as errors of hearing than of sight. In one interesting series in March 1205 charters are dated at Worcester on the 21st and 24th, at Woodstock on the 23rd, 24th, 26th and 27th, and a letter close at Woolward on the 24th.[64] Similarly the 'Woodstock' of 10 April, 1200 should probably be 'Worcester' since the court seems to have been at the latter place on the 9th, 10th, and 11th of that month.[65]

The charter rolls fortunately preserve sufficient evidence to enable one to secure a reasonably clear picture of the processes of their production. These documents were enrolled upon the recto of the membranes with some exceptions[66] and other administrative details on the dorso.[67] As can be seen in the following illustration the order of the charters does not follow the chronology of the dates of the charters (Table 2).[68] The documents of 22 September and earlier are 'by the hand' of the chancellor, Hubert, while those of 25 September and later are by the vice chancellors, Simon and John.

Two chance remarks in the rolls offer interesting clues to the solution of the problem of production of the rolls. In one the men of the hundred of Middleton are said to have carried off their confirmation charter before it had been enrolled.[69] This would seem to show that the roll was copied directly from the original charter rather than from a chancery draft.[70] The second item says that the charter of the abbot of Bec 'was written and sealed in Normandy in the fourth year of King John but it was delivered in the fifth year because he did not have money to acquit it before that time.'[71] Until payment was made the charter was evidently held in chancery. The order of

TABLE 2. Royal Charters Granted in the Period 31 August to 30 September, 1205

Membrane	Date	*Datum per manum*
11	12 Sept.	Hubert, archbishop of Canterbury
	22 Sept.	Hubert, archbishop of Canterbury
	25 Sept.	Simon de Wells and John de Grey
10	22 Sept.	Hubert
	25 Sept.	Simon and John
	26 Sept.	Simon and John
	7 Sept.	Hubert
9	31 Aug.	Hubert
	26 Sept.	Simon and John
8	22 Sept.	Hubert
	26 Sept.	Simon and John
	28 Sept.	Simon and John
	26 Sept.	Simon and John
	30 Sept.	Simon and John
	29 Sept.	Simon and John
7	3 Sept.	Hubert
	30 Sept.	Simon and John
	29 Sept.	Simon and John

the charters in the rolls is the order of delivery and to judge from it a good many persons did not have their money ready.

With the evidence above we may add the following item in the rolls about a charter:[72] 'This charter was made on 8 October in the presence of the king (and of three others named) and it was sealed by special mandate of the king.' The inference of the 'special' might seem to apply to the making of the charter, but it probably means only that the usual fee for it was waived and that the king's aged mother got her charter free. The rolls record another interesting document with fifteen witnesses duly listed. Then, to further strengthen the document seals were attached and the names of the owners of the seals added; fourteen of them were identical with the witnesses and appear in precisely the same order. The list of seals includes those of two men not listed as witnesses and probably not at court at the time of the transaction; their seals are out of their proper place according to their usual precedence. Apparently, the

witnesses had appended or had their clerks append their seals
at once and in the proper order, but the seals of the others were
added later in the vacant spaces on the charter.[73]

From the study of the royal charters no evidence emerges
which casts doubt upon the belief that the witnesses were
present at the place and date given in the charter, presumably
in such meetings as have been described by the historian of the
king's council.[74]

IV

Attestation of royal charters, as we have noticed, can be
controlled more readily than the local charter lists. It may be
said that in the course of an examination of a great body of
evidence for the lives of the writers of thirteenth century England no instance of 'constructive presence' appeared.[75] Although the general impression was that attestation was real
rather than 'constructive' control is difficult. Under the circumstances one may turn to evidence from legal records and
manuals of diplomatic practice for light upon attestation in
general and upon the evidence adduced to show 'constructive
presence' in particular. The evidence is discussed under the
heads of the function of the local charter, the customary practice relating to charters, and the possibility of 'constructive
presence' of witnesses.

The function of the local charter was not, as we might
expect, to convey property. This was done by livery of seisin.
The problem of the possession of property usually arose after
the death of the persons who had conveyed property since,
until his death, one had only to refer to the donor to learn
whether the possessor held as custodian, as vassal, or in some
other fashion. Suits for warranty of charter were frequent,
however. The purpose of the charter was well expressed in the
following charter clause:[76] 'Et ne successores mei hanc
elemosinam meam imposterum infirmare prevaleant pre-
sentem cartam sigillo meo munitam in libera potestate mea
propriis manibus optuli super altare beate Marie in monasterio
de Wardon.'

The local charter thus was drawn to meet a particular need, usually to protect the recipient of a gift from hereditary right. When a question of a holding came into litigation the presumption of the court were graded in favor of (1) hereditary right, (2) possession by seisin, (3) possession as a result of exchange or purchase, and (4) possession by gift. That is, a person who claimed that he had been given property had to show not only a valid charter ending the hereditary rights (if that were possible) but also he must prove that he had seisin. Land acquired by exchange or purchase might be lost through someone's prior right but in that case the purchaser was usually entitled to something of equivalent value.

If a recipient of a gift were disseised by heirs (as often happened) and then to prove disseisin he presented a charter which was at all open to question he might easily lose his right. Everything connected with the charter usually ran the gauntlet of searching inquiry because it so frequently interfered with the normal course of inheritance. Gifts were challenged with respect to the donor of the document or the document itself. The donor was too ill[77] or too young to know what he had done.[78] He was forced to do it or he had previously become a monk.[79] The seal of a document might have been forged,[80] or a true seal used by member of the family[81] or even by executors improperly.[82] Obviously it behooved the recipient of a gift to have it protected by as perfect a charter as possible by conforming to the customary practices regarded as necessary for the establishment of a sound charter.

In an age in which custom played so large a place in life we should expect that a common practice, especially one subjected constantly to judicial review, would develop along well defined lines even if we had not had a specific statement to that effect.[83] Furthermore we have in Bracton, who writes in the next reign, a very long and explicit statement of the way in which the parts of charters should be drawn. It is easy to see in extant charters that Bracton describes what actually was written. If Bracton is obviously describing actual practices here is there reason to doubt him when he discusses proper methods of charter witnessing?

Charter witnessing varied according to the status of the donor of the document. In the royal court, as we have seen, the dignity of the king required a group of men in attendance sufficient to satisfy the needs of ordinary attestation of ordinary royal charters. It had also the officials and clerks needed for regular and efficient administration, one of whose duties was the handling of charters. To a large extent this held true of the greater feudal lords, who had in their clerks and their retinues ample facilities for effective documentation. On the other extreme in social status there were the freemen grouped together in villages. One might expect a certain informality here based upon the fact that each one knew the other's business anyhow.[84] In between was the knightly class together with the persons who possessed a manor or a large part of one. They did not always have clerks available, and the ordinary freemen might not be considered sufficiently important to be used as witnesses in their major transactions. Thus they might have to bring in clerks to write their charters and if the transaction were of great moment they might feel it necessary to invite their feudal lords to witness it.[85] It happens that the evidence used to prove 'constructive presence' of witnesses comes largely from this class.

V

The history of the production of a charter included usually three phases at least after the preliminary negotiations (including the actual gift of which the charter was the confirmation) had taken place. These were (1) the making or writing of the charter, (2) the invitation to witnesses, and (3) the completion or publication of the charter (*confectio notae*). This was not necessarily the actual order of procedure. Indeed Bracton assumes (what was probably the common practice) that all things would be done under the eyes of the witnesses and thus probably at the same time.[86] He would have us remember that the essential point of attestation was the final act in which the acknowledgment of the gift and the acceptance of the gift occurred.[87] It was possible for witnesses to see this done for each witness separately, but this obviously was a very clumsy process.

Writing or Making of the Charter. The term 'to make a charter,' we might expect, could refer to all the acts incident to preparing and delivering a charter.[88] Yet it is clear that it was more generally used with respect to the manual act of writing the charter, since in a number of instances the term must refer to this narrower use of the term.[89] That we might use the term in this narrower sense we could assume, even if we had no other evidence, from the frequent appearance at the end of the witness lists of expressions such as 'Roberto clerico qui hanc cartam fecit' or 'Willelmo clerico qui hoc scripsit.' Since it is clear what Robert and William did or wrote we could infer what the 'making or writing of a charter' would be. The separation of the writing of the charter from the publication offers an obvious explanation of why occasionally the tenor of a charter and the witness lists are in separate hands[90] and why charters are sometimes preserved without witness lists.[91]

We introduce here the first of a series of documents upon which the doctrine of the 'constructive presence' of witnesses has been raised:[92]

> Karissimis Dominis suis, Willelmo comiti Warennie, domino Willelmo de Aubenio comiti Sussexie, domino Gileberto de Aquila, Willelmus de de Averenchis et Cecilia mater eiusdem, salutem. Quia ad cartas faciendas inter nos et abbatem et monachos de Ponte Roberti super manerio de Suttona iuxta Sefordiam presentiam vestram habere non potuimus, precamur et obnixe rogamus ut de cartis nostris in quibus ob securitatem obtinendum testes estis ascripti, testes esse velitis. Valete.

Of this Mr Haskins says, 'It was possible for a man to be asked by letter to witness a charter already made.'[93] The assumption that 'made' means delivery of the charter is by no means certain and in fact is probably less likely than that it means 'written.'

Invitation to Witnesses. By definition a witness was one who saw and heard,[94] or whose name had been placed in a charter.[95] There is, I believe, no evidence that one could legally witness in a constructive fashion. It was not enough that he said that he was invited to be a witness[96] and even less that his name had been inserted without his knowledge.[97] By attesta-

tion a witness accepted a legal liability to go to court, a liability
which frequently became a fact, especially if the charter was
unusual in any way.[98] It was, moreover, an expensive liability.
If called and not essoined the witness might be amerced.[99] If
summoned, in theory at least, he might be asked to fight a duel
for the integrity of the charter.[100] He had to be a responsible
person and one to whom the other side could not take exception.[101] In view of the responsibilities involved it is clear that
inviting witnesses was a serious business. The usual expression of invitation was apparently *rogare quod esset testis.*

Let us look now at the other two documents (to which we
add two more) which are used to prove 'constructive presence'
of witnesses.

> Robertus de Gurnay Willelmo de Tyth' (and eight
> others named). Precor vos quod sitis mihi testes quod feci
> monachis de Brueria escambium pro illa parte de Hidon
> quam Templarii tenent de me quam scilicet partem ipsi
> monachi de me quondam tenuerunt ad firmam. Va-
> lete.[102]

> His sibi amicis Rob. (and several others named) H.
> dei gratia prior de Cumbewelle et ejusdem loci conventus
> salutem in domino. Quum pro negotio domus nostre
> vendidimus dilectis fratribus nostris abbati et conventui
> de Ponte Roberti redditum annuum duodecim de-
> nariorum quos solebamus percipere de Henrico de Hot-
> legh et heredibus suis de dono Engerranni de Frecenevilla
> precamus vos quatinus huius vendicionis testes sitis. Va-
> lete. In huius autem rei fidem huic scripto sigilla nostra
> apposuimus. Iterum valete.[103]

> Reverendis dominis suis, domino Willelmo comite
> Warenne et domino Matheo vicecomiti Sussexie,
> Mathild. de Fressenvill, uxor quondam Reginaldi de
> Meinieres salutem. Obscecro (sic) vos sicut dominos
> meos karissimos, quatinus in cartis quas feci monachis de
> Ponte Roberti de terra de Fudiland cum pertinenciis, in
> quibus estis testes ascripti, testes esse velitis. Valete.[104]

> (To a series of men named) Petrus de Capella sa-
> lutem. Precor vos quatinus sitis testes de donatione illa
> quam feci deo et monachis de Saltreia de quinque acris
> terre et dimidia de terra mea in villa de Gamilenkeia in

perpetuam et puram elemosinam sicut carta mea testatur
in qua vos de eadem testes assignavi.[105]

If we assume, as some do, that these documents indicate
that the witnesses never saw the charters at all we still have
certain limitations to the practice as evidenced by them. In time
they would indicate a period in between the earlier custom of
personal presence of witnesses (as shown by phrases denoting
physical presence)[106] and of later personal attendance required by law because the courts tightened up on their rules of
evidence;[107] that is, a period covering a few decades on either
side of 1200. In area we can be certain only of Robertsbridge as
a center of the practice with two isolated instances elsewhere.
Of the five instances, two (Gurney and Combwell) mention no
charter and since none has survived they cannot be assumed
because persons could be asked to be witnesses to transactions
as well as to charters. Furthermore, if the practice of constructive witnessing were at all common we should have expected
that many acceptances of such invitations would have been
preserved.[108] They should have been of the greatest legal
value to the possessor of a charter whose witnesses had never
seen the charter and who would thus be forced to acknowledge in court that their knowledge of it was not too accurate.
None has survived! What have survived, moreover, are by this
interpretation converted into certificates of the non-
attendance of witnesses and one may well ask why monasteries should have kept evidence which the legal treatises of
the time regarded as endangering the validity of their documents.[109] Probably the most serious difficulty with this interpretation is the translation of 'quatinus sitis testes' as 'will you
say that you have seen and heard something which have never
seen or heard,' a definition which seems to be found nowhere
else than in this interpretation of these documents.

Another interpretation of the documents is that which the
editor of the Gurney document gave nearly a century ago
when he suggested that the documents were invitations to the
publication of the charter. Let us examine this suggestion. It
has at the outset the advantage of not straining the meaning of
'quatinus sitis testes.' Moreover, we can understand why
Robertsbridge and other houses might well preserve such

documents since they would indicate the donor's intentions and would thus supplement the verbal donation although naturally that would not be so valuable as a properly witnessed charter. This interpretation explains the lack of acceptances to such invitations to 'constructive presence': there was no need for them since the witnesses were actually present. By this interpretation these documents fit in a legal and proper environment since, as we have already mentioned, the parties of the documents were of precisely the social class which might find it difficult to secure proper witnesses easily and would thus be forced to invite witnesses by letter according to the custom of the time. Unless these are such invitations we have none of them.

There are objections to the theory that these documents are invitations to actual attestation. One is that excellent palaeographers and diplomatic specialists believe that they are invitations to be 'constructively present.' A second objection is that the documents give no date nor place, items which would be expected of invitations for the future. This is primarily a problem of diplomatic practice about which a cursory examination of the evidence is not at all conclusive,[110] although a more careful search of formularies and letter books might reveal evidence of value. A third objection is that some of the men invited to be witnesses were very prominent men who would hardly care to bother about such transactions. Most of the men named in the documents were apparently of the type of persons who would normally participate in attestation and other business of similar character.[111] In only two instances (Avranches and Fressenvill) were very important men invited and in both of these cases quite large grants of land were being considered, large parts of manors in fact. The gravity of the transactions would certainly have justified such eminent witnesses:[112] the grantor and grantee may even have gone into the presence of these witnesses and repeated their declarations as stated to be possible by Bracton.

Publication. According to Bracton the minimum attestation was two witnesses who swore without contradiction to the validity of the charter, but he also insisted that it was better for it to be done in some assembly, such as the hundred or county.[113] One court record states that a land transfer should have been confirmed by charter read before a particular hundred court.[114] The records show many instances of recitation before assemblies; in hundred and county courts,[115] in church,[116] in private courts,[117] in monastic chapters,[118] in unofficial groups,[119] and even in the royal court.[120] The number of accessible assemblies, the facility of publication and the legal punishments of failure to follow recognized procedure make it probable that most charters were read in assemblies before invited witnesses.

Suppose a charter were read in an assembly should all the names of those who were present be recorded as witnesses? The invited witnesses were naturally enrolled; in many cases, possibly in most, the entire charter with its witnesses was read before the group. The emphasis upon invitation suggests that the names of others should not be included—that this is the meaning of the 'et aliis' and similar phrases which usually end the lists. Probably also it explains the double list of witnesses which occasionally appears, one of which is said to be particularly responsible.[121] Later manuals also emphasize the necessity of acquainting witnesses with the contents of charters.[122]

The legal obligation of a witness was to give what evidence he had. Thus it is probably an unrealistic view to speak of 'constructive presence' at all, particularly in the thirteenth century. If the witness had been present at the making or writing of a charter his testimony was more valuable than if he had been at only the publication. If his name had been inserted beforehand in a charter and he had not been at the publication but had been informed later he could report what he knew. If the donor and donee had come before him and solemnly repeated the transaction he was in a better position to testify than if the other witnesses had told him. This can be seen in several cases before the courts in the early fourteenth century. In two cases witnesses said that they had been invited to be witnesses but that they had never seen the charter.[123] In a third case the witnesses admitted no knowledge at all.[124] The charters were declared invalid. In a fourth case witnesses stated that they had never seen the charter nor been at the ceremony of exchange of land for money in trust for the heir. In this case,

however, the donee had had seisin of his land and the donor
had told the witnesses what he had done. After the donor died
the donee was diseised, and the donee sued the donor's heir to
recover property of equivalent value. No one apparently denied that the donee's father had paid money for the land nor
that he had had seisin. Apparently the refusal of an equivalent
by the donor's heir was based upon the hope that the charter
was so bad that it would offset the donee's claims.[125] In this
she failed.[126] Yet, even here we notice that the man who had
failed to have the witnesses attend the proper ceremonies had
conveyed land fraudulently or carelessly so that the buyer was
later diseised.

In another and very interesting if involved case two charter witnesses testified that three years before his death Master
Geoffrey Gibbewin, while of sound mind, had made a charter
at the door of Oseney Abbey in favor of the abbey. A third
witness testified that the abbot had come to his home in
Oseney and had brought him before Geoffrey who then ac-
knowledged that the charter was his and asked the third witness to bear witness to that effect. The testimony of the two
witnesses should have been sufficient and the procedure in
regard to the third was proper, according to Bracton, if unusual and somewhat awkward. Then a few months before
Geoffrey died a certain Ovid with two canons of Oseney came
to the Bucks county court, asked freemen there to testify to the
charter's authenticity, and had the charter read in court. The
problem evidently hinged upon the intentions of Geoffrey
with the evidence hanging upon a pretty delicate balance. The
court decided in favor of the heirs but allowed Oseney a
substantial compensation,[127] possibly because Geoffrey had
lived there for a time.[128] The court believed that the abbot had
had seisin only as a custodian accepting the theory that a
hermit had acted for Geoffrey since the abbey had. This may
have been the decisive factor. Yet one has the feeling that the
unusualness of the procedure in regard to the charter probably
gave color to a suspicion that Geoffrey never really intended to
give the land to Oseney.[129]

The interpretation of documents as evidence of 'constructive presence' is supposed to be corroborated by the phraseol-

ogy about witnessing in the charters: 'Certainly from the end of the reign of Henry II the formulae which assert the physical presence of the witness grew steadily fewer until the old phrases are supplanted by the sterotyped *Hiis testibus.*'[130] An easier interpretation of the crystallization of phraseology of such phrases would seem to be that the practice itself had crystallized and that the local clerks were adopting the Hiis testibus of the royal charters. It would at least spare us the difficulty of having to believe that the more the words remained the same the more the practice changed. When witnesses of 1295 are reported 'knowing and hearing' a charter they were probably doing precisely what their ancestors in the reign of Henry II had done.[131]

From this study a few points stand out with some clearness. The control of the royal charters of King John shows witnesses where the charters say they are with as great accuracy as can be obtained. Although the charters were probably never challenged before their witnesses administrative routine apparently produced a high standard of accuracy of practice. The diplomatic practice of the local charters was evidently well defined and placed a high premium upon publication before witnesses in assemblies: so much so that probably most of the charters were prepared in this fashion. Witnesses were expected to see and hear charters: that they did so may be presumed. That they were usually together as groups is also probably true. Some witnesses placed beforehand in charters evidently did not appear at the proper time; others saw and heard the charter officially but privately. The number of these exceptions was probably small in view of the ease and facility of the regular method. Until evidence is presented actually showing that large numbers were absent we may presume that witness lists do represent definite groups summoned specifically to accept the responsibility of guaranteeing the authenticity of that very important document—the charter.

Notes

1. (1702), pp. xxxi–xxxiii.
2. *Facsimiles of Royal and Other Charters in the British Museum,* ed. G. F. Warner and H. J. Ellis (1903), nos. 68, 69.

3.   The term suggested privately by H. G. Richardson seems very satisfactory. To him and to C. R. Cheney I am indebted for criticism of the first draft of the article.

4.   For these references see G. L. Haskins, 'Charter Witness Lists in the Reign of King John,' SPECULUM, XIII (1938), 321, note 6. He has added no additional instances. Two other documents of similar character are noticed below.

5.   *Ibid.*, pp. 322–323. None of the charters or documents used to show 'constructive presence' is an English royal charter.

6.   See the list of my articles in SPECULUM, XIV (1939), 108, note 1.

7.   Haskins, *op. cit.* In private correspondence Mr. Haskins has made it clear that his criticism was upon the method. He holds that to prove order in a group of forty witnesses I must have millions and millions of charters each containing the names of all the witnesses. It shows that his language is sharper than his mathematics.

8.   The method (explained in earlier articles) is so simple that it should not need the *imprimatur* of learned mathematicians or statisticians. Suffice it to say that it was developed with competent mathematical advice and has been approved by the distinguished statisticians of the London School of Economics, Rhodes, Glass, and Kuczynski.

9.   Wendover has three lists. In the first the earls are mixed up with the barons and others, but not many of them are identical with persons in the list which I worked out. For the five (earls of Essex, Norfolk, and Hertford, constable of Chester, and Eustace de Vesci) there are seven misplacements in ten chances! (II, 114.) Wendover does better with the royalists of 1215: in 78 chances for misplacement he has 21 mistakes. If we take only the barons and lesser persons he has 20 errors out of 36 chances! (II, 117.) In his third list he makes only 3 mistakes in 190 chances in respect to a group which is scattered widely over the scale of social status. (II, 118–119.)

10.   Pp. xxxi–xxxiii.

11.   Haskins, *op. cit.*, p. 322.

12.   A point made in conversation by Dr. I. J. Sanders.

13.   A criticism by C. R. Cheney.

14.   About 1336 several witnesses were elsewhere than where the charters place them, but no attempt has been made to indicate the extent of the constructive presence in fourteenth century charters. H. C. Maxwell-Lyte, *Historical Notes on the Use of the Great Seal of England* (London, 1926), pp. 234–237.

15.   'History from the Charter Roll,' *English Historical Review*, VIII (1893), 736: *The Collected Papers of Frederic William Maitland* (1911), II, 298–309.

16.   *Op. cit.*, p. 321.

17.   *Op. cit.*, p. 322, note 6.

18.   *English Historical Review*, VIII (1893), 728. Maitland believed that no well-settled order existed in the lists, an observation which Mr. Haskins quoted with approval (p. 320). As a matter of fact the misplacement in the list which Maitland published is only about three per cent—the

highest degree of order which I have encountered in charter lists. This is a good illustration of the deceptiveness of appearances which are not tested.

19. Roger of Wendover, *Flowers of History*, ed. H. G. Hewlett (1887, Rolls Series), II, 78–80; *Rot. Chart.*, pp. 196b, 206b.
20. The list is in Wendover, II, 114–115; the last appearances before the rebellion are for Robert Fitzwalter, *Rot. Chart.*, 204b; for Vescy, 210b; for Clare and Mowbray, 210b; for Fitzwarin, 199b; for Kyme, 205; for Fitzrobert, 201; for Gaunt, 201b; for Munfichet and Mandeville, 204b; for Huntingfeld, 201; for Lanvalet, 206b; for Chester, 201b, 219b; and for Multon, 205.
21. Wendover, II, 181. For Warenne, *Rot. Chart.*, p. 221b; for Arundel, 209b, 214; and for Salisbury, 222b.
22. Wendover, II, 166–167. For Ulcotes, *Rot. Chart.*, p. 220; for Vipont, 214; for Lisle, 216b; for Lucy, 214; and for Albemarle, 221.
23. Wendover, II, 145; *Rot. Chart.*, p. 202.
24. *Rotuli Hugonis de Welles*, ed. W. P. W. Phillimore (London, 1909), I, p. ii.
25. *Rot. Chart.*, pp. 194b, 194 and 195 respectively.
26. *Ibid.*, p. 202b at London on 22 November; at Buggeden on 5 November and at Lincoln on 27 December. *Liber Antiquus de Hugonis de Welles*, ed. A. Gibbons (Lincoln, 1888), p. 73.
27. *Rot. Chart.*, pp. 203b, 204b.
28. *Liber Antiquus*, pp. 74, 75.
29. *Rot. Chart.*, pp. 210b, 213b, 214b, 217b; 214, 214b.
30. *Liber Antiquus*, pp. 75–80.
31. *Rotuli Hugonis de Welles*, I, pp. vi, 104.
32. *Rot. Chart.*, pp. 218b, 219b; Roger of Wendover says that these men, together with Thomas of Erdington, were royal proctors (II, 159, 161). The last named had gone to Rome and, to judge from his absence from the witness lists, was still there in the autumn of 1215. *Ann. Monast.*, IV, 401.
33. *Rot. Chart.*, p. 218b (and for the bishop, p. 219). For Neckam see my *Dictionary of Writers of Thirteenth Century* (Lincoln, 1936), p. 16.
34. *Ibid.*, p. 93.
35. Roger of Wendover, II, 81.
36. *Rot. Chart.*, pp. 194b, 194.
37. *Rot. Chart.*, p. 195; Wendover, II, 94–95.
38. *Rot. Chart.*, p. 195b; Wendover, II, 95, 96.
39. *Rot. Chart.*, p. 196.
40. The following terms are instances: Hilary and Easter of 2 John, Michaelmas of 6 John, Hilary of 7 John and Easter of 9 John.
41. *Rot. Chart.*, pp. 42b, 56b.
42. *Rot. Chart.*, p. 93; York Fines (Surtees Soc. no. 94), no. 17.
43. *Rot. Chart.*, p. 117; *Fines sive Pedes Finium*, ed. J. Hunter (London, 1835) I, 229, 308; *Arch. Cantiana*, IV, 281.
44. *Rot. Chart.*, pp. 133b, 120, 120b, 122; York Fines, nos. 208–232 *passim*.
45. Aslacton, *Rot. Chart.*, p. 136b; *Rot. Litt. Claus.*, I, 6; Melkesham, *Rot.*

242

242 TWELFTH CENTURY STUDIES

Chart., p. 140b, Hunter, I, 58; York, Rot. Chart., pp. 143, 144b, York Fines, no. 244.

46. Kenilworth, Rot. Chart., p. 144, Rot. Litt. Claus., I, 23; Feckenham, Rot. Chart., p. 145b, Rot. Litt. Claus., p. 23b; Woodstock, Rot. Chart., p. 145b, Rot. Litt. Claus., I, 24.

47. York, Rot. Chart., p. 162b, York Fines, nos. 251, 252; Winchester, Rot. Chart., p. 165, Clarendon, York Fines, no. 254.

48. Rot. Chart., p. 178, Hunter, I, 244.

49. Rot. Chart., p. 189b, Hunter, I, 255, York Fines, no. 456.

50. Hunter, I, 244.

51. Rot. Chart., pp. 177 (2), and 178. The problem is complicated by the 'constructive presence' of Fitzpeter at fines (see below).

52. These include the York instances mentioned below, the Worcester, Woodstock, Wulward problem mentioned in a later paragraph as an instance of clerical error and the problems of the next paragraph.

53. All four terms of 1 John except Easter when both the royal court and the curia regis were at London, all four terms of 2, 5, 6, 7, and 9 John with the exceptions mentioned below.

54. Rot. Chart., pp. 119b–122, 133b; York Fines, nos. 208–232; Rot. Litt. Pat., 38b, 39. The problem is complicated by the Leap Day (February 24) which may have been actually two days.

55. Only 'G' is given. Arch. Cantiana, II, 246; Rot. Chart., p. 50b. Fitzpeter was in London on 19–20 and 28 April, according to the charters. Rot. Chart., pp. 49b, 55, 51b respectively.

56. See Rot. Chart., pp. 127–132b; York Fines, nos. 233–234.

57. Rot. Chart., pp. 171b–173b. Cf. B. F. Davis, The Justices from 1166 to 1215 (Ms in Public Record Office Literary Search Room), pp. 55–56.

58. Rot. Chart., pp. 76b–100b passim.

59. Hunter, I, 29, 114; Archeologia Cantiana, II, 252; many more are listed in Davis, op. cit.

60. Chronica Magistri Rogeri de Hovedene, ed. W. Stubbs (London, 1871), IV, 141.

61. P.R.O. Fine, B.C. 25(1) 95/3, no. 13; Arch. Cantiana, II, 252.

62. A suggestion of Charles Johnson. The possibility that the justiciar's son, Geoffrey, might have been serving is ruled out by the son's age at the time. Curia Regis Rolls, III, 255.

63. For a careful comparison of originals and rolls see the charters in the Registrum Antiquissimum of the Cathedral Church of Lincoln, ed. Foster (Lincoln, 193), I, 128–142.

64. Rot. Chart., pp. 144, 145(3), 145b, and 145 respectively; Rot. Litt. Claus., I, 24.

65. Rot. Chart., 54; 44b–48b, 54, 55b.

66. Exceptions appear in Rot. Chart., pp. 31b, 134, and 207b. Note that the first exception is explained, 'Et ideo in dorso rotuli scribitur eo quod liberata erat die qua intravimus mare apud Sorham et–transmisit transcriptum ultra mare.'

67. *Rot. Chart.*, pp. 30–31b, 58–62, 96–104, 133b–134b, 165b–166b, 191b–192b, 187, 207–209b, 221b–222, 224.
68. *Rot. Chart.*, pp. 20–24b.
69. 'Homines domini regis de hundredo de Middleton habuerunt confirmationem domini regis de habendis libertatibus et consuetudinibus quas habuerunt tempore regis Henrici avi regis Henrici patris domini regis et homines illi apportaverunt confirmationem illam antequam esset inrotulata,' *Rot. Chart.*, p. 150.
70. H. G. Richardson has pointed out to me a curious error in *Rot. Chart.* (p. 111). The clerk apparently enrolling a series of charters with the same clause before the attestation ('sicut...testatur') put down the same witness list for all with the same data and place (Falaise, 27 Sept.) although the original of one (Round, *Calendar of Documents—France*, no. 556) shows that the last of the series had been made two days earlier at 'Boz' with a slightly different witness list.
71.\ *Rot. Chart.*, p. 117b. For other references to delivery and fees see *ibid.*, pp. 173b, 191. Maxwell-Lyte states that 'a charter in favour of the Bishop of Hereford was enrolled in 1241 from a draft which did not give the names of witnesses or the date.' The Latin upon which this is based reads, 'Et missum erat rotulo transcriptum sine testibus.' *Calendar of Charter Rolls, 1226–47*, p. 259. Does 'missum' mean a draft here? I should rather read it, 'And the transcript was placed on the roll without the witnesses.'
72. *Rot. Chart.*, p. 25b.
73. *Ibid.*, p. 129b. The additional names were those of Geoffrey, bishop of Winchester and Savaric, bishop of Bath, which appear among the names of the barons.
74. J. F. Baldwin, *The King's Council in the Middle Ages* (1913), pp. 13–15. His chief source is the *L'Histoire de Guillaume Maréchal*, ed. P. Meyer.
75. Russell, *Dictionary of Writers of Thirteenth Century England* (London, 1936). Note interesting coincidences of charters and other data under Gilbertus Anglicus (p. 39), Lawrence of Somercote (p. 82), Richard of Wendover (pp. 123, 124), Richard de Wicio (p. 127, note 3), Robert Grosseteste (p. 136), Simon of Langton (p. 154), Walter of Bibbesworth (p. 176), William de Monte (p. 196).
76. G. H. Fowler, ed. *The Cartulary of the Cistercian Abbey of Old Wardon* (Manchester, 1931), p. 53. The charter is given the tentative date, 1200–10.
77. *Curia Regis Rolls of the Reign of Richard I*, etc. (cited hereafter as *C.R.R.*), I, 257, 352, 387, 461; VI, 149, 218; IV, 43, 127.
78. *C.R.R.*, V, 15, 141–142, 272.
79. *Ibid.*, IV, 126, 149; VI, 347–348.
80. *Ibid.*, V, 144; VI, 40, 61, 177; VII, 305.
81. *Ibid.*, VII, 38.
82. *Ibid.*, VIII, 281.
83. 'Et Gillelbertus venit et congnoscit cartas: set dicit quod aliter fuerint

facte et alio tempore quam fieri debuerunt,' *C.R.R.*, VI, 303.

84. Of which the scene described below is a good illustration: 'Juratores dicunt quorum maior pars est de testibus nominatis in carta...dicunt... quod ad Pentecosten anno proximo preterito venit idem Rogerus et convocare fecit vicinos ad domum Roberti fratris sui...et ibi portare fecit predictum Symonem qui multum gravatus fuit infirmitate, et ibi legi cartam de feoffamento, et idem Symon quesitus si cartam et donum concederet, dixit quod sic, et dixit quod libere et benigne concederet quicquid vellent.' But Roger had not had seisin from the donor and lost the case, *Bracton's Note Book*, ed. F. W. Maitland (1887), II, 635.

85. Presumably the lord might object if the vassal gave land in frank almoign without his consent.

86. 'Debent etiam testes ad hoc vocari, ut sub presentia eorum omnia cum solemnitate procedant, ut veritatem dicere possint, si inde fuerint re-quisiti et eorum nomina debent in carta comprehendi. Et si in confec-tione carte presentes non fuerint, sufficit si postmodum in presentia donatoris et donatorii fuert recitata et concessa; et utilius et melius si locis publicis, sicut in comitatu, hundredo, ut facilius probari possit, si forte fuerit dedicta,' Henry de Bracton, *De Legibus et Consuetudinibus*, ed. G. E. Woodbine (1922), II, 119–120; ed. T. Twiss (1878), I, 299.

87. 'Si autem dicant testes quod presentes fuerint confectioni notae in quam utraque pars consensit donator et donatorius, hoc sufficit ad probationem licet presentes non essent ubi carta scripta fuit et assig-nata,' Bracton, *De Legibus*, ed. Twiss, VI, 141.

88. 'Et Johannes venit et defendit cartam et sigillum et dicit quod pater suus nunquam illam fecit?' *Bracton's Note Book* II, 1.

89. 'Set cartam nunquam viderunt nec interfuerunt ubi facta fuit, nec ubi ei seisinam fecit,' *ibid*, II, 238. 'Et ipsi iii jurati dicunt quod nunquam fuerunt in loco vel stallo ubi Radulfus terram illam ei dedit vel cartam illam ei fecit, *C.R.R.*, VI, 61. 'Juratores dicunt quod intelligunt quod predictus Henricus dedit predicto Gregorio . . . set non fuerunt ad cartam faciendam,' *C.R.R.*, VIII, 18.

90. Haskins, *op. cit.*, p. 322. Also P.R.O. Duchy of Lanc. Cart. Misc. II, fo. 25: R. L. Poole, *Studies in Chronology and History* (Oxford, 1934), p. 305.

91. A charter of Geoffrey, bishop of Ely, is without witnesses and seems to have had no seal, P.R.O. Ancient Deed B 39: pointed out to me by C.R. Cheney.

92. Henry Ellis, *Original Letters Illustrative of English History*, 3rd series (London, 1846), I, 25. P.R.O. A.S. 497. For it see also L. F. Salzmann, 'Mediaeval Witnesses,' *Sussex Notes and Queries*, V (1934–35), 120. Wil-liam's charter remains as Campbell Charter, IV, 3 in the British Museum. The charter of his mother is mentioned in confirmations at Penhurst Place. *Hist. Mss Comm.*, pp. 106, 148. The three men head the list of witnesses in the charter.

93. *Op. cit.*, p. 321.

94. Glanville, *De Legibus et Consuetudinibus Anglie*, ed. G. E. Woodbine (New Haven, 1932), p. 87.

95. Bracton *De Legibus*, ed. Twiss, I, 298; ed. Woodbine, II, 119.

96. 'Tres testes (dicunt) quod bene recolunt quod predictus Radulphus aliquando venit ad eos et eos rogavit quod essent testes in illa carta set cartam nunquam viderunt nec audierunt nec interfuerunt ubi facta est,' *Bracton's Note Book*, II, 238. 'Robertus de S. Johanne et alii testes nominati in carta requisiti si ipsi presentes essent ubi predicta Beatricia dedit eidem Thome terram illam, dicunt quod non interfuerunt set idem Thomas uenit ad domos ipsorum et rogauit quod testes in carta illa?' *Ibid.*, II, 284. Cf. also *ibid.*, II, 204–205 and Bracton, *De Legibus*, ed. Twiss, VI, 138.

97. *Bracton's Note Book*, II, 337; III, 668.

98. Cases in which witnesses were said to have summoned appear in *C.R.R.*, I, 97, 152, 342, 407; II, 26, 291; III, 265; IV, 148, 274; V, 29, 97, 111, 272, 277; VI, 61, 171, 218, 281; VII, 190; VIII, 117, 252, 376; *Bracton's Note Book*, II, 155, 168, 177, 178–179, 210, 221, 238, 277–278, 486; III, 204, 691.

99. *Bracton's Note Book*, II, 238.

100. Glanville, *De Legibus*, pp. 87, 142; *C.R.R.*, V, 144; VIII, 14.

101. *C.R.R.*, I, 315; II, 291; VI, 14; Bracton's Note Book, II, 210.

102. British Museum, Harley charter 43 B 17; edited by D. Gurney, *Record of the House of Gournay* (London, 1848), I, 614.

103. Hist. Mss Comm., Report on the Manuscripts of Lord de L'Isle and Dudley preserved at Penhurst Place, I, 95, L. F. Salzmann told me of this item.

104. *Ibid.*, I, 70. The charter is printed on p. 71. Its witness list commences with the abbot of Battle, the earl Warenne, and Matthew Fitzherbert and continues with several others. It is probably of the years 1215–17 according to the editor.

105. B. M. Harley Charter 83 A 45. The charter is *ibid.*, 83 A 51 and has precisely the same set of witnesses as the addressees of the other document which should mean, according to Mr Haskins' interpretation, that none of them saw the charter at all. The documents have been published in Warner and Ellis, *op. cit.* as nos. 68 and 69, who date them 'temp. Hen. II–Rich. I.'

106. Haskins, *op. cit.*, p. 321.

107. The evidence of the time of Bracton is, it seems to me, so conclusively against 'constructive presence' that it cannot be assumed at all then. In one way the really amazing thing about attestation and of charters generally is the fact that they remained in use in spite of the great advantages which fines gave in landholding.

108. One instance of such a document has been alleged which reads as follows (B. M. *Ms. Cotton, Vesp. F xv*, fols 210ᵛ and 218ʳ): 'Sciant presentes et futuri quod ego Reginaldus de Warenne et Reginaldus Brunus frater meus interfuimus inscripti testes ubi Stephanus de Scalariis dedit monachis de Lewes, etc.' *The Chartulary of St. Pancras of Lewes*, ed. L. F. Salzmann (1934), p. xviii. This is of the first part of the twelfth century when personal attestation is universally held to be the rule. For other similar statements of actual presence about which there

246   TWELFTH CENTURY STUDIES

is no doubt see Madox, *Formulare*, p. 4 and B.M. *Ms Harley 1063*, fol. 11ʳ. Professor Stenton directed my attention to the last mentioned item.

109. That even Robertsbridge did retain evidence disadvantageous to itself appears in the admission on no. 28 that if these documents were shown to the abbey's enemies, they would be more helpful to them than to the abbey. Hist. Mss. Comm., Penhurst Place, ɪ, pp. xviii, 48.

110. An examination of several collections, notably B.M. *Add. Ms. 8167*, failed to uncover a document of precisely proper type. Dates and places are given, for instance, when a knight sends notice to his man to have hospitality ready for guests (fol. 128ʳ), or when a knight invites a bishop to be present at the dedication of his church (fol. 174ᵛ), or when a friend is invited to a wedding (fol. 178ᵛ) while time and place are not given in letters asking a bishop to consecrate a clerk (fol. 168ᵛ), or even when a baron asks a knight to accompany him to a tournament (fol. 106ʳ).

111. The names of the persons in the Robertsbridge documents can be checked in the H.M.C. of Penhurst Place where it will be seen that most of them occur frequently as witnesses.

112. Notice that one charter in the Penhurst Report had evidently been published in the royal court in the early years of King John. *Ibid.*, pp. 59–60.

113. Bracton, *De Legibus*, ed. Woodbine, ɪɪ, 120; ed. Twiss, ɪ, 300. On the importance of the county court as an agent of publicity see W. A. Morris, *The Early English County Court* (Berkeley, 1926), pp. 136–139; on the hundred, H.M. Cam, *The Hundred and the Hundred Rolls* (London, 1930), pp. 112–113, 183–184.

114. 'Et dicit quod nunquam venit in hundredo ubi carta illa confici debuit, *Bracton's Note Book*, ɪɪɪ, 691.

115. *C.R.R.*, ɪɪɪ, 332; vɪ, 275; vɪɪ, 309–310; *Bracton's Note Book*, ɪɪ, 238; ɪɪɪ, 691; H.E. Salter, *Cartulary of Oseney Abbey* (Oxford, 1934), ɪɪ, 252; ɪv, 69; C.W. Shickle, ed. *Ancient Deeds belonging to the Corporation of Bath* (Bath, 1921, Bath Record Soc.), p. 3.

116. *C.R.R.*, ɪ, 22.

117. *Ibid.*, ɪv, 7, 317.

118. *Ibid.*, vɪ, 181.

119. *Ibid.*, vɪɪɪ, 125.

120. *Ibid.*, ɪ, 155.

121. D. C. Douglas, *Feudal Documents from the Abbey of Bury St Edmunds* (London, 1932), p. xliii. The suggestion that one list was not present does not seem probable especially since it includes a name which should be that of the charter scribe.

122. H. G. Richardson has most kindly pointed out the following references. 'Et preterea testes qui nominantur in carta debent precari a parte recipiente ut testes fiant,' Cambridge, Gonville and Caius Coll. *Ms. 205*, fol. 315; Univ. Lib. *Ms Mm i 27*, fol. 79b. Robert Carpenter, *ca* 1261, for whom see *Eng. Hist. Rev.*, ɪ (1935), 28. 'Et debunt omnes testes esse rogati et conscientes et formam pacti sive empcionis scientes', Camb.

Univ. Lib. *Ms Ee i 1*, fol. 225ᵇ. John of Oxford, for whom see Russell, *Dictionary*, p. 70. 'Et non requiritur quod omnes testes sint presentes set muniantur per illos qui sunt presentes. Attamen bonum esset quod essent presentes et potissime in civitatibus et burgis ubi major, ballivi et aliquando aldermanni ponuntur in testes,' Longleat, *Ms. 37*, Thomas Sampson, fourteenth century.

123.   *Bracton's Note Book,* II, 238, 284.

124.   'Set de alia carta et dono nichil sciunt, scilicet de dono secundo,'*ibid.*, II, 204–205.

125.   Relying upon the situation described by Bracton. 'Et tamen nihilominus valet, licet scriptura non intervenerit, dum alias habet probationes,' Bracton, *De Legibus*, ed. Woodbine, II, 108; ed. Twiss, I, 262.

126.   *C.R.R.*, VIII, 8.

127.   *Cartulary of Oseney Abbey*, VI, 177–179. This item was pointed out to me by C.R. Cheney.

128.   'Quod perhendinans in abbatia,' *Bracton's Note Book*, III, 204.

129.   *Bracton's Note Book*, III, 203–206.

130.   Haskins, *op. cit.*, pp. 321–322.

131.   F.J. Baigent and J.E. Millard, *A History of the Ancient Town and Manor of Basingstoke* (1889), p. 607.

CHAPTER 17

The Canonization of Opposition to the King in Angevin England

In 1215 the leader of the baronial army, Robert Fitzwalter, "styled himself piously and grandiloquently 'Marshal of the army of God and Holy Church.' " [1] While the human conceit that God fights on the side of the speaker is widespread and by no means confined to the thirteenth century, the basis for such an assertion is often worth seeking. In this case others who favored the anti-royal side believed the same. Thus the chronicler of Melrose stated,[2]

> It ought to be known that no one in his right mind ought to censure Simon (de Montfort) or call him by the name of traitor. For he was not a traitor but a most devoted adherent and faithful protector of the Church of God in England, a shield and defender of the kingdom of England.

In the Song of Lewes much the same feeling of divine approval of the anti-royal forces appears,[3]

> Victoris sollempnia sanctaeque coronae
> Reddunt testimonia super hoc agone;
> Cum dictos ecclesia sanctos honoravit,
> Milites victoria veros coronavit.
> Dei sapientia, regens totum mundum,

Fecit mirabilia bellumque jocundum;
Fortes fecit fugere, virosque virtutis
In claustro se claudere, locis quoque tutis.

The whole poem betrays a spirit of "moderate and deeply
moral and religious feeling" which was truly remarkable in the
moment of triumph.[4] This attitude should probably be considered along with the noteworthy series of contemporary
antiroyal leaders who were honored, partially at least, as
saints.

The first and greatest of these saints was Thomas Becket.
So great was his fame that it has tended to obscure the remarkable group of men who followed him. Hugh of Lincoln, Edmund Rich, and Thomas of Cantilupe were all rather ascetic
and were actually enrolled among the saints. Stephen
Langton, Robert Grosseteste, and Robert Winchelsey might
well have been saints: they were good men as well as able
scholars and political leaders. To their number may be added
Simon de Montfort and Thomas of Lancaster, both laymen.
These men provided much of the most effective leadership
against the king, and their acts have become a part of every
account of the constitutional history of the period. However,
they also seem to have given a particular type of leadership to
their followers which produced a remarkable *esprit de corps*.
Part of this was probably based upon the success of these men,
part upon their character: both had a strong appeal for the
English people. Because it was apparently in large measure the
political side of the careers of these men which led the English
people to give them the honors of sainthood popularly, we
may call them political saints.

The tremendous response of the English to the martyrdom of Thomas Becket was not wholly religious. The Archbishop was vain, rather overbearing, self-confident: in general, not a likable type of feudal prelate. His type usually
attracted rather unfavorable comment in the late twelfth century. Even his uncomfortable undergarments and violent
death, protecting the privileges of the Church, cannot explain
all of his popularity. The political situation seems to have been
partly responsible. By 1170 Henry II had reduced the baronage
to order and was taking back many of the privileges which the

Church had assumed in the troublous times of Stephen. The regular and effective collection of revenue made Henry's efficient administration distasteful to many who were already beginning to forget the evils of lax government. The rising boroughs found that Henry was slow to grant civic privileges. Many classes of Englishmen were thus willing if not actually anxious to devise some check upon the ever more powerful king. By his resistance and death Becket stayed the royal advance. The king's penance at the martyr's tomb was such as any Englishman could understand. In the person of Becket resistance to the king had been canonized.

Saint Thomas Becket had a singularly wide appeal. The Church did not forget that he had been Archbishop of Canterbury. In the time of Henry III, when the clergy threatened with excommunication those who would violate the charters of English liberties, they did it

> Auctoritate Dei patris omnipotentis filii et spiritus sancti et gloriose Dei genetricis Marie et bonorum Apostolorum Petri et Pauli omniumque Apostolorum beati Thome Archiepiscopi Martiris omniumque martirum beati Edwardi Regis Anglie omniumque confessorum atque virginum et omnium sanctorum...[5]

As Archbishop, also, he had been a feudal baron and had sat in court among the most powerful in the land. Since the baronial ideal was all too frequently a successful revolt, it is not surprising that the baronage should regard with favor a fellow-member who had defied the king so successfully as St. Thomas. Becket also possessed an appeal for the boroughs, for he was a Londoner by birth. Matthew Paris tells of the dream of a priest in 1243. The priest saw the martyr destroy the newly built walls of London and allege that these walls had been raised *in contumeliam et prejudicium Londoniensium.*[6] Thus in the veneration of St. Thomas Becket there existed an element of unity among three important classes of the kingdom. He remained the most popular English saint for centuries.

Next to Becket in time and apparently in popularity as a saint was Hugh of Avalon, Bishop of Lincoln. Genial of character, loving a joke, sincere in his ecclesiastical labor, and wide in his sympathies, many knew him as a friend. The Jews be-

wailed his passing as that of one who protected them during
the crusading hysteria of 1189–1190. He stood up manfully for
what he considered his rights against both Henry II and
Richard. In the latter case he voiced the protest of a considerable portion of England, and the king backed down.[7] Like
Becket, Hugh of Lincoln stands out as a successful rebel
against royal power. It was fitting that he was canonized in
1220 in the year of the great translation ceremony of St.
Thomas by a third member of this group, Stephen Langton.

With Stephen Langton have been associated the man-
oeuvers which led to Magna Carta, one of the greatest of
checks upon English royalty. Langton was an all-round
character—scholar, rebel, administrator—and in all of these
capacities he had notable success. It is needless to sketch his
career, but it should be pointed out that he was eligible for
canonization both on account of his character and of the miracles which followed his death.[8] He probably failed of canonization because King John had drawn him into a position of
hostility to Innocent III. Langton continued the tradition of
anti-royal leadership by the Archbishop of Canterbury.

In this he was followed by Edmund of Abingdon who was
of a very ascetic and contemplative nature. Archbishop Edmund was hardly the man to act as a political leader in
thirteenth-century England: he had not the vigor and practical
skill of a Langton. Had he continued to act as a leader throughout his life, he might have endangered the tradition of effective
leadership against the king on the part of the Archbishops.
Fortunately he elected to retire to Pontigny as Becket had
done. This act fulfilled a prophecy attributed to St. Thomas[9]
and probably strengthened the belief of many in the right-
eousness of the anti-royal forces. Like Becket also, St. Edmund was entered into the calendar of saints rather quickly.[10]
With St. Edmund may be considered Thomas Cantilupe,
Bishop of Hereford. Among the most likable of English prelates, he shared in the political controversy of his time, generally against the king, until he finally withdrew to France.
Although never an outstanding leader he bore a creditable
name as a politician, and in his canonization he is at least
partially a political saint.[11]

A leader resembling Langton in many ways appeared in Robert Grosseteste, Bishop of Lincoln. Always a great scholar, he undertook the care of the vast diocese of Lincoln with such energy that he appeared terrific to clergy and laymen. Such a robust character could hardly have been other than a leader in the anti-royal forces of England. His resistance of papal claims upon the English Church apparently prevented his canonization, although it was favored by powerful parties.[12] His tomb in Lincoln Cathedral, near that of St. Hugh, became famous for the many miracles occurring there.[13]

In Rishanger's chronicle there is an interesting account of Grosseteste's relations with Simon de Montfort. The Bishop was tutor to de Montfort's children and correspondent with members of the family. Parallel to Becket's prophecy for Edmund of Abingdon comes Grosseteste's reputed prophecy for the Montforts. Putting his hand upon the head of de Montfort's oldest son, the Bishop is alleged to have said, according to the chronicler, Rishanger,[14] "O my dearest son, both you and your father will die upon the same day and in the same way for the cause of justice."

Simon de Montfort was the greatest of the anti-royal leaders and his administration of the government marked the height of anti-royal organization in the thirteenth century. His appealing personality and sincerity made him an almost ideal incarnation of anti-royal feeling. It is not surprising that writers liked to recall his close association with Bishop Grosseteste. He was hardly dead before miracles were performed at his tomb.[15] Rishanger tells of the terrible storm with intense lightning and darkness which came over England when de Montfort died.[16] So great was the veneration of de Montfort that Henry III felt it necessary to forbid it and remind the people that the fallen hero was excommunicate at death. This passage from the Dictum de Kenilworth reads:[17]

> Rogantes humiliter tam dominum legatum quam dominum regem ut ipse dominus legatus sub districtione ecclesiastica prorsus inhibeat, ne Simon comes Leycestriae a quocunque pro sancto vel pro justo reputetur, cum in excommunicatione sit defunctus, sicut sancta tenet ecclesia; et mirablilia de eo vana et fatua ab aliquibus

relate nullis unquam labiis proferantur; et dominus rex
haec eadem sub poena corporali velit districte inhibere.

Prayers were written in his honor as well as a hymn imploring
his aid.[18] In a political song of the period he was compared to
Thomas Becket as we might expect:[19]

> Mès par sa mort, le cuens Mountfort conquist la victorie,
> Come ly martyr de Caunterbyr, finist sa vie;
> Ne voleit pas li bon Thomas qu perist sainte Eglise,
> Ly cuens auxi se combati, e morust sauntz feyntise.

In the reign of Edward I, Archbishop Winchelsey has
some claim as a popular anti-royal leader. So successful was he
that the king "could not wholly forgive the man who had
brought on him the greatest humiliations of his life."[20] Since
his name was offered with that of another anti-royal leader,
Thomas of Lancaster, in 1327, by petition to Parliament as one
for whom canonization should be sought, it may be assumed
that miracles had occurred over his relics.[21] The leaders of the
reign of Edward II seem to lack some of the finer qualities of
character typical of the earlier ones. Upon the violent death of
Thomas of Lancaster miracles occurred in profusion, even
though the king forbade his veneration.[22] For him an office
was composed in which the parallel to Becket in name and in
manner of death was stressed:[23]

> Gaude Thoma, ducum decus, lucerna Lancastriae,
> Qui per necem imitaris Thomam Cantuariae;
> Cujus caput conculcatur pacem ob ecclesiae,
> Atque tuum detruncatur causa pacis Angliae;
> Esto nobis pius tutor in omni discrimine.

A layman and excommunicate, suffering a political death
which to a very large part of Europe must have seemed justified, he lacked practically every qualification to rank as a
religious saint. His "martyrdom" was one of the factors favorable to the accession of Henry IV at the end of the century.

The English people had shown that they regarded a number of anti-royal leaders as saints largely on account of their
political activity. Each of these men had combated one or more
acts of the kings in which the latter seemed clearly in the wrong
in the eyes of many Englishmen. Precedent after precedent

254 TWELFTH CENTURY STUDIES

had occurred in which the anti-royal politician appeared on
the side of justice. For this reason the leaders probably came to
represent justice and even God. The growth of this theory
would be characteristically English in that it was based upon a
series of concrete acts.

There existed to a certain extent in the minds of Englishmen a kind of communion of these saints. The alleged
prophecies of Becket for Edmund and of Grosseteste for the de
Montforts are instances of this. So are the comparisons of de
Montfort and Lancaster to Becket. Certain other associations
would be easy to recall. Four of these men had been Archbishops of Canterbury. Two had been Bishops of Lincoln and lay in
its cathedral performing miracles. Langton had presided at the
ceremonies of 1220 for both St. Thomas and St. Hugh. Winchelsey and Lancaster were recommended as subjects for
canonization by a petition to Parliament. These saints were, of
course, before the public as effective leaders against the king.
Whatever their relation, both the feeling that the anti-royalists
represented justice and the popular canonization of anti-royal
leaders remain as facts in the thirteenth-century political situation. A number of questions arise as to their significance.

There are several indications that these facts combined to
produce what seems almost a cult of political sainthood—a
consciousness that this group represented justice and that in
their veneration justice was honored. Thus one account of the
miracles of de Montfort mentions that "miracula fiunt pro
Symone de Mounteforti et sociis suis," and later miracles
occurred at the tombs of two knightly followers of Lancaster,
who were killed at the same time as he: Henry de Montfort
(note the name) and Henry Wylyngton.[24] This suggests that
the English people were ready to grant the honors of political
sainthood to even the humbler martyrs. This fact, together
with the number of these saints and the regularity with which
miracles occurred after the death of each, seems to show a
fairly sustained emotional attitude. It would seem that an easy
and almost unpunishable way of showing hostility to the king
would be to invoke one of these saints. However, with respect
to this as well as in other regards, the lists of miracles and other
evidences of the attitude of the times need to be examined for
their political implications.

Excellent evidence of the character of the appeal of one of these saints remains in the early catalogue of the miracles of Simon de Montfort.[25] This list includes miracles wrought upon many ranks of society. Over one hundred persons are named in such a way that it is difficult to define their social status. There were, however, fourteen knights and at least six ladies. The city of London is represented by three citizens and the professions by a merchant, a carpenter, and a miller.[26] Perhaps the most astonishing feature of the list is the number of religious persons who felt themselves benefited by the excommunicate de Montfort. Of the nearly forty clerks mentioned, the most prominent was an abbot, and there were numerous monks, friars, and priests. Several of these had already visited the shrines of such orthodox saints as Becket and Robert of Knareborough. The clergy are of special importance because in their sermons they could easily give publicity to the saints by whose sanctity they were healed. In any event the clerks were normally men of authority and in positions to encourage the veneration of those who they felt deserved veneration.

The statements of witnesses are also very suggestive. For instance, there is the case of Ralph of Thanet to which all the isle of Thanet is called to witness.[27] Of the recovery of a certain Alice the whole village of Burton Novereis is witness and of Roger Horsman the village of Bocland.[28] So also the incredulous or curious may learn from all of the parish of Evesham of the cure of Olive of Leyminster; from the abbot and monastery of Winchcombe, the recovery of the monk, William de Sarle; and from the village of Hide in Kent of the good fortune of its vicar, Roger.[29] Thus the good news spread so rapidly that it is no wonder people flocked to Evesham, enabling the monastery there to collect accounts of more than a hundred miracles in relatively few years. The shrines of these men were obviously centres of dissemination of interest. However, crowds even flocked to an image in St. Paul's, London, which was thought to resemble Thomas of Lancaster.[30]

Another question is in regard to the effect of political sainthood upon the conduct of the struggle against the king. The political saints led largely by their moral and political advantages. What violence occurred was mostly on the part of the king. Becket, de Montfort, and Lancaster all died in the course of the struggle. Of the kings, Edward II alone suffered violence, and his death aroused only a flicker of moral enthusiasm. Even when de Montfort and his followers were taking power from the king, they retained an exemplary and even courteous regard for the persons of the royal family. May we not believe that it was due in large part to the "moderate and deeply moral and religious feeling" inspired by the political saints that the constitutional struggles so seldom descended to the plane of a bitter civil war?

One result of political sainthood was that it offset the charge which was laid against the anti-royal forces in the thirteenth century—treason. Outside of the island the position of the English anti-royalists was seldom understood. The Curia mistrusted Langton and Grosseteste and excommunicated de Montfort and Lancaster. Louis IX, as arbiter between the king and his opponents, could see only the royal side. In France those who opposed the king were feudal rebels: in England they might be saints.

The canonization of hostility to the king had a more permanent effect than the immediate one of offsetting the charge of treason. It tended to neutralize the supernatural attributes of royalty. The king signed his charter, "..., by the grace of God, king of England, lord of Ireland, etc.," and the phrase "by the grace of God" had more than a hopeful significance. Coronation with its ceremonies of anointment and consecration by the bishops lent ecclesiastical approval to the ceremonies and gave the kingship a kind of indelible character, almost episcopal in nature. In England as in France the king began to exercise thaumaturgic powers and healed the sick by his touch.[31] These were powerful advantages, but the canonization of the rebels was more than a counterbalance. Saints ranked higher than kings in the Middle Ages.

The English royalty might possibly have overcome this advantage of the opposition by weighting the balance of sainthood on their own side. This happened in France, as Professor Gerould has stated:[32]

> The Capetians might lack the energy and sagacity of
> the house of Anjou, for example, but they were more
> highly favored of Heaven than any other sovereigns in

Europe: and in the long run they gained solid power from such imponderables as miraculous unction and the gift of healing...Feeling is, after all, one of the great realities of politics in any age.

Since the Capetian dynasty regarded itself, and was regarded, as carrying on the succession of Merovingian and Carlovingian rulers, it benefited also, without much doubt, from the extraordinary and complicated growth of the *chansons de geste* in the second half of the eleventh century....It would be absurd to argue, of course, that the royal line of France fostered the growth of the Charlemagne legend in order to strengthen its own position....It is almost certain, however, that they profited from the popular fame into which the great emperor emerged.

The French were also aided by the prestige of Louis IX, the embodiment of justice, who quickly became St. Louis. Finally there was Joan of Arc who appeared as the incarnation of successful resistance to England. No doubt it was easy to believe in the divine right of a line of kings traced back to Clovis and Charlemagne, possessing a Louis IX, and aided miraculously by a Joan of Arc, and to feel in its steady increase of power a manifestation of divine approval.

In England somewhat the same development began. There were among the early Anglo-Saxon kings a number of confessors and martyrs, often with a strong local appeal, like Edmund or Oswald. None attained to the status of a country-wide hero. Professor Gerould has urged that the legends of King Arthur were encouraged as an aid to the Angevin dynasty by Geoffrey of Monmouth.[33] King Alfred was a great king—possibly too Anglo-Saxon to appeal to the ruling Normans. Edward the Confessor was a rather languid character. As late as 1245 Henry III paid his court poet to write of the lives of St. George and St. Edward.[34] In spite of these indications of attention to royal sainthood the cult never seems to have developed much strength. No legendary hero attained the place of Charlemagne in the imagination of the English, nor did any of the Angevins reach the saintly dimensions of Louis IX, and St. Charles I can hardly be compared to Joan of Arc.

The only Angevin candidates for political sainthood lived too long. It is possible that if Richard I had died before England had had to pay his ransom, or if Edward I had passed away by 1297, either one might have been enrolled among the saints and have raised by his death the position of royalty in England to somewhat the supernatural elevation of French royalty. Nevertheless, it would have been difficult for either of them. Against the background of Thomas Becket, Hugh of Lincoln, Stephen Langton, Edmund of Abingdon, Robert Grosseteste, and Simon de Montfort, the character of these crusaders would not have stood out as did that of Louis IX against his opposition. French royalty contended largely with more strictly feudal foes whose operations possessed little moral value. Especially in their supernatural attributes, the difference between the anti-royal forces of England and France is tremendous.

A final question we may ask is of the relationship of political sainthood to the development of Parliament. Since some of the saints helped shape parliamentary action, it is possible that they gave this institution some prestige. Was Parliament looked upon as the successor of the saints, and its spirit regarded as a continuation of their confident assertion of rights against the king? Did the growth of Parliament and of other effective means of dealing with the king cause the decline of political sainthood in the fourteenth century? Or was this decline a result of a lack of faith? Certainly England produced no saints in this century.

For any subject in such an ecclesiastical age as the thirteenth century the ecclesiastical and supernatural implications deserve consideration. The fact of the popular canonization of several anti-royal leaders, with no parallel canonization of contemporary kings, is certainly significant whether or not it was acutally part of a cult of political sainthood. This phenomenon was probably partly responsible for the dignified attitude of the anti-royalists. It certainly helped to neutralize the supernatural attributes of the English royalty by raising rebels to the status of saints and rebellion to the realm of sanctity. Its relationship to the rise of Parliament is uncertain and needs further study. However, the canonization of opposition to the king was one factor, possibly an important one, in elevating the anti-royal organization to a position of respectability and power in England.

Notes

1. W. S. McKechnie, *Magna Carta* (Glasgow, 1914), p. 34
2. Quoted by J. O. Halliwell in the introduction to *The Chronicle of Willian de Rishanger* (London, 1840, Camden Society), p. xxvii.
3. *The Political Songs of England, from the reign of John to that of Edward II*, ed. Thomas Wright (London, 1839, Camden Society) p. 73.
4. *Ibid.*, p. 71.
5. *Statutes at Large*, ed. O. Ruffhead (London, 1763−65), i, 21.
6. *Chronica Majora*, ed. H. R. Luard (London, 1872−83, Rolls Series), iv, 93−94.
7. J. H. Round, *Feudal England* (London, 1895), pp. 528 ff.
8. See *Dictionary of National Biography* under his name. In this study "miracle" means not the actual accomplishment of some exceptional act but acceptance of the act as accomplished. This is an arbitrary definition but the qualification of each statement might prove to be an element of complication and confusion in a study where the important fact is the belief, rather than the act itself.
9. Matthew Paris, *Chronica Majora*, iv, 74, 328.
10. For a list of biographies see Thomas Hardy, *Descriptive Catalogue*, etc. (London, 1871), iii, 87−96.
11. *Ibid.*, pp. 217−220.
12. See *Dictionary of National Biography* under his name; H. Wharton, *Anglia Sacra* (London, 1691), ii, 343; *Letters from Northern Registers*, ed. J. Raine (London, 1873, Rolls Series), pp. 87, 182.
13. *Annales Monastici*, ed. H. R. Luard (London, 1864−69, Rolls Series), i, 336, 344; *The Chronicle of William de Rishanger*, p. 7; *Flores Historiarum*, ed. H. R. Luard (London, 1890, Rolls Series), ii, 373, 393.
14. *Op. cit.*, p. 7.
15. *Chronica Monasterii de Melsa*, ed. T. Burton (London, 1866−68, Rolls Series), ii, 131. A very detailed list is printed as a supplement to Rishanger's chronicle.
16. P. 47 and also pp. xxxiv−v.
17. *Select Charters*, etc., ed. W. Stubbs, 9th ed. by H. W. C. Davis (Oxford, 1921), p. 409.
18. Wright, *Political Songs*, p. 124.
19. *Ibid.*, p. 125.
20. W. Stubbs, *Constitutional History of England*, 4th ed. (Oxford, 1906), ii, 161.
21. *Ibid.*, p. 387.
22. *Flores Historiarum*, iii, 206, 213, 347; *Vita Ed. II auctori Malmesberiensi* in *Chronicles of the Reigns of Edward I and Edward II*, ed. W. Stubbs (London, 1882−83, Rolls Series), ii, 290.

260   TWELFTH CENTURY STUDIES

23. Wright, *op. cit.*, pp. 268 ff.
24. *The Chronicle of William de Rishanger*, p. 104. T. Rymer, *Foedera, conventiones, litterae*, etc., ed. A. Clarke, F. Holbrooke, J. Caley (London, 1816–69), ii, 536.
25. Printed as a supplement to *The Chronicle of William de Rishanger*, pp. 67–109.
26. London citizens, pp. 102–103; professions, pp. 67, 79.
27. *Ibid.*, p. 68.
28. *Ibid.*, pp. 69 and 70 respectively.
29. *Ibid.*, pp. 70, 72, and 72 respectively.
30. *Flores Historiarum*, iii, 213. *Chroniques de London*, ed. G. J. Aungier (London, 1844, Camden Society), p. 46.
31. G. H. Gerould, "King Arthur and Politics," *Speculum*, ii, 43.
32. *Ibid.*, p. 41.
33. *Ibid.*, pp. 45 ff.
34. *Ibid.*, iii, 47, 56 item 2.

Index